Men at Play
A Working Understanding of Professional Hockey

After a year spent documenting the working life and daily routines of players for an American Hockey League team, Michael Robidoux found that most peoples' perceptions of hockey players' lives as romantic and glamorized are unrealistic. The majority of professional hockey players work in a closed and discriminatory environment in the lower tiers of hockey on semi-professional teams.

Players dedicate their lives to the goal of playing professional hockey and teams demand total commitment from their players, giving them complete control over almost all aspects of the players' lives. With the enormous labour turnover in the AHL and the surplus labour pool, players are extremely vulnerable: they must perform well or be replaced by the scores of other men willing to do the same job. With limited education and limited life skills, players seldom meet people who are not connected to the game and, when they do, they do so with trepidation. The constructed universe of the game consumes the players so that, in spite of any wealth they may accumulate, they often know nothing other than the game and have invested everything in an occupation where their services quickly become obsolete.

Very different from the sensational memoirs of those few players who make it to the top, Robidoux's Men at Play offers a bracing inside look at the dynamics of the fastest game on earth.

MICHAEL A. ROBIDOUX is assistant professor of kinesiology, The University of Lethbridge.

Men at Play

A Working Understanding of Professional Hockey

MICHAEL A. ROBIDOUX

McGill-Queen's University Press

Montreal & Kingston · London · Ithaca

© McGill-Queen's University Press 2001
ISBN 0-7735-2169-0 (cloth)
ISBN 0-7735-2220-4 (paper)

Legal deposit second quarter 2001
Bibliothèque nationale du Québec

Printed in Canada on acid-free paper

This book has been published with the help of
a grant from the Humanities and Social Sciences
Federation of Canada, using funds provided by
the Social Sciences and Humanities Research
Council of Canada.

McGill-Queen's University Press acknowledges
the financial support of the Government of
Canada through the Book Publishing Industry
Development Program (BPIDP) for its activities.
It also acknowledge the support of the Canada
Council for the Arts for its publishing program.

Canadian Cataloguing in Publication Data

Robidoux, Michael A.
Men at play: a working understanding
of professional hockey in Canada
Includes bibliographical references and index.
ISBN 0-7735-2169-0 (bnd)
ISBN 0-7735-2220-4
1. Hockey – Sociological aspects – Case studies.
2. Hockey players – Canada – Social conditions.
I. Title.
GV848.4C3R62 2001   305.9'7969   C00-901238-9

Typeset in Sabon 10.5/13
by Caractéra inc., Quebec City

Contents

Acknowledgments   vii

Introduction   3

1   Producing the "Self" in Professional Hockey   16

2   Repression, Incorporation, and Segregation:
The Evolution of Sport in Canada   32

3   The Meaningful Universe of Professional Hockey:
The Ethnography   50

4   The Game   65

5   The Practice on Off-Days   85

6   Entering into the Trade of Professional Hockey   100

7   Homogenizing Men in Professional Hockey   127

8   Power, Play, and Powerlessness   151

Conclusion   188

Appendix A   Profiles   195

Appendix B   Players' Salaries: Calculations for the 1999–2000
NHL Hockey Season   198

Notes   199

Bibliography   209

Index   219

Acknowledgments

I wish to acknowledge a number of people whose support and assistance were instrumental throughout the various stages of this research endeavour. Without the initial encouragement of Dr Martin Lovelace and the direction of Dr Diane Tye from Memorial University of Newfoundland, this project would never have materialized. I would like to thank the Institute for Social and Economic Research (ISER) for providing me with the critical funding during the field-work for this project. I am extremely grateful to the players and staff of the Troy Reds, who provided me with access to their work worlds for the 1996–97 hockey season. Special thanks also goes to Rick Morocco, director of player relations for the Professional Hockey Players' Association, for providing me with profiles for players in the American Hockey League (AHL), International Hockey League (IHL), and East Coast Hockey League (ECHL).

Throughout this project I have received invaluable editorial comments from Dr Mark E. Workman (University of North Florida), Dr Gerald L. Pocius, Dr Peter Narváez, and Dr Neil Rosenberg (all from Memorial University of Newfoundland). From McGill-Queen's University Press, I am extremely grateful to Joan McGilvray and Wendy Dayton for their editorial assistance. As well, I would like to thank Dr. Leonard Primiano (Cabrini College) for his critical insights, hockey artifacts, and a host of other resources.

Finally, I wish to express my deepest gratitude to my family, whose love and support make all things possible. Thank you.

Men at Play

Introduction

The game of hockey in Canada far exceeds the realm of pastime or sport; it has come to symbolize a way of life in this nation. Throughout the country, children and adults can be found playing hockey, in either its more vernacular[1] forms of pond, street, or ball hockey, or in its more institutionalized forms of play on rinks and arenas as part of the Canadian Hockey Association. Hockey has become part of the Canadian mythos, and media and artistic forms have celebrated and continue to celebrate its mythological status.

The political implications of hockey are also profound, inasmuch as the game has served as a national symbol for a country whose identity is constantly scrutinized by its own people. Few other institutions in Canada have the unifying potential of hockey, making it "one of this country's most significant collective representations – a story that Canadians tell themselves about what it means to be a Canadian" (Gruneau and Whitson 1993, 13). Perhaps the most celebrated hockey and, in turn, Canadian story occurred on 28 September 1972, when Paul Henderson scored the winning goal in the final of an eight-game series against the Soviet Union. In *September 1972*, a television documentary retelling the story of what was designated "The Challenge Series," former hockey star Phil Esposito remarks solemnly about the final outcome of the series: "It was done. We accomplished what we started and it will never be the same again" (*September 1972*, 1997). The documentary summarized the series as follows:

Team Canada arrived home to a heroes' welcome; Canadians rejoicing from coast to coast. There were twenty-seven remarkable days, never to be seen again.

That wasn't how it started; it all began as fun. But things changed. In one incredible month we renewed our love for more than just a game. [Inserted in the commentary is Paul Henderson's statement, "I don't thing we were ever more Canadian than we were on September 28, 1972."]

There is something about September, September of '72. Its magic will always live. (*September 1972* 1997)

As with all stories, however, hockey is a construction that has been cleverly manipulated by hegemonic forces in this nation. In order to gain an understanding of hockey as it is lived, much of its associated ideological weight must be deconstructed.

Recent works such as Laura Robinson's *Crossing the Line* successfully move beyond hockey's romantic/mythological framework, offering a new assortment of narratives that reveal the abusive and intrinsically violent nature of the sport, rather than its unifying potential. The scandalous information put forth in *Crossing the Line* provides a necessary, albeit disheartening, counter-discourse to Canadian hockey; not only does it challenge popular images of the game, it also removes the protective shell that has kept the general public from acknowledging the victimization and victimizing that occur in hockey contexts (Robinson 1998, 7).

The intention of this book is to provide a counter-discourse of its own, to provide another variety of narratives. But it is also intended to focus specifically on professional hockey in Canada. The objective here is to gain an understanding of hockey as an occupation, as it is "worked" – a view not generally shared by Canadians. By approaching a professional hockey community in this manner, it becomes apparent how traditional behavioural patterns acquired through the occupation influence individual competences within the group. Aside from the skills that are mandatory in playing the game of hockey, upcoming players learn traditional behaviours and roles in order to satisfy labour demands. The team atmosphere in which the players are immersed creates a perpetual environment of group interaction, scrutiny, and verification; players either thrive or struggle under the group's gaze, yet they are forced to perform their roles within the rigid boundaries predefined by existing team/group structures. Divergence from these unstated codes of behaviour is interpreted as subversive: it undermines the desired levels of group unity and cohesion.

My intention is to discuss how professional hockey players' identities are *shaped* and *defined* through the labour process. I have particularly emphasized the difficulties the individual faces working within an environment that both celebrates, and exploits, male physical supremacy and general elitism. Paramount, then, is the manner in which power relationships are generated and perpetuated within the group. An attempt is thus made to perceive male hegemony as "no more than a politically interested figuration" (Spivak 1989, 517), one subject to scrutiny and subsequent deconstruction. From this position, the pervasive discrimination within professional hockey can be properly weighed within its occupational context and addressed for what it is: a problem of production. These behaviours are suddenly less connected to the concept of sport, but linked instead to the ideological concerns of ownership and the owners successful use of sport (hockey) as a means of generating revenue.

In order to achieve these goals, I made arrangements that would allow me to immerse myself within a professional hockey community as a participant/observer, my aim being to conduct an ethnography of the group. Yet while an ethnography was performed and the project ultimately realized, an admission of failure must be conceded. The original arrangements made to enter the community did not materialize, and I was unable to gain the kind of access to the community originally envisioned. Moreover, I was unable to establish the rapport with the players that I had thought possible when starting the project; hence, throughout the research, I remained an outsider.

For most of the project, I struggled to overcome this outsider status. But I was simply unable to transcend the brutal fact that the professional hockey community is deliberately segregated from the larger society – a fact which, ironically, contributed to my overall research findings. My presence, while perhaps not a threat to group unity, was certainly intrusive, as verified by the players who nicknamed me "the spy." The research process therefore proved to be most revealing, for I conducted the study from an outsider's perspective, enabling me to appreciate the exclusive nature of this occupational group. It should also be stated, however, that although I was never part of the group, the players gradually did become used to my presence, to the extent that, during the early stages of the season following my ethnography, one of the interviewed players telephoned me at home to ask if I could provide him with some information about registering for courses at a local university. Clearly, a certain level of familiarity had developed, allowing me to gather a substantial amount of research data for this project.

GAINING ENTRANCE INTO THE ARENA
OF PROFESSIONAL HOCKEY

The professional hockey community that serves as the basis for this research was not haphazardly selected; it is an organization that I felt best suited my research needs. From the outset I had decided not to conduct a study of a National Hockey League (NHL) team, simply because the high-profile nature of NHL organizations would have made it virtually impossible for me to gain access to the players. I then decided that it would be best to approach an American Hockey League (AHL) franchise: while the AHL is closest to the NHL in terms of talent, style of play, and business operations, comparatively, it functions with relatively minimal fanfare and media attention. The distinction between the NHL and AHL is highly significant, and it must be understood that my research into one does not speak for the other. The important relationship between the two leagues that does exist needs explicating, however, and will be discussed further in chapter three. What does need stating here is that while a distinction must be made between the two leagues, the interrelationships and commonalities are such that one cannot be considered apart from the other.

Having made the decision to study an AHL team, I then had to decide which team to target and how best to make my approach. Without any connections to an AHL franchise, my choice of team was purely arbitrary: I would work with whichever one would agree to work with me. Before even approaching the team, however, I decided that my research must remain completely anonymous. I made this decision for three reasons. First, I thought that guaranteeing anonymity to both the players and to the organization might make them more willing to allow me into their environment to do my research. Second, I believed that those involved might be more at ease and more forthright in their dealings with an outsider who came in to study their community. Finally, because the majority of the people with whom I was working were local, national, and at times even international personalities, I considered it extremely important to conceal their identities. All study participants have therefore been given pseudonyms[2] and the team and its location have been similarly disguised. I then set out in search of an AHL franchise that would allow me to study it during its hockey season. My search began and ended with the Troy Reds.

When I first approached the Reds with my research proposal, I felt that my hockey background[3] would be a pivotal factor in gaining access to this hockey community; I therefore made a point of stressing it in my first interview with the team's director of operations. My first meeting with him – which took place in June of 1996 – seemed to confirm that my past experience in hockey was indeed of value, and undoubtedly it got me through this initial stage of my research quest. I left the meeting feeling confident that my research proposal had been well received, and that I was well underway in my attempt to insert myself into the Reds' organization.

My meeting with the director of operations was short and to the point. I presented him with a three-page document highlighting my academic and hockey career, along with a point-by-point summary of my research proposal. This research proposal was quite simple: I was seeking some form of employment (menial or otherwise), preferably within the dressing room, which would allow me to participate in and observe the players' formal and informal work routines. Ideally, I wished to conduct an ethnography of the work lives of professional hockey players; the only way I felt this could be done was to participate in the everyday events of the dressing room. Thus I volunteered to become an unpaid assistant to the Reds' training staff. Since I had witnessed dressing-room protocol for so many years as a player, I felt I already possessed a certain level of competence, which would enable me to perform any tasks asked of me satisfactorily, without interfering with the players or coaches.

I spent the majority of the summer attempting to verify my status with the Reds' organization. But it was not until towards the end of August that the Reds' athletic therapist Al Jones phoned to inform me of my situation. He was not especially optimistic. In fact, he was calling to tell me that having considered my proposal, he was sceptical about my proposition. With nothing to lose, I began explaining to Jones what I was hoping to accomplish with this project and stressed the potential significance of the research.

The more I talked, the more Jones seemed to become interested in the idea. Indeed, as the conversation developed, he began discussing other aspects I could consider and what he felt would be the positive implications of the research. From the outset I had realized that this phone call was my only opportunity to stave off rejection. Yet although by the end of the conversation I had managed to persuade Jones to assist me in my research endeavour, I had no concrete notion of the actual role I would play with the Reds' organization. Nevertheless, I was confident that I would have, at the least, limited access to the team.

I was unable to solidify my relationship with the team until October, when their season officially began. Although the Reds' season actually began in September, that was only as a part of the parent organization. Because the AHL is a farm system for the NHL, the players initially report to their respective NHL teams to attend training camp. Those players who do not fit into the NHL team's roster are then generally sent back down to the Juniors, or to their AHL (or any other minor league) affiliate. Thus AHL franchises only begin their seasons when the NHL training camps are concluded. I was thus forced to wait until October to resume communications with Jones; only at that point could I find out how access to the team would be managed.

An additional difficulty was that the Reds had recently hired a new coach, Dennis Murphy, for the 1996–97 season, and Jones was not sure how he would react to my presence in the dressing room. Since it is the coach who is in charge of what ultimately takes place in the dressing room, and Jones had only known him for a brief period of time, Jones was leery of making any unwelcome decisions. My fate, therefore, was in Jones's hands: it was up to him to approach Murphy and see if it was possible to provide a position that would allow me to observe and participate in the dressing room dynamic.

Jones phoned me on the sixteenth of October to say that Murphy was not in favour of giving me that kind of access to the dressing room. I suggested a variety of other possibilities, but all were dismissed. Evidently, Murphy felt my presence would be too intrusive and would affect the team negatively. Instead, I was offered the opportunity to observe the players in their natural work setting, which meant studying them while they practised and played their games. In addition, I would be permitted to approach the players for interviews or for discussions of any questions I might have. I would also occasionally be allowed access to the dressing room so I could observe behaviour during more informal time periods. Although the situation was not ideal, it allowed me to conduct an ethnography of a professional hockey team strictly as an observer. Certainly, this is not the ideal methodological approach, and I recognized that serious problems would arise out of it. It is necessary, therefore, to discuss briefly the strengths and limitations of my approach so that readers can draw their own conclusions from this ethnographic study.

THE DILEMMA OF ETHNOGRAPHY

The discernible imperfections of ethnographic research has become a source of contention for scholars. The postmodern, poststructural, deconstructionist debate has forced social scientists to re-evaluate the plausibility of ethnography, to the extent that those who continue to write ethnographies are often doing so apologetically and, subsequently, ineffectively, because of all the "navel gazing, self-doubt, equivocation about truth, and even obsessive guilt" (Cintron 1993, 380). The mere suggestion of "ineffective" ethnography is problematic because it predicates the possibility of *effective ethnography*: a possibility that is becoming increasingly dubious. In *Writing Culture: The Poetics and Politics of Ethnography*, the collaborative authors (Clifford and Marcus 1986) attempt to bring clarity to this debate by scrutinizing the concept of ethnography; subsequently, though, they reassert its effectiveness as a valuable contribution to the understanding of cultural behaviour. The result, however, has not been clarity, and the debate continues, leaving scholars to contend with the uncertainty of their own research and writing.

It would be beneficial here to reconsider the contribution of Clifford and Marcus to the growing trend of ethnographic scrutiny. In an attempt to address the concerns and scepticism related to the ethnographic tradition, Clifford and Marcus collaborated on a series of essays, providing varying perspectives on ethnographic writing and its value for scholars as a means of illuminating cultural behaviour. An overriding theme throughout the text is the admission that ethnographic writing is a form of fictional[4] discourse (Clifford 1986, 6). The intent is not to discredit ethnography, but to elucidate the limitations of any so-called scientific understanding of culture. Indeed, it is important to recognize that the imaginative forces at play in all ethnographic writing are not hazardous, but an unavoidable outcome of what is intrinsically an interpretative process. While Clifford acknowledges that what he has "been stressing may be a source of pessimism for some readers" (1986, 25), he asks if it is not also liberating to remove the pretence of a methodology that assumes people can be objectified through an ethnographic lens. His vision, however, has not yet been universally welcomed and, as with any postmodern discourse, the potential for nihilism – in this case ethnographic – is always painfully close. As a result, the *Writing of Culture* has contributed to a growing trend in anthropological discourse, among both postmodernists and modernists, that questions whether the partial reality of ethnography implies ethnographic futility.

In setting out to do my own research, I have been forced to grapple with this question. What exactly constitutes my role as an ethnographer? Am I even comfortable with the term? I began to question if what I was doing was, in fact, ethnography, or some other form of qualitative or descriptive research. Did my work in the field qualify as ethnographic? Were there time restrictions? Did I have to physically move into the community? Were there stipulations of which I was unaware? All these questions forced me to reconsider ethnography as a concept, and to re-evaluate my role as an "ethnographer," a term I have since come to accept with a certain degree of comfort.

Much of the controversy surrounding ethnography revolves around the concept itself. The problem is that the term is twofold: it "refers both to the *processes* for accomplishing it" and to "the *product* of that research, which ordinarily takes its form in prose (Wolcott 1990, 47). Thus, ethnography is composed of two equal parts: the observation and collection of data, and the articulation of what has been observed or collected through written discourse. Failing to provide one of these component parts therefore disqualifies the research as ethnographic, which means that research cannot come to ethnographic fruition until it is in its written form. It is here that the fundamental problem arises, in that this relationship is based upon transforming human experience, not, as what some wish to believe, on representing it. By its very nature, then, ethnography is a creative process that involves selecting aspects of culture (what affects this selection process will be discussed later) in order to communicate certain parts of what was selected in the form of a document.

If we consider the creative process further, it is evident that ethnography, as it is experienced by the reader, is at least four times removed from the actual cultural activity being studied. Initially, it is separated by the researcher's *selecting, interpreting,* and *articulating* of culture in some form of written discourse; then, it is *interpreted* by the eventual reader, removing it once again from the initial experience. The argument I am putting forth is not intended to contribute further to the postmodern problematizing of ethnography, nor would I argue it to be postmodern; in fact, Claude Lévi-Strauss wrote extensively about the degenerative reality of ethnography over forty years ago.[6] I would simply say that ethnography can be best understood as the displacement of experience, which forces ethnographers to communicate the experience as it presently exists in their mind. The result is a unique blend of the reader's imagination, the author's imagination, and the initial experience studied.

What then are the implications of a mode of scholarship that admittedly reinvents its subject matter in its attempt to convey its findings to an audience? What is gained by a research endeavour that is clearly fallible? Cultural dynamism is ambiguous and multifaceted, making it impossible to articulate in any definite or indisputable manner. Attempting to represent what in essence defies representation in an empirical and totalizing fashion is not only ineffective but dangerous. Perhaps, therefore, ethnography, which does not intend to represent but rather to interpret culture, is best suited for cultural exploration and commentary. Without pretensions of scientific precision, the ethnography does not speak for its subjects of study, but contributes to an existing, imperfect, human dialogue. In contrast to an attempt to achieve closure, ethnography opens itself up to debate, contradiction, consent, and potential conflict. Therefore, the indeterminacy of ethnography is actually its strength: its contested meanings generate further dialogue, and in its imperfection and contradiction it is as close as possible to being an "accurate" reflection of what is being studied.

Having said this, however, the onus is placed on ethnographers to recognize the limitations of ethnography; this, in turn, imposes upon them a still greater sense of responsibility. Because ethnography is essentially an interpretative process and a contribution to an already existing dialogue, the reader must be duly informed in this relationship. Readers must be made aware of the factors that have helped shape the ethnographic text, thereby allowing them to enter into this dialogue able to criticize and to accept or reject what is being discussed. It is imperative, then, that authors open themselves to their readers and relate how their individuality – personally and professionally (if a distinction is to be made) – makes *their* particular interpretation of culture unique. For example, in Alan Klein's ethnographic study of bodybuilders, he vividly reveals to his audience his own predicament entering a particular fieldwork setting: "I was convinced that there was not a bizarre or grotesque type of behaviour I hadn't seen, read about, or had told to me. Crossing the threshold of the gym door, however, I unexpectedly froze when it came to engaging the 'erotic' scene before me ... In retrospect, I felt like one of those subway-riding New Yorkers who, when faced with an ugly incident on the homeward journey, sits with eyes riveted on some inanimate object, denying it all in the hope that the obscene drunk or attacker will desist" (1993, 24). Through this colourful passage the audience immediately becomes aware of Klein's relationship with the culture under observation and his initial vantage point as a researcher.

In my own situation, the significance of being a white, Canadian, heterosexual male, and a former hockey player, who is doing a study of professional hockey culture, cannot be ignored. Undoubtedly, my perceptions of the community differ from those of individuals with a different ethnic, gender, or class background. My reception by the community also affects my perceptions of that community and their subsequent dealings with me. Moreover, the theoretical biases I bring with me as a scholar should be shared with the reader. It is through self-revelation that authorial authority is minimized, allowing for a more effective dialogue between the reader's imagination, the author's imagination, and the primary experience.

PLEASE CHECK YOUR BAGS, SIR

When I initially contemplated doing a study of professional hockey, one of the factors that contributed to my final decision was that I satisfied a demographic that would seriously increase my chance of gaining entrance into this exclusively male, predominantly white, and professed heterosexual hockey community. But along with this aforementioned identity, I was also part of a privileged male voice that has been a source of contention for myself and many others in the academic community who recognize the "need to reclaim the voices of those whose insights and experiments are absent from mainstream genealogies" (Bell 1993, 3). In response to this predicament, certain male ethnographers have attempted to remove their gender from their writing and appropriate a more recently valued female-centred discourse, to become what Les Back designates "proto-females" (1993, 217). But as Back correctly asserts, "'feminised' discourse is not the same as feminist social theory, because the former does not carry the political commitment of the latter" (1993, 217). How then does one resist perpetuating androcentric discourse without denying one's gender in the ethnographic process?

It was apparent early on that by reflecting on authorial representation I was indirectly distancing myself from traditional male discourse, without appropriating a voice not my own. A major influence of feminist theory has been its ability to successfully challenge the presentation of male ethnography as if it were generic or genderless. Thus the very act of men acknowledging their gender as it affects the outcome of their research has automatically decentred the male voice. Jonathan Rutherford explains that putting "masculinity into the picture" is really about "making ourselves 'seen,'" and "about making our ... masculinities a basis for discussion" (1988, 46). In other words, the baggage I bring with me as an ethnographer – in particular my gender – needs to be examined, in order to illustrate how it "informs and affects" the cultural activity I am studying.

To begin, the reader must understand that I was once part of a hockey community and still have professional hockey players as friends and acquaintances. Moreover, I enjoy watching and playing hockey in both its vernacular and organized forms; furthermore, I entered this ethnographic field of study only seven years after leaving competitive hockey. Is it not realistic to think that my experiences in this exclusively male domain would distinguish my perceptions of the community from those without this same background? By appreciating these concerns, the reader undoubtedly has a better opportunity not only to scrutinize what I am presenting through the ethnography, but to respond suitably to any authority I will undoubtedly claim. I agree with Kamala Visweswaran when she argues that "the reflexive mode emphasizes not what we know, but how we think we know," (1994, 80) and that this stance enables readers to assign their own value to what is being discussed.

THE LAYOUT OF THE WORK

It is within this context that I begin this series of narratives about the profession of hockey and the power relationships that players succumb to, and resist, in their daily occupational endeavours. To accomplish this task I have felt it necessary to first set my research in its proper occupational framework. Readers must understand that although this book is about professional sport, it is first and foremost an occupational study. Thus, it is of great importance to consider the relationship between professional hockey and work, and to relate how player performance within the industry expresses occupational identity and competence.

A historical narrative follows this section. There I trace the evolution of sport from its vernacular origins to its current status as a multi-billion dollar industry. By examining the manner in which sport has developed, readers can trace the threefold process of repression, incorporation, and segregation that allows sport to be perceived as a contested cultural entity. Indeed, the value of sport intensifies with the introduction of professionalization, and it is out of this professional framework that hockey in Canada is explored. Throughout the discussion, I have emphasized the various controlling forces and power relationships that contribute to a Canadian sport identity, and how these forces affect those individuals who engage, as players, in its execution.

The next three chapters are dedicated to the fieldwork conducted for this project. As already stated, this research was performed from the perspective of an "observer"; hence my access to the players was limited during the more informal periods of their working day, such as time spent in the dressing room winding up or down from games and practices. This is not to say that that the research was conducted from the vantage point of a spectator; in fact, this was the perspective that I wished to transcend in order to discuss the actual community of professional hockey as it is experienced and lived by the players. My intent, then, was to avoid discussing it as it is experienced by the general public; that is, as "spectacle." I was able to avoid discussing the community from a purely spectator's point of view by basing two of the three chapters on the players during practices, as opposed to during games. It is during practices, away from the crowds, that the players are seen working, both formally and informally, at perfecting their skills and simply expressing themselves within their occupational environment. Moreover, I consciously resisted discussing the spectacle of the sport in certain segments of the ethnography, despite its at times overwhelming nature. In chapter three, the only chapter dedicated entirely to the formal game of hockey, the concept of spectacle is addressed specifically so readers will understand why I have chosen not to pursue this aspect of professional hockey.

Finally, the last three chapters consider the observations made in the field about this particular professional hockey community. The fifth chapter, for example, examines the rituals currently in place to signify the transition the players make from being members outside of the community to members within it. The sixth chapter discusses the product of this transformation – in other words, what the players become as they enter the hockey community. Because this is an exclusively male domain, I explore the manner in which masculinity is expressed and lived within this group. I found that there are learned behaviours, perpetuating a pre-existing identity that players are pressured to assume on entering the league. While these structures provide players with a sense of security – in that they know what is expected of them as males, and as hockey players – they also provide the players with the sense of power as a unified body. The last chapter explores the players' perceptions or constructions of power and how these perceptions/constructions contribute to eventual exploitation and individual powerlessness.

CHAPTER ONE

Producing the "Self"
in Professional Hockey

While this book focuses on exploring hockey as it is worked rather than discussing the *sport* of hockey, the relationship between hockey and labour is not immediately obvious. Thus my reasoning for approaching a hockey community in this vein demands further attention. The difficulty in making the connection between hockey and "work" lies in the premise of play that underlies any professional sport. To *play* hockey professionally is to engage oneself completely in a working environment that is governed by the tenets of play; in other words, it is to work at something that in any other context is "essentially a separate occupation, carefully isolated from the rest of life, and generally ... engaged in with precise limits of time and place" (Caillois 1961, 6). The dictates of play demand that participants comply with the structure (or world) of the game; otherwise, the game will not be successfully realized. Of course, play theorist Roger Caillois, in his description of play, refers to what is intended to be a momentary departure from "the rest of life." Individuals who play for a living, however, are forced to abandon themselves to this principle, to the extent that the realm of play becomes their way of life. For professional hockey players, the notion of leaving or entering this "enclosure" becomes a very literal function, in that the game is not temporary, but rather, their livelihood.

This distinction between work and play does not simply clarify how players approach the game of hockey; instead, it situates players in the labour process, enabling us to better understand their *work* and their role as productive members of their community. Those who feel "playing" hockey is removed from "productive" labour and hence that it remains outside of a working-class framework, may take exception to this distinction. Thorstein Veblen, however, supports this notion by saying that occupations such as "government, war, sports, and devout observances" are essentially non-productive, because those who engage in these activities are not doing so to improve their economic situation, or for subsistence (1899, 40). The professional sport industry, though, undermines this premise, inasmuch as the professional hockey player works and plays for subsistence as well as for economic gain, producing millions of dollars for team owners, stadiums, and cities, as well as for the myriad businesses and agencies that market products directly or indirectly through the organization and/or the league. But of greater consequence is a more immediate product of this labour process, which Karl Marx and Frederick Engels both tell us is the ultimate product of any act of production; that is, the production of *self* (1972, 27).

THE PRODUCTION PROCESS

It is worthwhile considering this act of production further if we wish to truly gain an understanding of people and their behaviours within the labour process. It is unarguable that, through the act of production, the labourer expresses her- or himself as a working member of a particular community. But according to Marx and Engels, the ramifications of production exceed occupational iden-tification; it is the essence of human existence, they say, that is manifested through the production process (1972, 27). The empha-sis they place on production stems from their grounded understand-ing of human history. They argue that the basic principle that dictates all existence is the fundamental need for *producing* a means of subsistence, "which involves before everything else eating and drinking, a habitation, clothing and many other things. The first historical act is thus the production of the means to satisfy these needs, the production of material life itself" (1972, 27). As people engage in producing a means of subsistence, then, they are, in turn, producing the foundations that envelop them through the act of living; that is, the political, social, economic, and cultural con-structions. The very identifying of people and their responses to circumstances as the determining factor for not only historical development, but for the very existence of history, reveals an important idea: "As individuals express their life, so they are" (Marx and Engels 1972, 18). Or as Hannah Arendt puts it, the

basic formulation of production is based on the notion "that labor
(and not God) created man" (1958, 86).

It is this expression or production of self that is of enormous
interest to us here. If we can agree that "through the human historical process, we produce ourselves and our societies" (Williams
1977, 91), the physical products of our activities are only important
in so far as they are the consequences of human development. For
example, the mechanic who repairs an automobile is, in fact,
engaging in a process of defining the very essence of what it means
to be not only a mechanic, but also a person "enter[ing] into
definite social and political relations" (Marx and Engels 1972, 22).
In other words, occupations continue to serve as the essential means
of production, in that we define ourselves through our work.

Anthropologist Thomas Dunk points out that because the "neces-
sity of paid labour and the fear of losing it dominate the lives of
the working class" (1991, 41), workers are entrenched in the labour
process, struggling or thriving in a perpetual performance of the
self. The key term here is *struggle*. As Harry Braverman explains:
"The transformation of working humanity into a 'labor force,' a
'factor of production,' an instrument of capital, is an incessant and
unending process. The condition is repugnant to the victims, whether
their pay is high or low, because it violates human conditions of
work; and since the workers are not destroyed as human beings
but are simply utilized in inhuman ways, their critical, intelligent,
conceptual faculties, no matter how deadened or diminished, always
remain in some degree a threat to capital" (1974, 139). Increased
levels of control and systemization in the workplace inhibit people's
ability to express themselves through the labour process, to the
extent that Marx and Engels believe that individual expression is
nullified. In *The Communist Manifesto*, they lament that "the extensive use of machinery" in the workplace has denied the proletarians'
individual autonomy, and thus they become a mere appendage of
the machine (1888, 87). These comments are significant in that
Marx and Engels correctly assess the increasingly oppressive nature
of labour within a capitalist mode of production. However, what
needs stating is that Marxists and neo-Marxists alike have often
underestimated human agency, not to mention the human ability to
actively respond to growing levels of control and coercion.

The tension between worker and machine is considered in Robert
McCarl's influential essay "The Production Welder: Product, Process

and the Industrial Craftsman." In this study, McCarl explores the intrusive role of management personnel and their measures to maximize labour efficiency. As if directly responding to Marx's concern expressed in the passage above, McCarl cites an example where "management decided to try out a spot welding machine to take over a welding task previously done by hand" (1974, 251). With the introduction of this machine – which was actually an effective tool – the "boredom and lack of skill involved in feeding material into it forced the welders to revert to the old hand method whenever possible" (McCarl 1974, 251). The welders outright defied management by refusing to employ a work method that would serve to simplify the labour process. Moreover, the work that remained because of the men's rejection of the incorporation of the machine was a task that senior workers often avoided and generally consigned to junior workers. Why, then, would these welders risk the consequences of defying management to do more work (especially work that, by and large, was avoided by those in a position to do so)?

Quite simply, these welders were resisting the loss of control workers are increasingly experiencing in the workplace. With the increase of automation in the workforce, the workers' control is reduced; increasingly, they are alienated from the act of production. But by resisting worker alienation, the welders studied by McCarl were attempting to reincorporate themselves back into the mode of production, despite the fact that in so doing they were making more work for themselves. The work that was initially theirs, and therefore meaningful to them, was reacquired through their own subversive behaviour. The magnitude of these acts of subversion[1] is not only relevant in this individual circumstance; such behaviour sheds light on the dynamism within the production process itself and the flaw in Marx's understanding of the worker within it.

What must be clarified is that while the automation of labour might appear to serve the worker, it is in essence serving, first and foremost, the constant demands for increased capitalist production. These demands for surplus are not the product of the basic demands of the workers; they far exceed their needs. Thus, the value of production is reduced, inasmuch as the products of the trade no longer belong to those who are actually involved in producing them. From this, Marx concludes that the "product of labour is labour which has been embodied in an object and turned into a physical thing; this product is an *objectification* of labour" (1963a, 122).

Yet while the objectification of labour does occur, it is not a necessary conclusion. Marx fails to acknowledge the active role of the worker, whereby the reality of an objectified labour force is resisted through a means of personal expression. It is this creative aspect of labour which Michael J. Bell focuses on in his essay "Making Art Work." In his consideration of assembly-line workers in an automobile plant, Bell breaks down one particular worker's daily work routine. He shows that what appears to be an unconscious, automated labour process is, at least in this case, a "deliberate" and "self-conscious experience," which serves as "a display of style and expression that molds the individual pieces of the work process into a truly creative event" (1984, 220). What is apparent is that workers resist being alienated through the process of production; rather than serving as an intrinsically objectified performance as Marx suggests, their labour is a vital means of expressing both individual and group identity. The challenge is first to recognize where this expressive behaviour lies, and then to discover what is being expressed.

LABOURING IN A CAPITALIST CONTEXT

Before any kind of performance analysis is attempted, it is crucial to fully understand the context in which the performance occurs. Since I am considering an occupational community within a capitalist framework, the basic principles of capitalist production must be examined. We have already touched upon the conflict between the workers and the modern technological age in which they work, but this antagonism must be further elucidated so that the behaviours within the occupational group of our particular study – professional hockey – can be appreciated. Hence we must begin by exploring where the labourer fits within the capitalist system of production.

At its most basic level, capitalism is entirely based on producing surplus value at the expense of the working class. According to Sheila Cohen, it is a system of exploitation that essentially consists of one class employing "labour for less value than it produces" to guarantee the generation of profit for the hiring class (1987, 42). As alluded to earlier, however, the exploitative framework of capitalist production need not imply that labourers are passive victims of their material surroundings; rather, they can be individuals engaged in an oscillating process of conflict and consent. Workers, who are often unconcerned with debates of political policy and ideology, are conscious of their position within a system where "quantitative maximization of output and reduction of socially necessary labour time ... dominates managerial strategy" and hence, consciously and unconsciously, comply with and resist their role within the workplace (Cohen 1987, 43). This conflicting relationship becomes clearer when we consider the reality of power within a dominant culture: power lies within a class's ability to naturalize that dominance, creating the illusion that the existing power structures are somehow innate. The exploitation of labourers has become part of this reality, serving to reduce the natural conflict this unfavourable relationship generates and, ultimately, to establish and maintain capitalist hegemony.

The concept of hegemony is very useful, inasmuch as it implies a negotiation of power and subsequent consent to domination, rather than a group's outright submission to an overt execution of force. It should be stressed that hegemonic structures are never stagnant and are extremely difficult to maintain. Chris Rojek explains: "Hegemony is therefore to be understood as a type of domination which is based on the 'active consent' of the subordinate group" (1985, 31). Thus, the dominated class is constantly involved in a process of negotiation, concessions, threats, and pressures, thereby keeping hegemony in a state of flux. Michael Burawoy perhaps states it best when he writes that within "the labor process the basis of consent lies in the organization of activities as though they presented the worker with real choices, however narrowly confined those choices might be. It is participation in choosing that generates consent" (1979, 27).

The labour context must be understood as a site where workers accede to an exploitative labour process, but simultaneously resist servility. In fact, occupational environments are filled with subversion, as workers seek to regain degrees of power they relinquished on entering the unequal partnership with management. While subversive acts are diverse, they perform a uniform function, which is to oppose the formal structures of work (Dunk 1991, 7). Logically then, most acts of subversion occur within the *informal* processes of labour, where workers are able to establish "a new system of meaning" in which "they [the workers] are morally and intellectually dominant" (Dunk 1991, 159). But only by acknowledging the intrinsic conflict within the context of labour are we able to decipher this esoteric system of meaning; only then can we competently discuss performance within the workplace as a negotiation of power.

It has been stressed that the hegemony of a class is largely maintained by its ability to execute its power over those living in the dominated classes in a non-conflicting manner. In other words, the desired hegemonic structure would be for those in power to maintain their dominance without making it noticeable in everyday life. Without any specific imposition of power, thoughts of subverting aspects of authority are difficult. In the occupational arena, this naturalizing process of power is perhaps more easily achieved for the simple reason that employers are aware of the fact that workers are dependent upon having and maintaining a job for their basic survival. The unequal or exploitative relationship between worker and owner is generally accepted in capitalist societies as a "natural" relationship, one that only becomes contentious if the exploitation surpasses an accepted level of suitability. Maxims such as "It's just part of the job," arise in direct response to the undesired realities of the job, their very utterance suggesting subservience. Or, as one professional hockey player once said to me, "It's part of the game. And that's just the way it works" (Copper 1996).

The expression of dominance is often cleverly disguised as a basic life process, leaving few opportunities for workers to formally counteract. With this said, though, it is also true that the dominated classes are cognizant of their subordinate role, and that, in response to their situation, the same subtle behaviour that serves to challenge authority without having to assume a revolutionary posture can be found. As a result, much of the antagonism that exists within the unequal relationship of labour seemingly remains unexpressed. Yet as Cohen explains, the lack of formal resistance does not deny what she describes as a relationship bound in conflict: "The dialectic of structure and response within the capitalist labour process springs not from some externally delivered political awareness, a radical response by workers to the oppressive domination of management, but from the contradictory relationship inherent in the production process itself, that of exploitation" (1987, 41). The obvious difficulty for those studying these processes within the workplace is decoding behaviour that, by its mundane and everyday nature, appears to be purely benign but, in fact, is rich with subversion.

How then can a researcher begin to access behaviours that are so deeply disguised as natural life processes?

"READING" BEHAVIOUR

The difficulty in recognizing the significance of the mundane actions of everyday life is not unique to my situation. Indeed, other culturally related disciplines have recently begun considering the potentials and difficulties of looking at the familiar rather than the strange.[2] One problem is the apparent complacency surrounding these behaviours. But by reminding ourselves of the unarticulated political tension present in the labour process, we can recognize such behaviour as ideologically and culturally rich. It is precisely from this premise that Roland Barthes approaches everyday behaviour in his enduring work, *Mythologies*. In this book – an examination of the lived events of everyday life, from wrestling to plastic material culture – he discusses everyday behaviours as highly politicized occurrences. The work is in direct response to Barthes's "feeling of impatience at the sight of the 'naturalness' with which newspapers, art and common sense constantly dress up a reality which, even though it is the one we live in, is undoubtedly determined by history" (1957, 11). In other words, Barthes sets out to denaturalize life processes that have gone relatively unquestioned because of their innate guises; he also seeks to expose and interpret the multiplicity of meanings that are hidden within these routine performances.

Although the argument put forward by Barthes is not revolutionary,[3] the success of his analysis lies in the manner in which he accesses the ordinary. His approach draws from Ferdinand de Saussure's systematic approach to language, called "semiology." We need not, here, explore in detail the work of Saussure, except to say that it considers the representation of forms as distinct entities with their own intrinsic values. More specifically, semiology "is a science of forms, since it studies significations apart from their contents" (Barthes 1957, 111). Barthes carries Saussure's work with language over into the area of communicative acts such as "photography, cinema, reporting, sport, shows, publicity" (1957, 110). By considering the representation of the event separate from the event itself, Barthes says that the actual event can suddenly be "read" or interpreted as a multivalent text, rather than simply as the naive action it appears to be.

Barthes applies Saussure's linguistic semiology to the semiological analysis of non-linguistic forms of discourse. He begins with a simple linguistic phrase: "because my name is lion" (1957, 116). Barthes argues that this phrase, considered as a pedagogical tool for teaching elementary grammar, means not the result of being named lion, but rather "a rule about the agreement of the predicate" (1957, 116). The representation of the concept remains unchanged, yet its meaning has completely altered because of the new system of meaning (or in ethnographic terms, new context) in which the phrase has been expressed. Thus the representation of concepts is arbitrary, to the point that in different communicative situations, it signifies something quite different.

To further illustrate consistent representation and its inconsistent signification, Barthes moves away from a purely linguistic message and offers the example of a photograph in *Paris-Match*. (He employs the term "sign" as the physical manifestation of the representation.) His example is a photograph of a French soldier of African descent standing with eyes uplifted, saluting the symbolic colours of the French Empire. The literal images within the photograph are expressions of colonial loyalty (saluting to French iconography) and French superiority (those who were once conquered by France willingly stand in honour of French power). But in a new system of meaning, the same photograph may equally signify abject subordination, impoverished identity, and subsequent debasement as a result of French imperialism. The sign does not need to change for its signification to alter drastically and, ultimately, to represent an entirely different concept from the first. Hence, the vehicle employed to express meaning is separate from meaning itself.

The power of this argument is that it moves beyond a phenomenological understanding of hermeneutics; that is, the image is unique in every communicative situation, despite its consistency in form. Whereas the phrase "because my name is lion" is at one point a grammatical example, in another system of meaning, it is an explanation. The same form is in fact two disparate entities, rather than simply two different interpretations (although each entity on its own is ultimately subject to an indefinite number of interpretations). The same holds true in any labour context, depending on the manner in which the labour process is fulfilled. For instance, a construction worker resting her / his head atop of a shovel along the roadside is in a specific resting pose; however, in another system of meaning, the same pose can be a communicative device capable of multiple meanings, such as worker resistance or even subversion. In the preface to *Feminist Messages*, Joan Radner offers similar observations of women manipulating (both consciously and unconsciously) the polysemic codes of patriarchal discourse to communicate female-specific meanings. Radner argues that, with little to no male scrutiny, disempowered females – this can be translated equally well to workers in the unequal predicament of labour – "communicate a variety of messages to different segments of their audiences," because the "essential ambiguity of coded acts protects women from potentially dangerous responses from those who might find their statements disturbing" (1993, vii–viii).

These physical or linguistic expressions must not, however, be mistaken for the concepts they are representing. As researchers studying the mundane and the everyday specific to the workplace, it is essential to make these distinctions move beyond purely naive readings if we are to realize that expressions of labour can be anything – from a joke, to an expression of pride. Moreover, what is being communicated can *be* all of these things and more, not simply different interpretations of the same expression. The point is that we must seek to locate these other values ($x = y$). And that is achieved by acknowledging material representations – language, film, sport – as *vehicles* for manifesting concepts, not as the concepts themselves. Thus, the simple act of reading the paper in the morning at the breakfast table may be that of an individual acquiring information. Yet this same sign/event may represent a wife avoiding conversation with an uninterested spouse. At the least, the event is two separate concepts embodied within the same sign: the first in its very simplicity lends itself to a naive reading; the second (as real as the first) is disguised within the naiveté of the initial reading.

PRODUCING "HOCKEY BODIES"

It is here, then, that we can begin exploring initial "readings" of the primary product of professional hockey. We have established that the ultimate product of any labour process is the self. This formulation is revealed literally in the case of professional hockey, inasmuch as the occupation is based fundamentally on the "body." At its most basic level, hockey consists of groups of bodies attempting to physically dominate and overcome opposing bodies; at the same time, it demands that individuals consistently compete against one another for occupational survival. The competitive nature of the sport situates players in a position where they are fighting either to maintain their position on the roster or to attain a new position by taking another player's job. This volatile framework demands that players have some form of bodily edge over their official opponents, as well as their teammates. Players accordingly dedicate themselves to rigorous training regimes and shape or mould their bodies to best suit the demands of labour.

In North American society, where people often flee their place of work to engage in recreational activities to improve their overall fitness, a professional hockey player's intensive physical training regime may appear to be advantageous. Yet danger lurks, not with regard to physical exercise necessarily, but with regard to the overall process of producing bodies. If a player's success, and ultimately the team's, depends on a player's ability to maximize his own bodily potential, the value of the body becomes immeasurable. Moreover, it is a body that is repeatedly tested. Players build their bodies through weight-training programs, attempting to make them bigger and stronger. As well, they develop their cardiovascular systems through running and cycling exercises, seeking increased speed and greater endurance. Not surprisingly hockey strategies and discourse involve "taking out the body," "playing the body," "skating through your man," "crashing the net (hence the goalie)," and "finishing off your checks." Because hockey bodies are ultimately a destructive force that can either break or be broken, they receive a tremendous amount of attention. To ensure improvement and maintenance, professional trainers (athletic therapists and physiotherapists) are hired to treat hockey bodies and the barrage of injuries they face.

On one occasion during my fieldwork, I entered the Reds' treatment room where, lying across the table, was a player covered only with a towel. The player's leg – commonly referred to as a "wheel" – was being repaired through a series of manipulations: massage, stretching, and what appeared to be some form of electronic stimuli. This typical treatment-room scenario illustrates the attention players' bodies receive in order to be productive, as well as the physical manipulation the body endures to achieve this end. At the same time, it shows the players' need to submit their bodies to professional care in order to maintain their hockey player status.

In essence, what we are witnessing is the shaping and moulding of "docile bodies."

The term "docile body," introduced in Michel Foucault's work *Discipline and Punish*, encapsulates the professional hockey industry's use of the hockey body, and the players' willingness to be used by the industry. For Foucault, the body is the locus by which power, control, dominance, and subjection are expressed and exercised in sociopolitical relations. Although he argues that a body's usefulness is measured in terms of production (economic), he believes that "the body becomes a useful force only if it is both a productive body and subjected body" (1977, 26). Because the ability to subjugate the body is an obvious source of power and control, "disciplines" or precise methods exist to best invest the body with qualities suitable to the desired levels of efficiency and productivity.

Foucault's argument is illustrated through the example of the soldier who, by the eighteenth century "can be made" (1977, 135), or physically transformed from one state of being (peasant) into another (soldier). Through intense regimentation, those behaviours that make the soldier an identifiable entity – i.e., "to remain motionless until the order is given, without moving the head, the hands or the feet" (1977, 136) – become habitual. Critical to his argument is the belief that, as the soldier excels in assuming these soldierly qualities, the soldier inevitably becomes more obedient to controlling forces and, thus, more "docile." In other words, the soldiers' success, or mastery of this role, subjugates them further, because the role is based entirely on subordination: subordination to the occupational demands (the demands dictate behaviour); and subordination to the governing forces who design, monitor, and evaluate these demands.

By stating that the soldier is a subjugated being I am not denying Foucault's claim that docile bodies are active bodies, voluntary, and as Debra Shogan says, "knowing" (1999, 12). What I am arguing, however, is that through ideological representations of the body that romanticize, glamourize, and mythologize it from a Canadian hockey perspective, young males willingly experience what Foucault would say is "a policy of coercions that act upon the body, a calculated manipulation of its elements, its gestures, its behaviour" which either intentionally or not, satisfy a *use* for the industry that employs him (1977, 138). Soldiers, or to return to a sporting context, athletes, undeniably experience levels of control and power made possible by subjecting themselves to disciplines of excellence, and are subsequently celebrated within this framework. In fact, these male figures are often turned into heroes and placed upon pedestals for everyone to see. The very celebration of this masculine identity makes it an attractive identity to adopt, and thus, ensures compliance.

But quite clearly, this heroic status is a delusion; outside the athletic framework its validity is undermined. These heroic figures are ultimately characters in what Varda Burstyn calls "fictive narratives of heroic manhood that homogenize in fantasy and symbol a reality of diverse, contradictory masculinities that are often far from the ideal" (1999, 103). In the case of professional hockey, it is apparent that the heroic values placed upon players are largely superficial, and that the hockey player's ability to physically dominate an opponent has little currency outside the sporting arena. In fact, it is the hockey player's dependence on his body that denies him access to the very system of power that dictates his professional career, and to a certain extent his life.

In the preface to *Out of Bounds: Sports, Media, and the Politics of Identity*, an interesting statement encapsulates the dilemma: "There is something quite criminal about a system that subsumes disadvantaged young men in their prime, exposes them to a world few real people will ever see, and then after a few years of life-threatening performance tells them that their bodies are no longer able to compete with a group of younger bodies who are going through the same thing they went through years before" (Boyd 1997, ix). Although these comments are indirectly discussing O.J. Simpson's predicament as a fallen sport celebrity, they also provide general insight into the ideological construction of bodily authority. The privilege and power the body exacts in professional sport is merely a symbolic representation of the *bodiless* players controlling and using these bodies for capitalist gain. The illusionary nature of male power as expressed through the body is vividly revealed as the body erodes, overcome by younger, faster, and more effective bodies. Like a finely tuned engine, the player's body is driven to exhaustion, and, once the body expires, it becomes superfluous. Thus, the professional hockey player – more than any other labourer – is dependent on his body for productivity in his occupational domain. To a certain extent he is prisoner to his body and to the controlling forces shaping it. From a coaching and managerial perspective, a group of docile bodies is paramount for occupational efficiency and effectiveness; thus we see the "disciplines" in place to ensure so-called docility-utility refined to a science.

In his book, *The Game*, Ken Dryden draws our intention to the Italian term *"inventa la partitia"* (invent the game), which more often than not refers to the loss of individual autonomy in professional sport: "It is a loss they explain many ways. In the name of team play, there is no time or place for individual virtuosity, they say; it is a game now taken over by coaches, by technocrats and autocrats who empty player's minds to control their bodies, reprogramming them with X's and O's, driving them to greater *efficiency* and *work rate*, to move *systems* faster, to move games faster, until achieving mindless pace." (1983, 132). Dryden captures wonderfully the docile body of professional sport and the intentional mind / body division. As with the soldier, the hockey player is willingly "subjected, used, transformed and improved" (Foucault 1977, 136) to ensure personal and team success. The inevitable obedience that allows this process to take place reduces the player to a body – one that is bought, traded, drafted, and released – all of which has tremendous ramifications in an age controlled by the mind, not the body.

The fact that players willingly forsake their bodies to this exclusively corporal enterprise makes them inferior not only in terms of capitalist production, but also in terms of masculine hegemonic relations. The privileging of mind over body has been a repeated trope throughout Christian and modern scientific discourse. The body has historically been seen as a weakness – and at times a danger – which must be intellectually mastered. Failing to move beyond the body means existing in a manual capacity, vis-à-vis manual labour, and thus being diminished by intellectual modes of being. The result is an antagonistic relationship between hand and brain; they "become not just separated, but divided and hostile, and the human unity of hand and brain turns into its opposite, something less than human" (Braverman 1974, 125). Thus, power lies with the capitalist, the "body-less" entity who works not by hand, nor by tools, but "through his money which he uses as capital" (Sohn-Rethel 1978, 118). The hockey player, then, is the capitalist's antithesis: whereas the capitalist buys and sells labour power, the hockey player is bought and his labour power sold for profit. Moreover, this privileged position of the mind over the body is a patriarchal construct: men being associated with the mind, and women, with the body. The subjugation of women by men has been based largely on the premise that women are subject to their bodies and, consequently, to desire, passion, irrationality, and emotionality (Turner 1991, 17). By denying them intellectual authority, this (intellectual) configuration has conveniently positioned women outside dominant power relations. Working-class men, however, are similarly oppressed by this mind/body division, thanks to their dependence on their bodies, not their minds, for subsistence.

Because the male working-class athlete's occupation is based entirely on bodily performance, he, too, is defined by his body. But the reduction of the hockey player to a body not only occupationally diminishes him in the eyes of those who use him; he is diminished as well by his masculinity. In contrast to theories of the male athlete being emblematic of masculine hegemony,[4] I contend that these celebrated images of the male body are symbolic representations of an ideological construct, with limited value in masculine hegemonic relations. Masculine hegemony is based not on the body, but on rationalization and restraint. These refined qualities hold little relevance in the world of professional hockey, where passion and instinct dictate behaviour. Once outside the hockey enclosure, the physically dominant model of masculinity loses its validity, and these young men are often left with only physical dominance to compensate for their sudden powerlessness. The hockey player is thus often associated with power because of the authority his body commands. But it is this same bodily authority which positions the player outside the dominant power relations.

CONCLUSION

The task at hand is to consider the professional hockey labour process (which is comfortably hidden behind the sporting facade – behind the game) as a continuous performance of players or workers striving to express themselves as productive individuals, within a system of efficiency employed by management that exploits this artistry for capitalist gain. The resulting struggle itself can be perceived as two groups motivated by the desire to produce, but who generate two completely separate acts. It is here that a semiological understanding of expression needs to be more readily applied. Dunk astutely observes that the means for worker resistance are greatly restricted by the existing hegemony because "their cultural tool box is full of tools that were designed for other purposes by the system they are struggling against" (1991, 159). Thus, the struggle to be a creative individual within the hockey environment may often mean performing a task that involves incorporating the unique skills and precision for which the player is known, and ultimately creating a distinctive product or end that is interpreted, esoterically, as his own. The danger, though, is that while the creative act may be successful, the superior nature of the product or end, along with the effective manner in which it was achieved, actually caters to the demands of management, thereby reinforcing worker subordination.

It is evident that worker performance, and the labour process in general, is riddled with complexities. Through the act of production the worker, or in this case the hockey player, is potentially establishing himself as a creative human being, while simultaneously reinforcing his own subordinate position with management. This relationship generates further tensions and, in turn, a means of production imbued with political and ideological meaning that is rich with interpretative potential. It is critical, then, that we move beyond the mundane facade of formal and informal behaviours within the occupational setting; that we examine the means by which players resist their subordination and "create a meaningful universe in which they are morally and intellectually dominant" (Dunk 1991, 159). Once this is achieved, we can begin to explore the constructed universe of professional hockey by first examining its historical context.

CHAPTER TWO

Repression, Incorporation, and Segregation: The Evolution of Sport in Canada

As we begin to explore the phenomenon of hockey in Canada, we quickly realize the difficulty of the task at hand. As a symbol of Canadian culture and heritage, hockey must, one would think, represent in some way what it means to be Canadian. Yet given how hockey is played and/or watched, its symbolic value may seem unwarranted. How does a game known primarily for its violence and speed represent a nation known internationally as a moderator of violence and disputes and, moreover, as unreasonably polite? Does the game of hockey actually tell us anything about Canada or is it a convenient and non-threatening symbol representative of nothing but the relentless desire of Canadians to be inoffensive?

If we look at the historical development of sport in Canada, however, and the deliberate construction of a Canadian sport identity, it is apparent that hockey's symbolic value is not arbitrary. Moreover, it does inform us of Canada's national interests and sensibilities. In fact, the development of sport in Canada has been shaped largely by the desire to resist the imperial influence that continued to define Canada, and the need to formulate an identity of its own. Canada has continually sought cultural signifiers that would represent the nation as a self-defined and visible entity, and sport seems to provide the perfect vehicle. Sport and nationalism, therefore, are not separate entities in Canada; they need thorough investigation if we are to understand hockey and the associated political tensions. Similarly, it is imperative to explore the sources of Canadian sport and the way in which these "foreign" influences helped shape a contemporary sport identity.

SPORT IN THE VICTORIAN ERA

Canada was still very much part of the British Empire in the eighteenth and nineteenth centuries. As such Canada's political and social climate was inextricably linked to England.[1] Understandably, then, the development of sport in Canada reflected British sport policy, which, itself, was only beginning to emerge. During this period in British history, there was an increased need to establish a way of regulating popular sporting activities.[2] Previous attempts – by both political and religious factions – to control these popular forms of entertainment entailed restricting the events. These attempts were limited, however, in their effectiveness, although they did impose an ongoing process of negotiation and coercion, and ultimately modified these popular pastimes.

By the early 1800s, the English working class had grown in size and strength, forcing the existing hegemony to seriously consider working-class existence as a threat to power. With the events of the French Revolution still ringing in their ears, the bourgeoisie attempted to repress any challenge to authority. Of growing concern to the ruling classes was the increase in "free time" available to workers as a result of an industrialized workplace; this, in turn, produced "unprecedented material affluence" and an "expanding sphere of leisure time" (Jarvie and Maguire 1994, 12). The concept of leisure was not in itself threatening, for capitalist thinking and the church recognized the value of less oppressive work schedules and healthier working and living environments as a way of ensuring a more productive and devout working community. The perceived "danger" was that people assuming more control over their non-Labour-targeted hours would likely turn to the immodest, but traditional, pastimes of dance and drink (Wheeler 1978, 192). The ruling classes soon realized, though, that the successful maintenance of hegemony could be achieved not by denying leisure activities, but rather by influencing their expression; in this way they could successfully control how the majority of people experienced leisure.

To maintain control of working-class recreation, dominant groups sought to incorporate leisure activities that were culturally relevant, but lacking in the unruliness and so-called immorality of traditional pastimes. The ruling classes sought to establish activities that would reinforce the bourgeois values that validated the existing power structures (i.e., political, religious, and gender hegemonies). Among the venues best suited to these objectives were popular sporting pastimes (i.e., football), once considered socially unacceptable and anti-bourgeois, but now suddenly deemed a "social cement" and a "useful safety-valve" (Hargreaves 1986, 34). As well as being a highly valued means of entertainment for the working classes, these sporting pastimes could be easily co-opted as the embodiment of a British, nationalistic, patriarchal and bourgeois culture. In essence, the dominant classes appropriated the popular form of entertainment they had failed to abolish on several occasions (Bourdieu 1993, 342)[3], using it as a disciplinary measure. For those working-class males permitted to participate in these activities, sport evidently provided a viable alternative to time spent working in unsuitable working conditions. It also provided a vehicle for both individual and collective fulfilment, made possible through industrialization.

One must realize, however, that the incorporation of sporting activities into the dominant culture necessitated a sanitizing process. Such a process saw traditional forms of play altered – in some cases drastically – and stripped of the "rough play" that often involved heavy alcohol consumption and extreme violence. The games traditionally played were loosely organized events located in unspecified physical spaces. Generally devoid of official rules and/ or governing bodies, they had no definite time frame (Jarvie and Maguire 1994, 12). If dominant classes were to assume control of these cultural performances, it was essential that the performances be regulated. Thus the concept of vernacular sport was replaced with an "elaborate system of regional, national and international organisations," in which sport "became more specialised, bureaucratised and its values oriented around individual achievement" (Jarvie and Maguire 1994, 12–13). This regulating process did not, however, result in working-class activities being incorporated into the dominant framework; instead, the success of regulated sport in Britain transformed these activities into a bourgeois pastime, one suddenly denied to the working class. What was initially an attempt by the oligarchy to *share* in these activities now became a divisive enterprise, which saw working-class activities become the exclusive property of the dominant classes.

The development of sport in Britain comprised – and still does, as it continues to develop – many complexities and individual circumstances unaccounted for in this simplified presentation of events. I have stressed the unfolding of these developments in a tripartite structure involving repression; incorporation; and, finally, segregation. To illustrate this threefold process, let us turn briefly to the development of football in Britain, which, in its original form, was perceived as a threat to the social order. Eileen Yeo explains that football prior to the eighteenth century was "a traditional Lenten sport played on Shrove Tuesday and Ash Wednesday" (1988, 138), often involving over a thousand participants. She adds that the game consisted of carrying (not kicking) the ball across *town*, and that games were seldom decided "in less than 6 hours of rough horseplay, brawling and drinking up and down the public streets" (1988, 138). Undoubtedly, the customary gathering of a riotous mob greatly worried both government and church officials. Not only could such an immense mass of individuals not be controlled, but the footballers, with tempers and spirits already high from the drinking and playing, were perceived as posing that much more of a threat to revolt. Measures were needed, it was decided, to prevent these events from occurring.

Officials soon recognized, however, that the abolishment of this so-called game could be a formidable task. Initially, the dominant classes curtailed these events so as to physically prevent people from participating. Laws were constructed that banned such events, and areas were policed to ensure that laws were upheld. However, local populations reacted violently to these measures. As John Hargreaves writes, situations often "developed into battles between a section of the local populace and troops and constables" (1986, 23). Hence, the first stage of the development of football was well underway when authorities committed themselves to repressing all football activity. But resistance to this initial stage was overwhelming, and it was not long before an ulterior means of dealing with this "dangerous" behaviour was implemented.

The stringent measures against playing football soon produced more tension than the actual games themselves. The decision was made to remove the aspects of the sport deemed threatening to the established order of society, rather than try to abolish the games themselves. In order to make this possible, football was incorporated into the dominant culture, where the games could be properly regulated and behaviour controlled. In effect, the game of football, scrubbed of its violence and brutality, came to be understood as a successful method of social control. The affinity the poorer classes had with the game made it easy for the dominant classes to attract participation; with football as a highly disciplined and orderly affair, the game came to embody the desired principles of the existing hegemony. By acting on the desires of the people and providing them with a regular diet of football (or any other sport), the dominant classes could apparently fulfill people's wants, while providing a much needed alternative to life within the workplace. Moreover, through the incorporation of football into mainstream activities, employers could monitor their employees' behaviour outside the factories; church officials could monitor their parishioners' so-called free-time; and government officials could deflect the implied threat to social order posed by unruly mobs.

In fact, the strategy to incorporate football into the dominant culture had such positive results that the sport soon became the exclusive property of upper middle-class males. Because the game idealized a model, masculine, bourgeois Victorian sensibility, the game was soon seen as worthy only of the British elite. Suddenly, the brutish vernacular game of football had been transformed into a "gentlemen's" activity that prepared young males for the ruling classes. And these skills were not required of working-class individuals. Playing a school sport was "conceived as a training in courage and manliness, 'forming the character' and inculcating the 'will to win' which is the mark of the true leader, but a will to win within the rules" (Bourdieu 1993, 343). Football required individuals to work well as a team, to display qualities of team leadership, to develop physical superiority and a certain ingenuity – all of which now became highly valued. As well, schools adopted the game as a vehicle for expressing Christian morality and British nationalism, and, soon, the football "tradition" – as it was conveniently called – had become an institutionalized endeavour, completely removed from the streets of its origin. Thus was British sport heritage built on "a class-divided society" (Baker 1979, 242) – one that accentuated rather than healed its divisions.

To reiterate: while this representation of the transformation of football from a potentially subversive vernacular game to an institutionalized bourgeois activity may be oversimplified here, these sporting developments were undoubtedly the result of a dialectical process that shaped a British sport identity. In effect, what might appear to have been a deterministic tripartite process was, in reality, an intense struggle between dominant culture and emergent or residual cultures. Both sides employed a series of compromises and coercive techniques. In effect, then, the development of sport as a hegemonic process entailed the constant modification of power relationships in order to secure ruling-class dominance. In addition, the threefold undertaking described here was a dynamic process. In fact, out of the final stage of segregation would come another stage of incorporation, one that emerged due to class resistance and the economic value of sporting contests.

SPORT HEGEMONY IN CANADA

The influences of British imperialism on sport development in Canada were obviously critical in shaping Canada's sport identity. For one thing, only the British elite participated in organized sport; the working class and various ethnic groups such as French Canadians were excluded: "Avant les années 1890, une minorité de francophones partage avec ses concitoyens de langue anglaise le goût du sport" [before the 1890's, a minority of francophones shared the taste for sport with their English-speaking countrymen][4] (Janson 1995, 31). This does not suggest, however, that Canadian sport is simply the product of British sport policies. In fact, as stated at the outset of this chapter, much of Canadian sport is the product of the early settlers' conscious rejection of a British sport identity. This resistance is made clear by the discarding of certain sports and their replacement with other more local forms of play and, subsequently, a sporting repertoire more suitable for Canadians. Ironically, the process involved in establishing sport in Canada as a prominent Canadian institution virtually mirrored what was taking place in Victorian England. As a result, although the content of Canadian sport differs from that of Britain, their development and ideological value have proved to be analogous.

As with British sport history, two very distinct forms of play manifested themselves in Canada by the mid-nineteenth century: the lower working class engaged in forms of vernacular play, while the upper middle classes engaged in more organized sports such as cricket and curling. This vernacular participation is highly noteworthy. Sport historians have tended to suggest that the lower classes did not engage in these more modern, formal forms of play because of lack of "time" to play. The Howells, for instance, argue that "the common man, forced to work for others for his living, had little time for recreational sport" (1981, 55–6). It is true that working-class individuals could rarely engage in organized sport because of the specified time frames in which games were played; however, the lower classes were not denied access to the realm of play. In fact, vernacular play was intricately woven into the fabric of the working-class and peasant society and was deemed highly valuable to both individual and community life (Gruneau 1988, 12).

Acknowledging that sport was a valued pastime for a much larger segment of the population is important for two reasons. First, it dispels the notion that only the wealthy were involved in these forms of sporting activities; second, it indicates that a general interest in sport existed alongside the desire to participate in recreational events. The measures taken by the bourgeoisie to implant organized forms of play into working-class life can thus be perceived as a response to a desire evinced through mass participation in vernacular games. But the ensuing bid to remove time constraints for the working classes was not simply a move to allow people to engage in indigenous sporting pastimes; rather, the so-called play was seen as a positive way of creating a healthy labour force. Thus, work schedules were altered, the thinking being to allow for more consistent "participation in exercise and sport," which would correct the "pallid appearance of the working man" (Howell and Howell 1981, 56) and, ultimately, introduce a means of maximizing work productivity. Ironically, it was the more indigenous vernacular games, not the organized games imported from Europe, that came to represent what was soon to be constructed as a truly Canadian sport heritage.

In effect, what took place was a process whereby vernacular forms of play were appropriated from the working classes by Canada's elite, and ultimately reintroduced to the working classes, but in the form of organized games. The games initially played by merchants, soldiers, and governments officials were games that had been played in Europe and gradually imported into Canada. Games such as cricket and curling, which exemplify the so-called civilized British and Scottish forms of play, contrasted with the "crude" and "dangerous" indigenous games that originated in North America. Alan Metcalfe explains that members of the upper and middle classes were perturbed by the often crude and violent nature of Canada's vernacular games; organized sports such as cricket served as a suitable alternative, then, to these improper exhibitions (1987, 17). But attempting to establish cricket as an official sport of Canada involved more than simply the introduction of a game; it was an attempt to maintain British hegemony. Hegemony, however, is never static and, despite the powerful reactionary measures implemented by Canada's upper and upper-middle classes to establish cricket as Canada's national game, cricket never gained the popularity hoped for by the colonial aristocracy.

After reaching its highest levels of popularity in the 1860s, cricket – and subsequently a uniquely British ideology – was successfully challenged by the pressures of "social change." The dominant culture within Canada was suddenly forced to respond to new emergent cultures and their desire to establish a Canadian identity, rather than one imported from Britain. Emergent groups within Canada, recognizing the value of using sport as a vehicle for establishing national pride and unity, ultimately appropriated what was essentially a British means of establishing these goals. In effect, the ideological significance of one sport (cricket) was rejected and replaced with an alternative sport seen as relevant to the Canadian population. Thus, even while Canada was officially being born as a dominion, Canadian businessmen – such as Montreal dentist George Beers – had begun a movement that strove not only to "express a clear sense of their own Canadianness" (Gruneau and Whitson 1993, 41), but to return to the "folk" and to discover Canada's sporting identity; the movement also sought to reject all previous negative perceptions of these vernacular forms of play. Indigenous games, rather than being perceived as uncivilized and improper, were suddenly seen as reflecting the brutal conditions of life in Canada and, thus, as character-building experiences. Indeed, Beers advocated lacrosse as a game built on the "Canadian" experience. Lacrosse was viewed as a game that "reflected the harshness of their [the early Canadian settlers] environment and was used as a vehicle to gain momentary escape from a life of hardship and toil" (Metcalfe 1987, 16).

The political motivations behind the movement to incorporate the game of lacrosse into the dominant culture were simply astounding. Lacrosse itself – an appropriation of a game called "baggataway" that was played by Canada's First Nation Peoples – was the perfect vehicle for resisting British hegemony and establishing a new "Canadian" identity. In 1867, George Beers made no

attempt to conceal the ideological worth of lacrosse, nor his political agenda to champion it as the new national game of Canada.
In fact, he overtly articulated his efforts in a series of articles that
not only enthusiastically supported the playing of lacrosse, but also
argued against those who supported cricket as Canada's national
pastime. Articles such as "A Rival to Cricket" and "The National
Game" generally expressed the same sentiment as that in the following passage taken from the *Montreal Gazette*: "As cricket,
wherever played by the Britons, is a link of loyalty to bind them
to their home, so may Lacrosse be to Canadians. We may yet find
it will do as much for our young Dominion as the Olympian games
did for Greece or cricket for our Motherland" (Beers 1867). For
Beers, the game of lacrosse served as the perfect metaphor for the
tenuous existence of living in Canada's hinterland; the physical
demands of this aggressive and often violent game embodied what
Beers envisioned as truly Canadian.

Up until the end of the nineteenth century, lacrosse was being
touted as Canada's national game. As well, through Beers's initia-
tives, exhibition games were set up in Britain not only to show off
Canada's new game, but, more importantly, to show off what it
meant to be Canadian. The exhibitions themselves were greater
"inventions" than this newly constructed Canadian identity. In
order to make the lacrosse metaphor complete, for example,
matches were staged between Canada's sporting elite and selected
First Nations Peoples decorated in ceremonial dress. One description of this carefully constructed event is as follows: "The teams
played sixteen games during their month-and-a-half swing through
Ireland, Scotland, and England. The order of ceremonies was
repeated for each match. The natives were escorted to centre-field
in their playing costumes, which consisted of red-and-white striped
'guernseys' (jerseys or tunics) and knickers, with white hose; blue
velvet caps overlaid with much ornamental bead work and topped
by two or three scarlet feathers ... In addition all the natives wore
earrings and many silver-coloured rings" (Morrow 1989, 60).
Morrow also noted that when not playing the games, the aboriginal
players were encouraged to remain in their costumes and were
"urged to hold snowshoe races on the grass, to dance 'war dances'
or the 'green corn dance,' or to hold mock 'pow-wows'" (1989, 61).

There is a certain irony in this expression of "Canadian nationalism" since baggataway was initially perceived by Canadian sportsmen
as reprehensible, behaviour not only unfit for gentlemen to engage

in, but dangerous in that it posed a threat to British colonialists. Legends of First Nations Peoples using baggataway as a means of overthrowing British power are rampant. Morrow recounts the tale of the Fort Michilimackinac attack on 4 June 1763 as follows: "The two teams conspired to use the contest to mask an intended attack on the British fort. Having drawn the officers out of the fort to view the game, at a prearranged signal Ojibwa charged the fort, killed over seventy soldiers, and took many others – including Alexander Henry – prisoner" (1989, 46). It was precisely this subversive aura surrounding the game that appealed to Beers; if used properly, he believed, the subversiveness of lacrosse could serve as the perfect vehicle to challenge British dominance, allowing the new emergent culture to prevail. But in order for lacrosse to become a vehicle for this so-called new Canadian agenda, the game had to be seen as a suitable pastime for the bourgeoisie. In fact, the development follows the already delineated threefold process – repression, incorporation, and segregation.

The transformation of lacrosse from an indigenous vernacular form of play to an institutionalized pastime illustrates the process of incorporation rather well. In this case, the game was drastically transformed – baggataway no longer existing as such and lacrosse emerging as the property of Canada's sport enthusiasts. In essence, the game of baggataway was colonized. Or as Beers put it: "Just as we [Canadian colonialists] claim as Canadian the rivers and lakes and land once owned exclusively by Indians, so we now claim their field game as the national field game of our dominion" (1867). In order for Beers to incorporate lacrosse into bourgeois culture effectively, the vernacular characteristics of baggataway, all remnants of aboriginal influence, had to be erased. Unlike other indigenous games, lacrosse was redefined through written rules and regulations that removed all undesired aspects of the vernacular game and gave it a uniform and easily identifiable structure. The game of lacrosse was no longer the property of First Nations peoples; it had quickly become a symbol for a new Canadian identity. But once again, the consequence of incorporation is apparent: rather than bringing two disparate cultures together, it actually enhanced the existing division between the First Nations peoples and the new Canadian elite.

It should be noted that although the result of the incorporation of lacrosse was the segregation of cultures, and ultimately of classes, this segregation process was not passively accepted. The rejection of First Nations' and later working-class players from league play did not stop these players from playing lacrosse. Both groups resisted being barred from the game, and their impact was clearly felt as they repeatedly challenged upper-middle class teams for supremacy in the sport.[5] However, this resistance was met by further restrictions, introduced to better regulate who could play and who could not. To achieve this, lacrosse league officials cleverly focused on the very qualities that had once made lacrosse a desired cultural expression: its rough and often ferocious nature. Violence was suddenly presented as not only a detestable remnant of the First Nations' influence on the sport, but as something that persisted because of the participation of First Nations' and working-class teams. In order to remove the violence, it was decided that these two groups must be barred from the sport.

To ensure this divisive step, and to make the sporting coup complete, league officials introduced the discriminatory framework of amateurism, thereby removing all remaining participants "unworthy" of playing this Canadian game. Their argument was based on the notion that "the incidence of disputes, violence, and undesirable conduct on the field of play could mean only one thing – some players were not gentlemen. The truth of this observation was given substance by the presence of Indians, who always played for money and, by race alone, could not be gentlemen" (Metcalfe 1987, 195–6). Therefore, amateurism – which evolved from the principle of prohibiting the payment of money for play to a "discriminatory system based on money and/or occupation"[6] (Metcalfe 1988, 47) – guaranteed that only English-speaking males with enough money and leisure time to engage in play would be able to compete. Despite measures introduced in the 1850s by some employers to shorten the work week, thereby allowing employees to engage in play on Saturday afternoons (it was forbidden to play sport on Sunday), the working class had little time to participate in organized sports and recreation (Howell and Howell 1981, 111). Organized sport was now geared strictly to people who did not play for money, and who also never accepted monetary value of any kind for playing, coaching or teaching, or organizing a sporting competition (Metcalfe 1988, 47).

The result of these regulatory measures ensured an exclusive membership, at least for a temporary period in the sport community; that is, a white, male, English middle- or upper-class hegemony.

In effect, while the British hegemony was successfully circumvented, a new hegemonic structure had been introduced that was, in essence, identical: a class-based sport program that legitimized its existence through participation in these events. But this period of absolute power was brief. The measures taken by early Canadian sport enthusiasts were unable to withstand the changes taking place in a period of massive social and economic change.

If the success of lacrosse in Canada was achieved by marketing it as the game of the people, thanks to the implementation of amateurism by Canadian sport officials these same people were quickly excluded from the game. Despite repeated attempts to gain access to the sport, entrance remained difficult. Those unable to play responded by participating in a new, exciting, and more accessible alternative: hockey. Unlike lacrosse officials' rejection of professional interests, hockey organizers took an alternate route. They succumbed to the lucrative potential of professional sport. By the twentieth century, therefore, lacrosse had lost its national appeal and hockey had taken on the mantle of Canada's national game (Morrow 1989, 67).

THE BIRTH OF HOCKEY

Pinpointing the actual birthplace of ice-hockey[7] is a contentious matter and, to date, no consensus has been reached. It is generally agreed, however, that "hockey-like" games have been played for centuries. The debate thus hinges on the actual point in time at which the game became what we presently understand hockey to be. Only then can the site of the first game be established. Various theories exist, identifying places such as Montreal, Dartmouth, Windsor (Nova Scotia), or Kingston as the place where hockey was originally played. Other investigators argue that Canada's First Nations' youth have been playing "hockey-like" games since the seventeenth century.[8] Records show that Huron boys played a modified form of lacrosse on the ice that had many similarities to the game of hockey. But as Donald Guay correctly states, "Ce n'est pas le hockey que l'on joue" [it is not hockey that they were playing] (1989, 34). In fact, both aboriginal peoples and European settlers were playing several games that involved hitting a ball with wooden sticks. As with this First Nations game, however, these were more closely associated with their original forms – lacrosse, bandy, shinty, and hurley – than with hockey.

Over time, these earlier games were modified, such that a new game developed. Although the exact moment when the game was "born" is still unclear, hockey historians usually agree that the first "formally" played game of hockey took place in Montreal, on the third of March 1875, and involved a group of McGill University students at the Victoria Skating Rink. It can be argued that this date is somewhat superficial, since the rules drawn up for this "new" game derived from a host of pre-existing sports. In essence, hockey was bricolage, a series of sporting pastimes re-ordered and recontextualized to better suit athletes whose landscape was frozen six months of the year. Neil D. Isaacs explains that when "the game [hockey] was described by the McGill University *Gazette* in 1877, the word 'checking,' borrowed from lacrosse, was used for the first time. And when W.F. Robertson and R.F. Smith codified the first set of rules at McGill in 1879, there were other borrowings. Robertson used terminology from field hockey ... and they transferred many of its rules to ice, incorporating rudiments of lacrosse and polo, while the 'on-sides' aspect allegedly was borrowed from rugby" (1977, 25). Clearly, the game of hockey was the amalgamation of a variety of vernacular and modern games formulated to fit the regional climates, landscapes, and sensibilities of Canadian males in the nineteenth century.

In addition to simply appropriating these more informal games, however, the students of McGill helped initiate a process by which the game became more structured, bound by rules and regulations, more solidified as an organized sport. In turn, the men from McGill were able to standardize play by agreeing on standard playing surfaces, equipment, and rules, thereby establishing the necessary order for "play" to exist. Consequently, the first public exhibition in 1875 of *one localized version* of the game of hockey had a miraculous effect: official recognition of hockey as a legitimate sport in Canada. Suddenly, what was once a vernacular pursuit, existing "only through its variant forms of localized play" (Simpson 1989, 171), became a game played by those who could afford (in terms of money and time) to occupy themselves in more instutionalized forms of leisure. Once again, however, there was fierce public resistance to the suddenly exclusive nature of hockey. In addition to resistance by working-class, French Canadian, and aboriginal groups, a new and emergent entrepreneurial sector of the population was challenging the amateur athletic hegemony. Hockey, unlike lacrosse, evolved alongside the emergent economic climate in Canada. An entrepreneurial spirit crept into the game, thus paving the way for a drastically modified Canadian sport milieu.

PROFESSIONAL HOCKEY IN CANADA

The incorporation of sport into first British, and later Canadian, bourgeois society was made possible by introducing sport as a vehicle for social control and the promotion of proper, masculine bourgeois values. By the turn of the twentieth century and with the increase of industrialization in Canada, however, two basic discoveries were made. First, through industrialization and the shorter workweek, people now had more opportunity to participate in formal leisure activities. Second, active engagement in formal leisure activities meant a new population of consumers willing to spend dollars in this rapidly growing leisure industry. Emergent capitalist principles were encroaching on traditional bourgeois values, and sport ideology in Canada was forever changed. Significantly, tremendous pressure was put on "amateurism throughout the twentieth century," along with the increase and development of "commercialized leisure and entertainment opportunities" (Gruneau 1988, 30). Speculators quickly sized up the game of hockey as a lucrative commodity. In order to capitalize on the emerging mass consumer markets, it was essential that there be a reassessment of the value of sport.

By the early 1900s, the ideological implications of sport had drastically altered and the dominant classes had begun to legitimize their interest in sport in terms of capitalism. Resistance to amateurism was no longer restricted simply to those who wanted to play the games; it came as well from spectators who wanted to see the best players on the field. More importantly, fans wanted to see their teams win. And that desire ultimately led to the payment of professionals. With a deep labour-pool eager for action and an already established fan base, sport was transformed from a pastime into a financial enterprise. Profit-making became the focus of sport in Canada and professional hockey teams quickly became "incorporated." The new corporate identity of professional hockey was realized.

The early stages of the "professional revolution" saw players reaping the rewards of what was clearly an open market. The introduction of professionalism spurred the development of a variety of professional and semi-professional leagues that needed talented players to sell their product. The first professional hockey league was the International Hockey League (IHL), which ran from 1894–1907. Around this time other leagues emerged, inadvertently creating a bidding war for the players and subsequently driving one another into financial ruin. Thus, without any regulatory measures, players would simply play for the team that paid them the highest salary. This quickly bankrupted smaller markets and often the leagues themselves. Out of this came the Canadian Hockey Association, organized late in 1909, which "set out to regulate salary expectations and made an attempt to clean up the professional game" (Simpson 1989, 86).

After many failed attempts and the birth and death of many teams and leagues, cartel structures were put into place to ensure minimal economic competition between parties with shared sport and economic interests. By 1917, with the formation of the National Hockey League, professional hockey was well on its way to becoming one of the most lucrative sport enterprises in the world. The success of the National Hockey League was made possible for the simple reason that the cartel structure put into place by owners and the league allowed the NHL to establish a monopoly of the hockey industry, dating from 1926.[9] The dividends of such an arrangement are enormous, for the implementation of a cartel returned power to the owners, while seriously reducing the players' bargaining rights. As a result, league officials and owners secured absolute control over all aspects of their product. With this control, however, came a total abuse of power. The NHL and various team owners agreed on terms that gave them autonomy over every aspect of their business. And as Rob Beamish points out in this lengthy passage, there were many benefits reaped by the owners as a result of their monopoly:

They have the power to determine membership in this exclusive league. Competition for facilities such as stadiums, parking, and food concessions is also reduced. Owners have sole access to live and televised spectator markets and they can work out various revenue-sharing schemes to maintain the stability of the league. The team owners' monopoly position enables them to influence the media concerning how sport is covered and at the same time the owners can decide, as a group, how they will market their product – is it a spectacle of speed, skill, or violence, for example?

Finally, the monopoly position enjoyed by the owners allows them to establish the length of the season, the number of exhibition games, the timing and length of training camps, and the structure of post-season play. (1988, 143)

The advantaged position of owners produced, in turn, a long history of player-worker exploitation which, until recently, has gone unchecked.

One of the few works that attempts to expose the exploitative history of the professional hockey industry is David Cruise and Alison Griffiths's book, *Net Worth: Exploding the Myths of Pro Hockey*. Much of *Net Worth* focuses on the establishment of the Players' Association – the National Hockey League Players' Association (NHLPA) – and the collective attempts made to empower the players in this exploitative labour environment. Cruise and Griffith trace the progression of player representation to the contemporary labour situation in hockey. They contend that although the status of the professional hockey player is much improved, power still lies with owners, who use such noble terms as "loyalty" and the "love-of-the-game" as weapons against player empowerment. As stated earlier, one of the benefits of a monopoly is the ability to control perceptions of a product through media and marketing. In the case of professional hockey, the game has been mythologized to the point that professional hockey players are immersed in what is likely the most profound contrivance of dominant culture in Canada. Martin Laba points out that hockey in Canada has come to signify the very heart and soul of Canadian existence; that it ultimately serves as a Canadian myth, as a narrative that portrays the game as "a natural outgrowth of the daunting challenges of Canadian geography and climate, as organically rooted as snow, ice, forest, prairie, rock shield, and the myriad of the country's other geographic and climatic facts" (1992, 343). The implications of playing professional hockey are enormous, as the players become active agents in the perpetuation of a constructed mythology, created not only by the media, but by hockey corporations who remind us daily through the presentation of their product (advertising, franchise paraphernalia, game broadcasts) that hockey is a cultural institution of great value to Canadians.

What then could be more desirable than these players fulfilling their boyhood dreams, and helping to express what it means to be truly Canadian, just by playing hockey? Similarly, how could players rationalize resisting an occupational opportunity that magically reaffirms an already troubled Canadian identity? How is resistance even possible, when the players believe that they are fortunate individuals participating in a wonderful game that serves as an organic outgrowth of Canadian culture, geography, and climate? According to Cruise and Griffiths, when budding hockey superstar Eric Lindros pronounced that he "won't be dictated to" and warned, "don't go off on some belief that I'd play the game for nothing, because I wouldn't" (1991, 356), he generated as much anger and outrage from hockey fans as he did from owners. Moreover, these so-called selfish sentiments of Lindros are not commonly shared by many players. They, too, have bought into the mythology of Canadian hockey. Or, as former professional hockey player and current AHL head coach Bob Carlyle explains: it is essential that players play for "the love of the game and play for the fun of it, not the money part of it," and that one needs "passion for the game" to be able to "just come in and play, and sometimes play when you're not healthy. Sometimes play not looking at the money aspect of it" (Carlyle 1997).[10] Despite the existence of players' associations and players' agents, the romantic perceptions of hockey in Canada, and of sport within the larger North American context, keeps professional hockey hegemony intact.

From its earliest stages, the domain of sport has been highly contested terrain. Its value is immeasurable, as it served, and still serves, as a vehicle of subversion, social control, recreation, regional and national identity, political as well as capital gain, class unity and class division, and popular entertainment. Out of these various configurations has arisen a Canadian sport identity that tends to be defined through the game of hockey, which in essence is the amalgamation of sporting (vernacular and formal), cultural, political, and capital interests in Canada. The game's multifarious origins have made its ownership both impossible and ubiquitous. And thus, it is claimed by all Canadians. The sport has been a means of empowerment for the lower classes, in that the games provided people with the opportunity to participate in a universe that was constructed and governed by the people themselves. The affinity the masses have had with hockey has also made it advantageous for existing hegemonies to assume control of sporting activities, thereby removing any potential threats to its existence and, once acquired, serving as a means of coercion. The overwhelming "love of the game" has prevented participants from being excluded from the sport. But at the same time, the "love of the game" has enabled dominant groups to establish public involvement on their own terms.

As hockey has developed into a commodity, it has taken on a whole new set of meanings that are quite removed from its specifically Canadian framework. More particularly, although hockey is undoubtedly Canadian, the game of *professional* hockey is undoubtedly corporate. The professional game is a business and a literal manifestation of capitalist exploitation. The huge profits and powerful corporate players running business operations have left the players struggling to retain some form of control of the game and, in turn, of the labour process. But as will become evident, the players have constructed their own "system of meaning," their own "meaningful universe" (Dunk 1991, 159) through their struggle for autonomy; this has allowed them to function outside the corporate and business world of sport. The upshot is that they have successfully constructed a world where they are morally and intellectually dominant yet, much like the ostrich with its head in the sand, highly vulnerable. In the following chapters, I explore the constructed universe of one professional hockey team and the ramifications of existing within this exclusive domain.

CHAPTER THREE

The Meaningful Universe of Professional Hockey: The Ethnography

A professional hockey game is a shared event between three primary groups: the participants, the fans, and the owners. Each party is integral to the sport's existence, and their relationship to one another is both conflictive and symbiotic. Yet despite being essential to one another, each party experiences the event uniquely and ultimately transforms it into something other than the basic sporting text. For the owners and associated corporations, professional hockey is a vehicle for financial development: it is a commodity. For the fans, the game is spectacle: a dramatic event where people generally cheer for the same victorious outcome in every performance. For the players, however, hockey is both a performance and a vehicle for financial development. But more importantly, it is a means for occupational survival. The players' success or failure in the sport dictates their place within the labour process, and, in this highly competitive environment, stability is rare to non-existent.

In order to gain an understanding of this community as it is experienced by the players, I spent seven months studying the team in its working environment. Much of the ethnography focuses on the players while they were at practice, as opposed to during the games. During these more informal periods, it was possible to observe the players – not only working on their skills to prepare themselves for games, but also interacting with one another in a more social manner. I sat right next to the players' bench, where I could hear them as they conversed with one another; I was able to observe how the players collectively and individually responded to the tasks the coaching staff had assigned to them; and, quite simply, I watched the players as they interacted formally and informally with one another. When looking for information about the job or about their individual situations, I approached the players after practice and asked them questions. Only two times throughout the season did a player not comply with my request.

Throughout this chapter and the following two, I present information that reflects my observations over the course of the seven-month research period. I also discuss the players as seen engaging in their profession. I have limited these chapters primarily to description so as to provide readers with a deeper understanding of details of the trade and the players' roles within the labour process. Within this descriptive discourse, there is an emphasis on hockey as a "real" lived experience, as opposed to merely a game or a form of entertainment. I have therefore chosen to focus on those behaviours that tend to separate the players from those individuals outside this occupational dynamic.

I must add that I have limited the next three chapters primarily to what was observed in my first week out in the field. I made this decision for three reasons. First, detailed descriptions of the patterns of behaviour specific to this occupation are needed so readers can comprehend my more general observations made over the course of the seven-month period (discussed at length in chapters five, six, and seven). Second, the occupational demands are largely repetitive – schedules and daily routines are preplanned and followed rigidly – which means that a discussion of the team's weekly routines speaks roughly for the entire season. Finally, because my first week in the field was the most intense, I was able, after additional time and reflection, to sort out and balance those initially vivid details of my surroundings. It is important to stress that the remaining seven months of fieldwork research was not discarded; I have used this knowledge as the basis for the final three chapters, which present a closer inspection of the players and the constructed universe in which they work.

THE AMERICAN HOCKEY LEAGUE

Before considering the team studied for this project, we must first examine its overarching professional league. As stated from the outset, I made the decision to study an American Hockey League (AHL) team because of its close affinity to the National Hockey League (NHL) – the dominant professional hockey league worldwide. It would have been virtually impossible for me to gain access to an NHL team because of the intense fanfare and media attention each receives; the AHL, therefore, was a convenient alternative. But in order to acquire a proper understanding of the AHL players' status as professional hockey players, we must look at the relationship between the AHL and NHL. The AHL was the product of a union that took place in 1936 between two nearly defunct leagues, the Canadian American League and the Canadian Professional League. Although the AHL produced some exceptional teams that NHL Hall of Fame player and coach Al Arbour has claimed were as talented as NHL clubs,[1] the AHL has always been understood to be a minor league which, for the players at least, functions as a means of entry into the NHL (Halloran 1986, 24).

Up until the 1970s, the two leagues operated separately from one another. But with the formation of the World Hockey Association (WHA) in the 1970s and its attempt to usurp the NHL's hockey monopoly in North America, the AHL's existence was suddenly in jeopardy. The WHA began poaching players from the AHL, draining all the talent from the league, and forcing the NHL to intervene to protect its own interests. Various NHL franchises began purchasing AHL franchises so as to strengthen AHL player stocks, and, in return, the NHL used the AHL as a developmental league, or "farm system." The parent organizations eventually assumed financial responsibility for signing the majority of AHL players to contracts, which relieved struggling AHL teams of the burden of paying their players. In return, the NHL clubs owned the rights of the players and could call them up to the parent club at any time. This move ultimately provided the NHL with more depth, while offering further protection from the WHA's attempt to challenge hockey supremacy.

Since merging with the NHL, the AHL has gone from six to nineteen teams, located primarily in central and eastern Canada and the United States. The diversity of players has also increased, which means the percentage of Canadian-born players continually decreases as the professional hockey market globalizes. In 1999 approximately sixty-eight percent of AHL players were born in Canada; fifteen percent were born in the United States; and seventeen percent were born outside of North America (primarily Russia, Sweden, Czech Republic, and Finland). As the AHL grows, so too does its relationship with the NHL; while NHL parent clubs continue to provide the necessary financial framework for teams (especially in smaller markets) to exist, the AHL continues to serve as the dominant developmental system for NHL teams. The Recent statistics from the AHL indicate that sixty-seven percent of NHL players at one time played in the AHL, and that by "next season the AHL will grow to include an unprecedented 22 teams, all of them primary NHL affiliates" (*Canoe* 1998). It is the close NHL-AHL association that attracts players to the AHL, and this despite the marginally higher average salaries players can receive playing in the International Hockey League (IHL), one of six other minor professional hockey leagues.

In North America approximately 2300 active, professional minor league players play in a range of professional leagues. The AHL and the IHL are the two premier leagues in terms of talent, financial compensation, and status. During the 1999–2000 season the AHL average salary was approximately $55,000 (US). In the IHL, players made approximately $60,000 (US) a year.[2] Along with higher salaries, players in these two leagues also receive benefit packages quite similar to those within other occupational contexts. Each league provides players with individual pension plans, worker's compensation, and a variety of insurance coverage such as medical, dental, and life insurance made available to the players through the Professional Hockey Players' Association (PHPA). This association was established in 1967 to serve as the sole bargaining agent for certain professional leagues not represented by the National Hockey League Players' Association (NHLPA), an association geared exclusively to NHL players.

In addition to the AHL and IHL, the PHPA represents one other league: the East Coast Hockey League (ECHL). The ECHL marks the beginning of the third tier of professional hockey. As the calibre of hockey declines, so, too, do the players' earnings: the average ECHL salary for the 1999–2000 season of $15,682 (US) was substantially less than that of their AHL/IHL counterparts. Players in the ECHL do, however, receive many of the benefits received by AHL and IHL players, thus placing them in a better position than the remaining 1100 players in the Central Hockey League, the United Hockey League, the West Coast Hockey League, and the Western Pro Hockey League. Salaries in these leagues are comparable to ECHL salaries, but players are without any labour protection and have little to no bargaining power. In fact, of all professional hockey players, those in the CHL, UHL, WCHL, and

WPHL have the most precarious existence, as well as the most limited opportunities for advancement.

Because careers are generally short-lived, the issue of salary is an obvious concern for minor league players. The American Hockey League, the focus of this study, is the optimal minor league to play in, yet the average age is only twenty-three. Indeed, of the 430 AHL players in the 1999–2000 season, only eighteen were over the age of thirty, which means players have limited time to break into the National Hockey League. But the odds against this happening are great. Players more often than not cannot move beyond their minor league status and must retire early from the game, or, in the odd case, extend their careers in the AHL (or another minor league) or in one of the European leagues.[3] Thus, the majority of minor league players never gain access to the enormous financial packages received by the NHL players. Compared to the NHL average salary – for the 1999–2000 season it was just over one million dollars (US)[4] – minor league salaries are low and players do not have the financial security often associated with professional athletes. This makes it that much more critical for players to take advantage of the close ties that exist between the NHL and the AHL. This also explains why the AHL continues to be the most appealing minor league in which to play.

Undoubtedly, the minor leagues should not be mistaken for the NHL. Each league has a history and identity of its own and each is a league unto itself. Yet having said this, it must be understood that the AHL, in particular, is an extension of NHL hegemony, in that its primary function is to produce a surplus talent pool from which NHL organizations can feed. The team studied for this project, the Troy Reds, is a team typical of any other AHL franchise in terms of payroll and talent. But it is also a farm system for one of only six Canadian organizations in the NHL. Clearly, then, the AHL cannot be fully discussed apart from the NHL, despite the distinctions between the two.

ENTERING THE ARENA
OF PROFESSIONAL HOCKEY

My experience with the Reds began officially on Tuesday morning, 22 October 1996. That first day, extremely anxious and apprehensive, I had no idea what to expect. Al Jones, the Reds' athletic therapist, had told me that the team practised every morning between ten and twelve and that I should introduce myself to him on that particular day. He said he would be the only one standing behind the players' bench at the beginning of practice and would have time to talk to me. At 9:45 a.m., I entered the arena, my backpack containing the indispensable notebook, pens, a hand-held tape recorder, and two sixty-minute tapes. I waited in the stands for Jones to arrive. A few players were already on the ice, stretching and playing with pucks, seemingly oblivious to my presence. The rest of the arena was empty, except for maintenance staff and one other gentleman, who did not appear to hold any official position with the team.[5] After selecting a seat down by the Reds players' bench, I tried to *see* a professional hockey arena, as if for the first time.

I should state, briefly, that before entering into this fieldwork setting, I had worried, as an ethnographer, about the dangers of conducting research in an already familiar environment. Having grown up within a hockey culture, I was already acquainted with the professional hockey landscape. What would it be like entering this domain now, from a researcher's perspective? How effective would I be in this role? Much of my uncertainty dissipated, however, as I entered and slowly took in an environment that I had never really questioned before. By simply introducing myself to this setting that I had taken for granted for twenty years, I was suddenly seeing it again, as neither member, nor stranger. Comfortable in my unfamiliarity, I soon found myself scribbling notes about this extraordinary environment.

My plan was to scan my surroundings without getting up, and to record whatever images entered my field of vision. Soon the layers of advertising that littered the building overwhelmed me. The arena itself was literally saturated with corporate advertisements and/or promotional strategies. Encircling the uppermost level of the building – where the walls and ceiling meet – large fluorescent signs trumpetted forth such messages as Don Cherry's Restaurant, Molson Canadian Light, Canadian Tire, Hostess Chee-tos, Chrysler, Pepsi, and Labatt's Blue. On the walls below were still more signs, among them the Molson Cup Three Stars Award and the Chrysler AHL Standings boards. These last served as focal points, not only because of their size, but because of the significant information each contained. Moving down into the aisles and sections, one could see, emblazoned on each individual stair, the word "Subway."

Above the ice were penalty boxes, their backdrops advertising Thrifty and Re/Max Real Estate. The boards surrounding the ice were similarly filled with company advertising, running the gamut from Dominion, Tim Horton's, and Molson, to the Royal Bank, and many other more local corporations. The ice surface, the locus of all activity, had a corporate presence inserted between the Reds' logo and the circles and lines necessary for playing the game of hockey. Present, too, were advertisements from the local mall, the telephone company, and The Gym.

After sifting through all the corporate imagery, I was drawn next to the enormous clock cum scoreboard suspended from the middle of the stadium's ceiling, over centre ice. Shaped somewhat like a cube, the clock/scoreboard has four identical vertical sides. It displays the progression of time during the game, the current score of the game, and the penalty situation of each team. When games are not being played, as on this particular morning, the clock/scoreboard emits only a red digital reading of the time of day – 9:52 – with all other areas of the board unlit. As I considered the current time, the significance of this ominous scoreboard began to dawn on me: I had entered a cultural context that was "out of time."[6] During the context of a hockey game, the tiny red digital reading of standard time is erased, replaced by a large, bright white digital reading of "hockey time," which governs behaviour for three twenty-minute stop-time intervals. As the significance of this literal and symbolic sign impressed itself upon me, I realized that my perceptions of my environment had begun to be shaped by the other-worldliness of my surroundings.

I looked to the sheet of ice where more players had gathered to begin their warm-up routines. The ice seemed almost magical after the warm October day I had left on entering the arena. Its shiny bluish-white surface with its symmetrical lines of blue and red was almost surreal. In fact, it was a simulacrum, in that it represented ice in its appearance and texture only – all stadium ice is actually an advanced formula of water, chemicals, and temperature transformed into an ice-like surface that its manufacturers argue is better than *real* ice. Jet Ice, for one, claims that its "thinner ice with a faster freezing surface ... produces less snow and improved hardness," which is not only good for the ice, but for the customer who enjoys "improved energy bills and easier maintenance" (Jet Ice). This "perfected" ice-surface became even more surreal when I realized that the winter-like conditions existed at a time of year incapable of supporting a frozen landscape. It is here, then, in a world that defies the order of time, and where nature has been successfully reinvented and perfected, that the players are engaged in the labour process.

By this time I had seen Jones standing behind the players' bench and was waiting for an appropriate time to approach him. Although by now a bit more relaxed because my presence seemed of no concern to anyone, I was nevertheless apprehensive about approaching Jones. Not only did I not want to interfere with his work, I did not want the coaching staff – who had already expressed concern about my presence – to think I was interfering with Jones or the practice. At a moment when he did not appear to be busy, I stepped up to the bench and introduced myself to Jones. Shaking my hand, he asked if everything was okay. I said yes and explained that I would just be sitting, observing, and taking notes for the first few days. I told him of my wish to acquaint myself with the surroundings before I approached anyone with questions. He said that was fine and that if I needed anything, or needed to talk to anyone, he would help me out. He told me that the team had a game that night so practice would be relatively short. He also said that if I wished to come to the game, I should knock at his door by 6:45 that evening or give him a call just prior to coming, to make arrangements. I thanked him, saying that I would be going and would see him later. I could think of nothing else to say, so I left and returned to my seat. I sat back down with a sense of relief for the encounter had been relatively casual. Realizing that my relationship with the Reds was precarious, I was comforted knowing that my actual presence had not jeopardized my uncertain status.

Just before 10:00 a.m., the entire team moved onto the ice, along with Head Coach Dennis Murphy and Assistant Coach Sam Dig. The players were wearing full equipment and their practice jerseys. On the front of the jerseys was the team logo; on the back was CCM lettering, more corporate sponsorship. As the season progressed it became apparent that every visiting team that played against the Reds had either this corporate sponsorship emblazoned on the back of their practice jerseys, or a Bauer logo.[7] At ten o'clock, coach Murphy blew one short, loud blast on his whistle, and the practice officially started. The players immediately skated to the centre-ice circle and fell down on their hands and knees. A fellow teammate led the group in a series of stretching exercises. Although brief

murmurs of discussion and occasional laughter were heard as the
players stretched, they seemed for the most part somewhat uninterested. As if detecting the group's lethargy, the individual who led
the stretches started slapping his stick on the ice, calling out loudly,
"Come on boys!" Getting up from the ice, the players responded
with brief cheers, echoing the initial encouragement, and skated into
position for the first warm-up skating drill.

PRACTICE DRILLS ON GAME DAY

The first skating drill had the players skating hard up the middle
of the ice and turning either left or right once they reached the far
end of the rink. Having eased up and caught their breath on the
turn, the players then skated along the boards back to their starting
point. They then converged again up the middle, before sprinting
back up the centre of the ice. During the drill Assistant Coach Sam
Dig yelled encouragingly to "pick it up!" and the players
responded, putting their heads down and pumping their legs to pick
up speed. At 10:07 this drill ended, followed immediately, after two
brief commands by Dig, by another drill.

The frequency of the drills – which during a ten-minute span
began at 10:13, 10:17, 10:19, 10:21, and 10:23 – produced a
driving intensity. One drill ended, only to allow another one to
begin. The transition from one drill to the next meant stopping the
players, informing them of what was wanted next, and getting them
into formation so the next drill could begin. The players rarely
stood still, moving with minimal instructions such as Murphy's
holler "Red in this corner and white in this corner here!" As if by
instinct, the drills were carried out.[8] A generic name – "flow-drills" –
is given to these types of drills, designed to keep the players in
motion at all times. The drills involve the players skating with the
puck, passing the puck, and then receiving the puck "on the fly"
in some patterned fashion.[9] I was amazed at how complex the drills
appeared – some I had never seen before – yet they were performed
with incredible fluidity.

One drill in particular seemed always on the verge of chaos,
although it was performed with such precision and timing that it
rarely broke down. Although I have attempted to explain the drill,
readers are advised to see Figure 1 to appreciate the illusion of
chaos that the drill creates.

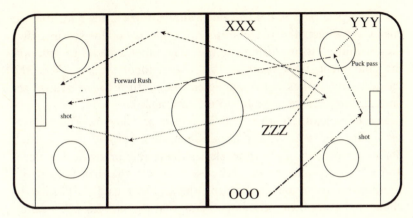

Figure 1
Illustration of a complex flow-drill.

The drill was carried out from both sides of the rink. For the sake of clarity, however, I will focus only on the one group (consisting of players X, Y, Z, and O). The players divided up into four sections: one section located along the high boards (designated X in Figure 1); a second section in the corner of the same high boards as section X (designated Y in Figure 1); and a third section on the middle of the blue line (designated Z in Figure 1). Another section was located directly opposite players X, alongside the boards across the ice (designated O in Figure 1).

The drill began with player O coming down along the boards and shooting a puck at the net (a goaltender in the net tries to prevent player O from scoring). Once the shot is taken, player O circles away from the net and heads up the ice along the opposite boards. As he turns up the ice, player Y passes a puck which player O receives on the fly. Players X and Z go into motion at the same time as player O shoots the puck. Their routes are basically a criss-cross pattern: player X skates into the end zone and just before reaching the face-off circle, he turns away from the boards and skates up towards the centre-ice area. Player Z skates into the same end zone but turns towards the boards so the players pass one another as they make their turns. The timing here is essential in that as they begin heading up the ice, player O must receive the pass from player Y. Once the pass has been successfully received, player O, who is directly behind players X and Z who are rushing up the ice, passes the puck up to one of the rushing forwards. Player O then joins the rush after the pass is made, which allows for a three-man rush to ensue. (In effect, the players are executing an offensive rush that they would perform during a game.) The line then tries to score on the goaltender, who waits at the other end of the ice. Once the scoring attempt has been completed, they return to the group, get back in line, and prepare to do the drill again.

The complexity of this drill is in fact an illusion. The players really only have to worry about their own specific role. If each player starts at the right time, skates the rigidly predefined pattern, and effectively passes and receives the puck, the drill is virtually foolproof. The intent of the drill, then, is to create an illusion of chaos and complexity, the hope being that the players will confuse their opponents and thereby overcome any line of defence their opponents can muster. However, the element of surprise has been seriously undermined in professional sport since the introduction of videos (teams gather before every game to watch videos of their opponents). Reds defenceman Steve Toll, in an interview later in the season, explained to me that with the video and TV, "we play back a lot of our games and find mistakes that we don't remember all the time. And we look back and check over the mistakes and go over them and try to correct them, and work on them ... maybe before the game on Tuesday and Wednesday. [If] we have a team coming in, we'll look over some of their players and watch a little bit of the video tape of what they do – say on a power-play or penalty killing, and, you know, special teams. And we go from there and see what we're going to do against them" (Toll 1996). Despite the fact that the fundamental principle of hockey – to score more goals than the other team – never changes, it has become increasingly difficult to carry this out. Drills must therefore be constantly modified and developed if a team is to maintain its edge over another, or successfully defend against another team's strategies. I was impressed by the team's tremendous efficiency and speed, as I sat watching the series of drills unfold.

THE INFORMAL PRACTICE

By 10:23 a.m., the team had gathered into a circle at the centre of the ice and begun again the stretching done at the opening of practice. The group then broke up. Some players went to the bench to grab a water bottle and talk to one another while taking a drink. Others grabbed pucks and began shooting or performing other manœuvres. Although the coaches remained on the ice, it was evident that the formal, organized practice had concluded and the players now had an opportunity to practise individual skills. Some practised their shots; some worked on their backward skating; some practised passing to one another; still others practised skating in circles and other agility manœuvres. The practice was no longer operating at the high intensity evident under the coaches' direction. Although this was my first practice, my general interest in professional hockey meant that I was already familiar with the reputation of certain players and the roles they played on the team. I took special notice of the veteran starting goaltender, Paul Proux, who took time to go over to rookie goaltender John Dent and, through his mask, say something while Dent took a brief break from stopping pucks. Through Proux's gestures, it was evident that he was offering Dent advice on how he might make a save; Dent nodded his head and Proux skated away. Players resumed firing pucks at Dent, while Proux stood and watched the rookie's attempts to stop the shots.

Individual players began to leave the ice half an hour after the practice had officially started (10:30 a.m.). Although some players remained on the ice, by 10:43 only four players were left, along with the rookie goaltender. The two coaches had stayed on the ice as well and began putting these players through various conditioning drills. Interestingly, the four remaining players wore grey jerseys, with the exception of Dent, while the rest of the team wore either red or white jerseys. The red jerseys were worn by the forwards and the white by the defence. Since the colour of jersey signified the position a player played, I assumed that for some reason these players were not playing in the game scheduled for that night. Jones later informed me that the grey shirts were worn either by players who were hurt and were trying to work themselves back into the lineup, or by those who had not yet made it into the lineup and were working their way onto the team – at this point, they served as extras. Moreover, inasmuch as only one goaltender can play in goal at any one time, the goalie not playing is considered a backup and is automatically assigned to this group. These five players, then, were working to get themselves into game shape and were going through arduous physical conditioning.

These conditioning drills were largely endurance drills, as opposed to the short quick drills worked during official practice time. The players were required to skate as hard as they could for intervals of a minute to a minute and a half. They skated in pairs, which allowed one group to rest while the other skated. The conditioning was deliberately set up to best simulate the physical demands of a game situation. Hockey is a sport that forces the players to exert themselves to their maximum for shifts which last, ideally, for approximately a minute to a minute and a half. As soon as one line exhausts itself, its members return to the bench and another line, fresh and ready to go, steps onto the ice. A professional team usually has three primary lines, as well as a fourth line, sometimes referred to as a "utility line," which generally serves more of a defensive, and occasionally an intimidating, role. Players therefore have about five minutes to rest between shifts. The game is essentially anaerobic, which means it requires high-intensity physical activity for relatively short periods of time. These four players in practice were getting their bodies into "game shape" through intensely anaerobic workouts that had them bent over and gasping for breath at the end of each interval.

Even from my seat, I could see the sweat pouring off the players' faces and steam rising from their helmetless heads. At the beginning of each skating session, one of the only two African Canadian/ American[10] players on the team – Ted Simms – shouted encouragement to his skating partner and to the group that followed him. Dent left the ice after about five minutes of skating and headed to the dressing room to join his teammates. The remaining four continued doing drills, with both coaches still present and still yelling encouragement. Head Coach Murphy was the most vocal and called each player by first and last name as he went through the drills: "Come on Pat Smith! Come on Ted Simms!" Both Dig and Murphy engaged in brief banter with the players in-between skating intervals and while the players caught their breath. By 10:53 the players were clearly exhausted and were labouring to maintain any kind of stride. By skating in pairs, however, no one player could stop exerting himself; otherwise, his partner would eventually pass him, create an obvious gap between them, and ultimately make him look inferior. On the other hand, neither player tried to skate ahead of the other; if one partner was slower, the other could keep pace without having to exert himself any more than was necessary. Consequently, the players finished each interval within a few strides of one another, virtually every time.

THE EXIT

Assistant Coach Dig left the ice at 10:58 and Head Coach Murphy yelled, "Okay Todd Jones, that's it!" The players immediately broke from their partners and cooled down in their own way: Pat Smith keeled over and fell to the ice as if completely exhausted; Ted Simms grabbed some pucks and started shooting them into the net; Sid Zeal lay down on the ice and began to stretch; Todd Jones went to the players bench, sat down, and drank water from the water bottle. Seal and Jones were the first to leave the ice and go to the dressing room. Simms then stopped shooting pucks and went to the bench to drink some water. Smith put the pucks that had been shot into the net on top of the net. He then joined Simms on the bench, but at the opposite end. They did not speak and continued to sit as if waiting for something. For close to five minutes, the players sat there just drinking water; at 11:05 Smith got up and went to the dressing room. As soon as he stepped off the ice, Simms followed him out. Practice was officially over.

I have dwelt on this departure in detail because of the overt meaning of this seemingly mundane behaviour. As I watched the players vying to be the last one to leave the ice, I was reminded of a passage from *The Game* in which Ken Dryden articulates wonderfully the significance of leaving the ice last. The passage reads: "Larocque and I are competing again ... So today he is among the first on the ice, and certainly will be the last one off. It is bound to be noticed ... The net is empty. Larocque and I skate towards it, easily at first, then like two kids reaching for the last piece of cake, with disinterested single-mindedness. When I realize that only an embarrassing sprint will get me there first, I angle away and skate to the dressing-room. Larocque has won. But by leaving the ice first, I have reminded him that I am still the number one goalie" (1983, 152). The act of staying longer – even if it is only for a matter of seconds – communicates much to fellow players and coaches. To stay longer signifies to teammates – and it is hoped to coaches – that you want it more than the next guy and are willing to go that "extra mile." At the same time, the ability to leave early, as Dryden explains, communicates power over fellow teammates.

Just as the two players for the Reds vied to be the last player to leave the ice, veteran goaltender Proux did not take any extra practice after the first half hour; moreover, he was one of the first players to leave the ice, while his junior – in experience and skill – remained on the ice trying to prove himself to coaches and teammates. Until Proux's place as number one goalie is challenged, he can decide whether to stay or leave.

I sat and wrote down these and other thoughts before closing my book. The game-day practice had concluded for me as well. But as I mulled over what I had just seen, I became increasingly fascinated by the highly competitive nature of the players. By watching the players practise on this day, I had witnessed the briefest of collective labour tasks demanded of professional hockey players. Game-day morning is used to prepare for the game to be played that night, when the players must raise their levels of intensity. With all this in mind, I began to look forward to reentering the arena that night. The next episode – the game – would reveal a whole new system of meanings.

CHAPTER FOUR

The Game

The Reds' home games – unless played on Sunday – always began at 7:30 p.m. That starting time is quite standard throughout professional hockey. Not only does it allow for those who work during the day to go home before heading off to a game, it also means that parents can take their children along. With the early start, games do not usually extend much beyond 10:30 p.m.

The Reds' games were held in a stadium which, including standing-room, held approximately 4,000 spectators. Tickets ranged from sixteen dollars and fifty cents for a seat, to nine dollars for a standing-room ticket. Because it is an old stadium, one of the smallest in the league, it no longer suits the needs of a professional hockey franchise in the contemporary sport era. In fact, the city of Troy will lose the Reds unless a new stadium is built. Already, the Reds' parent organization had made it clear that if a new stadium were not funded – either publicly or privately – by the end of the team's immediate term in the city, the team would be relocated to another city before the end of the millennium.[1]

THE ARRIVAL

I arrived at the stadium at 6:45 p.m., as Al Jones had suggested earlier at practice. I had been instructed to go around to the back of the arena, to knock at a door, and to ask for Jones. However, there were at least four entrances that could have been the door in question. Unsure which door was the right one and angry that I had not paid closer attention to the instructions, I rethought Jones's directions and vaguely remembered him saying something about "Exit Three." I was relieved to see that each entrance had a number.

To my right was one with a sign that read "3." I knocked on the door and was greeted by a security officer. I asked for Al Jones, and the officer motioned to me to stay put. He walked to another door and knocked. Someone I had never seen before answered and looked at the officer as he called past him into the room: "There's someone here who says he knows ya!" For a few seconds I stood awkwardly in the doorway, until the officer motioned me to come forward. I saw Jones, who gave the security officer a knowing nod, at which point the officer left to return to his post.

Jones stopped his work and came to greet me. Already I felt intrusive. A player who had been lying on his stomach and receiving Jones's attention looked up to see who was being let into the arena. The two other men in the office – equipment manager Joe Sell, and assistant trainer Lou Penn – also eyed me curiously as I stood in the doorway. Jones's greeting did nothing to put me at ease, for it was apparent he was busy. He rushed through more instructions, explaining that because the arena generally sells out for the Reds' games, it was important that I find a place in the standing-room section, rather than a seat in the assigned seating. After offering advice as to the best place, he quickly sent me off in the right direction. I said thanks and after walking past the players' dressing room, through the blue curtains that act as a partition between the Reds' dressing-room area and the public space of the stadium, I headed up the hallway to find myself a spot.

A few paces up the hall was a stairwell that I knew ascended to the standing-room section. At that point I was relieved to be in the arena; although Jones was obviously rushed in his dealings with me, he had been courteous and accommodating. I walked up the stairs and into the upper layer of the arena, where I could overlook the entire stadium. The arena was virtually empty, except for stadium staff and officials and approximately thirty spectators scattered throughout the seating area. I found the spot where Jones had suggested I stand to watch the game. The view was impressive. As mentioned earlier, the stadium is quite small for a professional arena; even from the top level, therefore, I was able to see the ice surface perfectly and still be relatively close to the action. Once again I began acquainting myself with my surroundings.

The stadium was fully lit at this point, unlike during practice when secondary lighting illuminates the ice surface. At my level, I was surrounded by vendors setting up for the imminent onrush of

people. At every corner of the upper level was at least one concession stand, with a variety of fast foods and drinks such as popcorn,
peanuts, pizza, hot dogs, nachos, ice cream, and French fries. In
addition to the concession stands, numerous individual vendors
were stocking their trays with products to sell up and down the
stadium aisles. The obvious point of all this was to allow fans to
purchase food items without leaving their seats during the game.
Some individual vendors were even now attempting to sell to the
few people already in the building. Starting time was still forty-five
minutes away. Upbeat popular music – from country music to the
latest top-forty dance tunes – played loudly through the arena's
sound system. The mood was one of expectancy, as people slowly
began to enter the stadium.

THE GAME PREAMBLE

With approximately thirty-five minutes to go until game time, I
realized I could roam through the building with little interference.
I decided to travel along the top level until I reached the front of
the arena and then venture down to see where the general public
was entering. At the main entrance, a large crowd had already
assembled around the ticketing area. Some people were buying
tickets, while others stood chatting with one another as they waited
for the game to begin. Vendors were selling Reds' programs and
tickets for a 50/50 draw to be held later in the evening. All vendors
wore red aprons and hats in the colours of the Reds' uniforms. A
store called Redswear, directly adjacent to the main entrance, sold
Reds' merchandise. There customers leafed through paraphernalia
associated with the Reds' team: hats, jerseys, track suits, underwear,
sweaters, and T-shirts; children's wear; and posters, calendars,
mugs, and sticks. Although many females were present, both as
spectators and staff, there were more males, and people of all ages
mingled easily.

I worked my way into the crowd and purchased a program published in association with the AHL called *Reds' Magazine*. Every AHL
organization throughout the league publishes a similar magazine,
directed towards its own franchise. The contents of this particular
issue included brief articles on topics ranging from Reds alumni to
humorous individual player profiles. There were also the special
features found in every issue, such as a listing of the Reds' schedule

and team records. Thirty-three of the program's forty-four pages displayed individual advertisements, forty-four in all. The pages without corporate representation contained promotional strategies for the AHL and the Reds. The most interesting was a letter entitled "From the Office of the Mayor of Troy," which read: "As we enter a new year of hockey, it is unfortunate that so much controversy has taken place concerning the Reds and the stadium. The Reds' players are our friends. They have done much to enliven our city and in return they have become very attached to the people of Troy ... I would also like to thank the many sponsors who support their Troy Reds and the charities they support" (1996–97a, 7).[2] Only three weeks earlier, a local newspaper had printed an article in which the author had criticized the Reds' non-presence in the city: "How many Troy Reds stick around the city when the season is over? Besides the stadium and the [local tavern], have you ever seen any of the Reds hanging out around town? ... The Reds are simply a gang of athletic mercenaries, and the entertainment they provide is nothing more than an amenity" (*Articulate* 1996, 8).[3] This kind of critical commentary was not found in the *Reds' Magazine*, it being ultimately a promotional tool for the AHL and the Reds' organization, as well as for the many corporate sponsors. Because the Reds are the focus of the magazine and the Reds' fans consider it a desirable commodity, it has been a highly useful marketing tool.

I eventually made my way back to my standing spot for the game and waited until 6:50 p.m., when the Reds' opponents, the Mustangs, took to the ice for their pre-game warm-up. The Mustang players skated onto the ice to scattered boos from the fans starting to accumulate in the stadium area. The Reds took to the ice one minute later for their pre-game warm-up and were greeted with cheers from the two hundred or so fans. Each team performed various warm-up drills at its own end of the ice. The two warm-ups were similar, in that they consisted of a variety of shooting drills that had the players stretching out and the goaltenders loosening up. Although the drills were intended to establish the flow achieved during practice, they were extremely basic in order to guarantee the players high levels of success. The drills took various shapes but all basically achieved the same end: long shots on the goalies; shots on the fly from the slot area; and three-on-two drills, in which the goalie had three attackers coming his way while two defencemen tried to prevent a shot on goal. The warm-up lasted for exactly twenty minutes, timed by the giant clock that hung above the ice surface. The clock, fully lit at this point, was dictating the opening events. After warm-up, the players left the ice and the Zamboni arrived to begin cleaning the surface. Again, twenty minutes came up on the scoreboard and a countdown started. The game would get underway at the allotted time.

It was during this twenty-minute interval that the fans began to pour into the arena. As the crowd swelled, announcements sounded over top the popular music, which had increased in volume. The announcer, on behalf of the Reds, thanked the corporate sponsors and, more specifically, a list of approximately ten sponsors for their support. Then, after the corporate acknowledgments established by the American Hockey League, the announcer read a number of regulations directed to the fans. Loosely paraphrased, the message was: "The American Hockey League requires us to inform you that anyone found using foul language, consuming alcoholic beverages, or engaged in unruly behaviour will be asked to leave the premises."

Television sets dotted the top level where I was standing, situated roughly thirty feet from one another. The televisions would air the local community channel's coverage of the game, thereby allowing spectators to watch aspects of the game they could not see live at the stadium; for example, a replay of the action, or a moment missed because of something or someone obstructing their view. This evening, as highlights were shown from the game the night before, excitement stirred the crowd. The fans continued to pile into the arena. Just before 7:30, the secondary lights were turned off, illuminating the ice surface still further and setting the stage for the teams' arrival on the ice. The Mustangs, the first to step out onto the ice, were booed vociferously; I heard screams of warning around me: "Watch out Jones! You're gonna get it tonight!" These jeers were quickly replaced by a booming cheer as the Reds skated out onto the ice. As they entered, a voice boomed over the loud speaker: "Here are your Troy Reds!" and the song "Welcome to the Jungle" by heavy rock band Guns N' Roses blared from the speakers. My own experience as a hockey player had shown this to be a popular accompaniment to a team's initial appearance on ice. And it continues to be a popular anthem for many professional teams as they make their grand entrance. As the

fans of Troy came alive to the thrashing beat of the song, they
called out to their favourite players skating round the ice in a last
warm-up effort before the game got underway.

For less than a minute, the players sprinted around their halves
of the ice in clockwise fashion. Then all the players – except for
each team's six starting players – went to their respective benches.
Both teams' starting players lined up on their respective blue lines,
the two goalies standing in the vicinity of their nets and the game
officials positioned along the centre red line. All awaited the national
anthem. Because both teams were from Canada, only the Canadian
national anthem was sung, in both English and French. The speaker
announced the anthem, explaining that "tonight's national anthem
is provided by [local sponsor]. To sing our national anthem is
[female singer]." Before the last line was sung, the fans broke out
into cheers, making it barely audible. The anticipation had reached
its peak: the anthem was concluded; the red carpet unrolled for the
singer was rolled back up; the players assumed their respective positions; and the referee blew his whistle, raising his arm to call the
players to the opening face-off. The puck was dropped, prompting
the players into action. The game had officially begun.

SEEING THROUGH THE SPECTACLE

My intention here is not to relate the game, but rather to direct
attention to particular events that help explain the nature of this
occupational endeavour. Because of the sheer spectacle of sport, it
is easy to forget that those actually playing the game are engaged
in an experience that to them is very real. For the players, success
or failure is not simply one team winning or losing, but the very
basis by which their occupational identities and, in turn, their
livelihoods are defined. Because the ramifications of the game differ
so greatly for the players and fans, the game is naturally experienced in completely different manners. I was struck by this dichotomous experience when a man about fifteen rows below me yelled
at Reds forward Jerry Wall, "That's it Wally, kick his ass!" He
wanted Wall to seek revenge on a Mustang forward for an incident
that had occurred in a previous game between the two teams.[4] With
the fans encouraging him, Wall skated over to the Mustang player
and attempted to draw him into a fight.

For the fans, Wall's actions were simply part of the hockey spectacle. Perhaps more than any other sport, hockey is a physical game that often relies on violent behaviour as a means of defeating an opponent. Consequently, if a player throws a bodycheck at another player, it is not uncommon for the player who receives the check to retaliate. Tempers often rise and shoving matches and fist fights may result. Fans, from the safety of their seats, are accustomed to this violence; it is a fundamental element of the spectacle of hockey. For the players, however, violence is real: the act of beating someone up, or getting beaten up, is not staged or fabricated; the players suffer real consequences for their actions. I do not wish to imply that the players are not conscious of the performative value of their behaviour. But their performances are only a means to a highly tangible end. The stark division of experience caused me to interpret the events in terms of this dichotomy.

In this particular incident, a fight did not occur. The Mustang player rejected Wall's challenge. But the Mustang player's refusal to fight angered the fans, who screamed at him for not facing the battle; it also served to validate Wall, who had successfully stood up for a "just cause." The incident was not over for the players, however, as they continued to batter one another physically and endure the hostile conditions of the game. The many fans, when not screaming for vengeance, were now purchasing sodas and popcorn, clapping to the music during stoppages in play (stoppages of *time*), and participating in the antics of the Reds' mascot, "Chester." The presence of Chester succinctly articulates the disparate experiences I am attempting to describe.

Chester is a person dressed up in a bird's costume, his enormous head accentuating his already absurd appearance. He wears a Reds jersey over his costume and his job is to move through the stadium, providing humour for the fans and prompting them into cheers. On this night, he had throngs of children following him wherever he went, and during lulls in the game's action he actually stole the fans' attention. I watched this intentionally ridiculous figure gyrate his hips to the popular songs playing over the speakers and, at one point, fall atop a glass partition that wedged up between his legs, leaving him writhing on the ice in agony (fabricated, I hope). The humour generated by his wild antics and surreal persona contributed to the whole carnivalesque atmosphere. His presence suspended reality for the fans: not only did they accept his presence, but they enjoyed engaging in the physical dialogue he created.

I use the term "carnivalesque" deliberately here, drawing from Mikhail Bakhtin's discussion of medieval carnival in *Rabelais and His World*. In this work, Bakhtin introduces the term "ritual spectacle" for events such as carnival pageants and "comic shows of the marketplace" (1968, 5). He describes this ritual experience as a period of collective mockery and absurdity in which participants are both the subjects and the recipients of the joke. In contrast to romanticism, medieval carnival is a celebration of grotesque realism where the essential principle is degradation; that is, "the lowering of all that is high, spiritual, ideal, abstract; it is a transfer to the material level, to the sphere of earth and body" (Bakhtin 1968, 19). The exaggerated and absurd bodily imagery is not individualized, however. Rather, it is shared: "This laughter is ambivalent; it is gay triumphant and at the same time mocking deriding. It asserts and denies, it buries and revives" (1968, 11); yet "it is also directed at those who laugh" (1968, 12). As the carnival participants lose themselves in the laughter and the spectacle, the carnival becomes a lived experience embraced by all. According to Bakhtin, there is a profound effect of this collective laughter: it "expresses the point of view of the whole world; he who is laughing also belongs to it" (1968, 12); that is, festivals offer people the means of seeking harmonious union with the world around them.

Whether these wondrous celebrations provided the healing function with which Bakhtin has credited them is questionable. But it has been argued – largely from within an earlier Freudian framework – that the absence of medieval carnival has left a void. By the nineteenth century, a new Victorian sensibility had characterized the value of these celebrations as grotesque and absurd; gradually, they were pushed to the periphery of society. The once celebrated behaviours of carnival were suddenly seen as too vile and extreme for the bourgeoisie, and, consequently, images "of bodily life, such as eating, drinking, copulation, defecation, almost entirely lost their regenerating power and were turned into 'vulgarities'" (Bakhtin 1968, 39). The catharsis brought on by the collective laughter of grotesque realism was no longer possible, and "many of the images and symbols which were once the focus of various pleasures in European carnival have become transformed into the morbid symptoms of private terror" (Stallybrass and White

1986, 174). Perhaps it is an overstatement to claim that the banning of carnival has prevented the masses from achieving oneness with themselves and with nature; it is nonetheless evident that the desire to celebrate the carnivalesque has remained.

This paradoxical situation, where society is both disturbed by carnival and longs for it, has encouraged the substitution of mimetic glimpses of carnival in its stead. These glimpses, referred to as "sentimental spectacles" (Stallybrass and White 1986, 183), were more temporary activities and were *viewed* by the general public. A shift had occurred: the only reputable involvement in these activities was that of the spectator, and laughter was directed *at* the performers not *with* them. In a contemporary context, it is the sporting event that provides us with the mimetic glimpse of carnival, the sentimental spectacle. It is important, however, to make the distinction between the spectacle of modern sporting events and the ritual spectacles that Bakhtin describes in *Rabelais and His World*. Today, no ritual or healing significance attends the sporting event; it is spectacle in the purest sense of the word, signifying "tastelessness and moral cacophony" (MacAloon 1984, 246). But it is because these forms of behaviour are suspect and regarded as being outside of proper bourgeois values that they arguably satisfy, at least temporarily, the voyeuristic urge of the masses.

Of critical significance, here, is the spectacle nature of professional hockey. Here the athletes represent the essence of the spectacle of the sporting event, yet at the same time are psychologically removed from it. Mind you, the players' behaviour is "spectacular" only in the larger sporting industry context, that is, their performance on the ice makes the spectacle possible; their experience is hardly "spectacular." Whereas the actions on the ice serve to provide the audience with the mimetic glimpses of carnival, the actions more immediately serve to satisfy the demands of labour. However outrageous or exaggerated the behaviour may at times appear to those outside the game, the ramifications are real, and the players' livelihoods depend on them. Clearly, the spectacular nature of hockey is an exoteric construction, one outside the players' frame of reference.

This dichotomous experience revealed itself wonderfully to me as I witnessed Chester the mascot's status dissolve as he left the framework of the spectators and attempted to make contact with the players. For the fans who laughed and shared in the banter

Chester provided, he was "real." But for the players returning to the ice for the third period, Chester was invisible. The players skated right past him, intentionally refusing to acknowledge his presence, despite Chester's offering of an outstretched arm for the players to "high-five" him on their way out onto the ice. The parodic figure was a wonderful juxtaposition to the players, whose intense physical and mental activity was hardly frivolous or facetious. For example, the Reds' goaltender, Proux, at the beginning of each period, just before play gets underway, stands in his crease, bent over, head down, talking furiously to himself. In this crouched position, he moves his feet back and forth, as if skating on the spot, and bounces rhythmically to each shuffling leg. This ritual is done each game, three times a game, as his teammates skate by him and touch him ceremoniously with their sticks. Each player has a specific spot(s) on the goalie to touch; each has a specific manner in his approach to this touching; and each will touch the goalie a specific number of times.

It is important to realize that the players are the focus of the circus-like atmosphere, but at the same time are removed from it. To emphasize this juxtaposition still further, the coaches walk past Chester onto the ice, wearing suits and ties. Those players not dressed for the game wear similar formal attire. The players' demeanour on the ice, their clothing, their passion, all express the seriousness of the "playing" of hockey. Yet I perceived this almost as a contradiction to the intensity of the jocular tone within the stadium. The carnivalesque qualities that surround the game are misleading, as they poorly represent the occupation of hockey. Thus, while it is important to acknowledge the spectacular nature of hockey, I would be doing a disservice to the players if I pursued a study of their occupation in this vein. For this reason I have chosen not to dwell on the carnivalesque nature of the game, although as an outsider watching from the stands, I must at least acknowledge its presence.

It may be difficult for people to look at grown men wildly chasing a rubber puck around artificial ice – and beating one another up in the process – as anything other than spectacle. But if we return to the initial example cited, of Jerry Wall attempting to seek retribution for the previous night's infraction, perhaps we can shed some light on the matter. First, it needs reiterating that the more extreme the behaviour on the ice, the more that behaviour tends to function as a heightened form of entertainment for the fans who, as in the last example, are heard screaming for the vengeance Wall can only give them by proxy. But as Wall talked about the events in an interview with me the next day, he described his theatrical behaviour in pragmatic terms. He began by reminding me that at the end of the previous night's game, "the guy jumped me, and did what I call a gutless move." It was this move that provoked the following response:

It was my first shift of the night. It was an icing call and he [Mustang player] went back to touch the puck. And I came up right beside him and said "Let's go."[5] There were no officials around, and I called him on. I went up to him face-to-face and I said "Do you want to go?" And I asked him a few times throughout the night if he wanted "to go" and he just left. And I don't know if he was backing down or if he had some sort of situation that he got suspended. I'm not sure, but you know, it's not always going to happen in one game. You just put it in the back of your mind, and then you can get the guy ... I wanted to get it done on my first shift of the hockey game, but you know it just never happened with him. Obviously he didn't want any [laughs] part of it. But I am sure, you know some time – I mean we play these guys twelve times throughout the season and it will happen some time. (Wall 1996a)

But in addition to "paying" the player back, Wall discussed the significance of his actions as contributing to his success as a hockey player: "I think it is something I have to do, to create my own room on the ice. You know, I'm not the greatest skater and I'm not the worst skater. But certainly if I can do that kind of stuff it gives me more room on the ice, and you know, they're not going to come and bump me and get in my face as much. So if I create those kind of situations, hopefully it will make some other players back down; we don't want them to get away with stuff like that" (Wall 1996a). Violence on the ice can be seen as a highly expressive text that may help establish a player's identity, assert a player's presence on the ice, or serve as a means of retribution. But violence always serves a utilitarian function. Without violence, Wall would be largely ineffective on the ice and would likely not have a position on the team. For the fans, however, violence is an extension of the game they pay to watch; it has no physical bearing on their lives.

The dichotomous relationship I am stressing here becomes even more apparent if we consider a specific point in the second period of the game. The Reds were leading the Mustangs by a goal, and the tension from the initial ruckus in the opening minutes had subsided, leaving a certain complacency among the fans. Suddenly a shot deflected off a Reds player's stick and travelled right into the stands, hitting a woman directly in the mouth. The woman's head dropped into her lap, while a man beside her began frantically waving his one arm in search of aid. With his other arm, he was trying to console the woman. When she lifted her head from her lap, it was apparent that she was bleeding profusely and was in tremendous pain. The crowd watched in horror as the woman received first aid attention; all that was heard was the quiet murmuring of the audience. The play on the ice resumed in normal fashion, but I could see that at least seventy-five percent of the people at my end of the arena were watching with concern as the woman was treated and, finally, taken away.

As I watched all this take place about a hundred feet away from me, I thought about an earlier incident in the period. Reds defenceman Colin Best was knocked to the ice by the punch to the face he had received while fighting a Mustang player. The fans' response to this incident could best be described as that of disappointment as they witnessed a player from "their team" lose a fight. The significance of this response did not register until later, when I was comparing it to the crowd's reaction to the unexpected blow to the woman's face. There had been no noticeable concern that Colin likely would need stitches to repair the cut on his face. Yet even if the severity of the woman's wound was greater than that of Colin's, it seems that the shock expressed by the crowd was more because the woman should never have been hit in the first place. Colin, on the other hand, as a professional hockey player stepping onto the ice, willingly opened himself up to the intrinsic dangers of the game. The fans, from their supposedly sheltered vantage-points, felt they were paying to see the ramifications of players' voluntarily placing themselves in this predicament. When the two worlds collide, however, the result can be devastating: the horror with which the fans watched this woman in her predicament is the horror of spectacle and reality coming together as one.

PLAYER PERFORMANCE

As the game continued to unfold, the players busily attempted to execute the strategies they had been practising throughout the week. The game moved at a ferocious pace, and the players were forced to perform to their utmost potential. The score was tied halfway through the first period. Coach Murphy was on the bench, reinforcing his players, but also reprimanding those who erred, using deliberate physical gestures such as finger pointing or waving his arms as if in disbelief. The Reds at this point in the season stood high in the standings; they also had a better record than the Mustangs, which meant that they should have been ahead in the game. Failure to do so meant contending with angry coaches and an unforgiving media, and often the ridicule of spectators. Repeated unsatisfactory play meant changes; ultimately, certain players would lose their jobs.

This game, while played with sufficient intensity to allow both teams to remain competitive, lacked the emotion evident on other nights. The Reds were expected to win and, at this point, were meeting expectations. Scoring opportunities were few, but when they occurred a goal generally ensued. As the game progressed, it became apparent that Murphy was encouraging this "boring" style of play, a style without risk. The players were playing a close checking game and only attempted to score on opportunities provided by the Mustangs – in other words, they sought to capitalize on Mustang mistakes. Murphy is a former NHL hockey player who is relatively new to the coaching scene. His playing career was based on a defensive, disciplined game, and his limited success had been made possible by a strong work ethic, as opposed to exceptional skills. It is not surprising that his team used a similar philosophy when they frustrated the Mustangs who, all night, were unable to generate any kind of offence.

The Mustangs' frustration as a team was gradually expressed through individual actions. These actions – such as players and coaches losing their tempers and subsequently acting out in outrage, both physically and orally – need further consideration. The first incident – the verbal assault of the referee by Mustang head coach Paul Martin after a dubious call made against his team – is a familiar scene in hockey, one in which the coach, while standing on the players' bench, puts a foot on top of the boards and leans to the ice hollering at the top of his lungs. In most cases, the referee, or whoever is being verbally accosted, ignores the barrage of name-calling and criticisms and the coach regains his composure after a few seconds. In this particular situation, however, Martin continued to scream until his face grew red; he proceeded to the doorway which led onto the ice, as if he wanted to physically attack the referee. At that point the referee saw that Martin was completely out of control and that his behaviour had to be stopped. The referee called a double-bench minor penalty on Martin, which meant that his team would have to play with a player short for the next four minutes of the game. His outburst did not change the referee's previous call; moreover, the Mustangs were worse off because of the additional penalty minutes they had to serve.

Why then did Martin unleash such a relentless attack upon the referee when he was aware of the repercussions of such behaviour? It was not as if his team did not have a chance to win the game; they were only trailing the Reds by one goal. Was it possible that Martin actually lost control of his temper and could not prevent such an outburst from occurring? Or was this a staged performance that had a significance other than what I perceived from the stands? For example, was it a motivational strategy? If we look to the next incident, we see the players erupting in much the same way: they became overwhelmed with anger. The situation occurred as the Mustangs were scored upon for the fifth time in the game. Immediately after the puck entered the net, two Mustang players, one after the other, broke their sticks: one over top of the goal crossbar, the other against the glass behind the goal. The player who smashed the glass then proceeded to the bench, screaming at himself – or so it seemed from where I was standing – and later at his teammates who went to the bench after him. Neither player received penalties for his conduct, but their actions were equal to Martin's in magnitude. As I stood and watched these expressive acts that fall outside the players' frame of reference, the players appeared almost childlike, whether sincere or not.

Once again, however, the division of experience was clear. Those watching the "game" (like myself) were seeing it as something outside of everyday life. But for the players, the experience was real; thus, "playing" was real. Despite the work the players put into excelling at their occupation, their trade is based on the premise of play – "activity standing quite consciously outside 'ordinary' life as being 'not serious', but at the same time absorbing the player intensely and utterly" (Huizinga 1950, 13). The players' behaviour within their trade is consistent with this premise; the elements of play have not been removed from hockey even though the players are engaged in highly serious activity and, as play theorists Huizinga and Caillois would argue, are clearly not play-ing.[6] Thus, the extreme nature of their actions was congruent with the playfulness of the game itself, although, as mentioned, the game is the player's reality and therefore subverts the nature of play. In this regard, the player who risks injury to prevent a rubber disk from entering a mesh cage is no more engaged in play than the player who bangs his stick on the ice because he did not score a goal. Yet their actions are motivated by the nature of their occu-pation, which has as its foundation, play. Hence the players, although engaged in intensely playful behaviour, are not playing.

To illustrate further, let us look at the antithesis of the temper tantrum – the elation expressed after making a great play, or perhaps after scoring a goal. When the Reds scored their third goal early in the second period, Reds defenceman Steve Toll skated approximately thirty feet and jumped on Jason Dodd, the goal scorer. After hugging and banging Dodd on the helmet, Toll pro-ceeded to inflict the same affections on the rest of the players involved in this particular scoring play. Could Toll really be that excited by the fact that they had scored a goal, or were his actions staged for motivational reasons? Whether staged or sincere, the point is that his behaviour is consistent with the intrinsic playful-ness and ultimate non-reality of the game, despite the fact that the behaviour stemmed from reasons that were far from playful. Thus, coach Martin can lose himself in an emotional outburst yet, once penalized, is able to recover his composure and carry on with his duties. Or Toll can celebrate a goal with frantic enthusiasm and, two minutes later, be found sulking in the penalty box for taking an unnecessary tripping penalty. The entire game necessitates this seemingly excessive behaviour. If this approach were not in place, the very premise of grown men chasing a puck around contained artificial ice would cease to make sense.

AUDIENCE PERFORMANCE

It was this element of play that seemed to draw the fans into the game. Between periods, while the so-called game was temporarily on hold, the spectators were drawn still further into the world of play by the clever promotional strategies of game organizers and corporate sponsors. Two breaks occur within the three-period structure of a hockey game; they allow the ice to be cleaned and resurfaced while the players go to their dressing rooms to rest and receive further instructions from coaches. These twenty-minute time periods of non-activity are timed by the scoreboard clock. The breaks in the action allow fans to go to the restroom, purchase food or beverages, or peruse the latest Reds merchandise on sale in the stadium. For those who remain in their seats while the ice is being prepared to be cleaned, game organizers have developed various "entertainments" which also promote corporations that financially support the Reds. Contests, for example, have been set up that allow fans to compete for a wide range of prizes. That night, during those forty minutes (two twenty-minute breaks), six games were played. I will discuss the first three, which occurred during the second twenty-minute break.

The first event was a generic contest that has been played during virtually every Junior and professional game I have ever attended. This time it was sponsored by a grocery store chain, but the structure of the event is identical regardless of corporate sponsorship. During the first period two fans had been selected from the crowd through a predetermined selection process; they were taken onto the ice along with a male announcer; a female assistant; and Chester, the Reds' mascot. The announcer, who was wearing a microphone headset, narrated the events to the audience. He and his assistant were wearing Reds track suits. Chester happily harassed the contestants and played to the audience to keep them interested in the events taking place on the ice. The people selected – a middle-aged man and a young woman – were escorted to the centre ice area and introduced to the audience. At the other end of the ice, in front of the goal, two men were setting up a board with three holes cut out at the bottom. The middle hole of the board, which was covered with grocery chain logos and advertising, was larger than the two outside holes.

The object of the game was to shoot a puck into one of these holes from the area where the contestants were standing, the monetary prize being greater if the puck goes into one of the smaller holes. The first contestant, the man, was given a hockey stick, and a puck was then placed on the ice in front of him. The other contestant stood and watched; she would go through the same steps in a few minutes. The contestant holding the stick stepped up to the puck and attempted to shoot it towards the net; however, the puck, although it came close to hitting the hole in the right-hand corner, ended up missing the net altogether. The audience moaned as the puck grazed the outer post. Then the woman was handed a stick and she, too, attempted to shoot the puck into one of the holes. Her shot was straight but without enough speed, and it stopped about ten feet short of the net. Again the fans moaned. The contestants' second shots had some success: the man put his shot into the middle hole while the woman again missed the net. The contestants then agreed to take a third shot, this time playing for double or nothing. The first contestant, who had won fifty dollars on his one successful attempt, was now playing for one hundred dollars; the woman was playing for fifty dollars. Contestant one shot the puck but missed the holes and lost his money. The woman, however, shot the puck straight down the centre of the ice into the middle hole. The fans cheered and laughed at the sudden turn of events. The announcer, having congratulated and consoled them so the entire crowd could hear, directed them off the ice with his assistant. As they departed, two more contestants were on their way in.

The next contest, a more theatrical event, had the contestants competing directly with one another. As the event was sponsored by a regional gas and service-station company, it had a service-station theme. The two contestants – selected in a fashion similar to the first two – were placed on the right- and left-hand side of the ice. Each faced a piece of Plexiglas, a bucket, a squeegee, and a gas tank on the ground. About thirty feet away stood another pail. The contestants were given a jacket, a hat, and a pair of gloves that local service station attendants would typically wear while on the job. The announcer yelled "Go!", the music started to play, and the contestants began putting on the apparel. Once suited up, they walked hurriedly – they are instructed not to run for reasons of safety, though some still do when the announcer's back is turned – to the first station, where they took the squeegee and began washing the Plexiglas. After wiping the glass, they grabbed the gas tank and sprint-walked over to the pail, where they began pouring the contents of the gas tank into the container. Once this was finished they sprint-walked back to where they had started, now the finish line.

The man who was trailing in the competition began to run to the finishing line but slipped, lost his balance, and just barely kept himself from falling. He ended up in second place. The audience, who had been cheering for both, broke into laughter at the slapstick antics unrolling before them. At the conclusion of the race, these contestants, who were competing for twenty-five dollars, shook hands and the announcer announced the winner. After receiving a big round of applause, the contestants were directed off the ice. As they made their way through the doors, a shiny new Chrysler van was driven past onto the ice. This marked the beginning of the last event in this particular twenty-minute break.

The van, after being driven in a circle around the ice, was parked in the middle of the rink, still clearly in view for all to see. A gentleman stepped out of the van and was introduced as the sole contestant for the next competition; he was playing to win the van. As he was greeted by the announcer, he was put into a headlock by Chester the mascot, which seemed to embarrass him slightly. The spectators laughed. As was the case in the first event, a board had been set up at the far end of the ice; this time, though, the board was labelled with Chrysler logos and slogans, along with a centrally located, painted-in goalie, with a tiny hole between his feet. This event followed the same format as the first competition, although this time the contestant had to shoot the puck from about fifty feet further and into only one, tiny hole – the hole being only a fraction larger than the puck itself.

Once again, the contestant was handed a hockey stick and a puck was placed in front of him. Before shooting the puck, the man took time to aim. This time, the fans were more attentive than they had been during the other events, likely because of the enormous odds against winning, as well as the large prize up for grabs. At first, as the puck headed for the net, the fans began cheering in anticipation; seconds later, however, the puck began to curl away from the net, missing it completely. For a brief moment a murmur of disappoint-ment could be heard from the fans, but their moans were trans-formed instantly into cheers when it was announced (as always happens during this event) that Chester, the mascot, would now try to shoot the puck into the hole for the contestant. If Chester could put the puck into the net, the contestant would win the van. Although the contestant had one more chance at winning, his hope this time was riding on the birdlike character with the enormous head. It was not surprising that after much clowning and exagger-ated aiming, Chester shot, fell to the ice, and missed the net by close to ten feet. Once again laughter ensued.

The contestant was escorted back to the van and driven off the ice. Although unsuccessful at winning the van, the contestant seemed to be thoroughly enjoying himself as he waved to the fans. All of this took approximately ten minutes, leaving ten minutes for the Zamboni to resurface the ice. Game organizers, aware of the tedium that results from watching the Zamboni being driven in circles for ten minutes, had instructed Chester the mascot to remain on the ice and create havoc for the Zamboni driver, until the game resumed play.

THE RESULT

The game ended with the Reds winning five goals to three. The players gathered together after the final horn had sounded and shared brief, congratulatory embraces. They were not overly zealous in their praises of one another, and they were not especially elated by their victory. They were satisfied with a job well done and the fact that they had been rewarded with a victory. The Mustangs' demeanour was not much different. They were less emotional than the Reds as they came together to support one another. They had not played poorly and, overall, looked at their performance positively. They had, however, lost. And that is always difficult to accept for the players, who understand winning as the essence of their occupation. I spoke with various Mustang players after the game and asked how they responded to the loss. One player explained that "from a personal angle, it's always tough when you lose. Even sometimes, if you have a real good game, it won't get to you as much as a – well you know, a horseshit game [laughs]. If you have a really bad one, you have a hard time sleeping for a couple of days, until the next game basically. So it's really tough" (Bélanger 1996). The Mustangs' goaltender expressed similar sentiments:

Well, sure it's hard. It's disappointing, but I think I have to concentrate on what I can do on the ice. And I think there's always [a] place for better nights, but tonight, I think I did my job quite okay. We gave up a lot of shots and we weren't lucky. And the other goalie made some good saves. But I just try to concentrate on my stuff. And do what I can do best and that's stopping the pucks – as many as I can … If I think I gave up a soft goal, for sure I'll be mad at myself. But tonight, I was happy with my game – but when you lose, it's always frustrating. For the past two years I had a winning team: we were winning a lot. So when I lose I get mad, but I have to concentrate on what I can do, and if I play well, then that's a big part of my game. (Boland 1996)

The players are well aware that they have a long season ahead of them and their behaviour after the game – both as winners and losers – illustrates the pragmatic approach they take to playing. In winning, the Reds were able to briefly enjoy their success; in losing, the Mustangs were forced to regroup and prepare for their next game. If the losers had been unable to make the necessary adjust- ments and losing became consistent,[7] the losses would take on an even greater significance and the players' jobs would suddenly become precarious. Thus, off-day practice sessions become key. Teams use this time to practise new strategies, perfect the old, and work on physical conditioning so as to be even better prepared to go through the ritual just described all over again. For the Mus- tangs, however, it would be with the intention of achieving a different result – a victory.

CHAPTER FIVE

The Practice on Off-Days

The professional hockey player's week during the season consists essentially of a pattern of two-days stints: the "game-day" and the "off-day." Where these days fall within the week is immaterial, for players' routines are fashioned around whether or not there is a game that particular day. Moreover, the term "off-day" is a misnomer since players do not actually have the day off. Instead, players are required to show up for practice and engage in on- and off-ice activities, such as physical conditioning and group viewings of previous game performances. The term "off" is nonetheless significant, for the practice never goes past one o'clock, and players are generally free to do as they please for the remainder of the day.

The first off-day[1] practice I attended occurred on Thursday 24 October, and I arrived at the rink as I had for the game-day practice, two days earlier. I sat behind the Reds' bench and immediately began taking notes. The players were all out on the ice by 10:00 a.m., stretching under the direction of team captain Darren Feld. Instead of wearing the red and white jerseys of game-day practice (or the grey jerseys worn by those not in the lineup), the players wore white, green, blue, red, and grey jerseys. Again, the grey jerseys were worn by those who were either recovering from injury or were not ready to play in the lineup, while the other colours represented where players "fit" within the team. The white jerseys continued to be worn by the defence, but the forwards were divided into lines, with their colours representing the specific line on which each would play.

The three players wearing red jerseys were on the first line, which meant they played on the team's top line. The blue jerseys were worn by the second line and the green by the third, the numbering

of the players' line corresponding to their status in terms of productive value. Team lines are not permanently fixed, however, as
players who cease to produce on the ice – in terms of scoring goals
– are demoted to a second or third line and replaced by a teammate
who provides the team with an offensive contribution. The division
of skill between lines may not be as great on some teams as others,
but there is enough of a discrepancy on virtually every team to
privilege one line over the next for extended periods of time. The
different colour jerseys demarcate this distinction of status wonderfully: if one line suddenly moves from second- to first-line status,
its members assume the colour of the first line, while the former
first-liners wear the jersey of their new ranking.

LEARNING THE SYSTEM

Once the players finished their stretching, Murphy called out to
the players, who immediately assembled into formation for the
first drill. The drill was basically a warm-up exercise for the
goalies; it involved the players skating up the length of the ice
with a puck and shooting it at the net from the blue line. I noticed
a series of events during this drill that need explication. The first
involved defenceman Toll who, as he skated down the ice, shot
the puck at goaltender Proux. His shot was high and caught Proux
in the shoulder area. The shot was not particularly hard, but its
height and less protected site meant that Toll had broken a basic
precept in hockey, which is to avoid putting your goaltender's
safety at risk. Proux's response was to skate out to Toll with his
stick raised, poised to strike him. I was not sure if it was only a
threat, but as he approached Toll yelled, "Sorry fuck!" He was
apologetic for his carelessness, but also upset that Proux had
taken such an aggressive stance. Proux returned to his net to face
more shots but continued to admonish Toll, who had taken his
place in line to carry out the drill. Less than a minute later, Toll
skated down towards Proux to take another shot; this time,
however, he gently rolled the puck towards Proux, who simply
brushed it to the corner. Toll's exaggerated restraint was his way
of apologizing to Proux in a manner that he could not express
orally. I subsequently wrote in my field book, "Actions make
amends, not words."

Although the off-day drills unfolded as they had during game-day practice, they were generally more physical and more intense. The drills also included body-contact checking, which again increased the intensity with which the drills were performed. A real emphasis was placed on speed and power, and in one drill in particular these two aspects were especially apparent. The drill was straightforward in that there were simply two lines at one end of the rink. In one line forward players faced forwards, while a second line of defence – about ten feet ahead of the first – faced backwards. From a standstill, the forwards sprinted up along the boards, trying to get to the other end to take a shot on goal. At the same time, the defenceman skated backwards, parallel to the forward, until he reached the centre ice area, where he attempted to prevent the forward from getting a shot on goal. As the forward cut to the net, the defenceman tried to physically remove the forward from the puck. Usually that meant a high-contact situation with one or both players crashing into the boards. The drill was highly explosive and, at one point, two players collided with the goalpost, knocking the net and sending rookie goaltender John Dent flying. Ted Right (the elderly gentleman who watched all the team's practices) groaned in excitement at the collision and said to me over my shoulder, "There's no fooling around, is there!"

In order for the drills to be performed at such a ferocious pace, they were all highly repetitive. The drills were designed so that players could repeat the same action over and over again, to the point of performing it instinctually. The rigid patterns and timing forced the players to be aware of their exact spot on the ice at all times, as well as the position of their line-mates. In other words, to allow for optimum team performance, the players practised playing in systems that regulated their behaviour on ice. Because each player is considered a component of a larger system, each individual aspect of the game must be practised until they come together as a whole. By the end of practice, then, drills were conducted in which all the component parts were working as one; this meant performing drills designed to get an entire line and defence pair carrying the puck from one end of the ice to the other, with the intention of scoring.

The precision of player positioning was most apparent in one particular drill. The drill was done without a puck, and without words. Murphy simply pointed to where a hypothetical puck was located, and all five players were required to skate to an exact spot on the ice where they should be if a puck were actually in that area. My field notes contain the following points:

- crucial positioning is being practised today
- one drill positions a line at one end with Murphy, who points to an imaginary puck in a specific position
- the five players skate to the positions on the ice where they should all be at that specific time
- the whistle blows and Murphy points to a new imaginary puck in a new specific location – again, formation on the ice changes
- this is the mechanization of the game that constrains players' actions and thinking. (Field Notes, 24 Oct 1996)

The intent here is to make playing the game as simple as possible by structuring play and, ultimately, making play predictable. As I watched the players come together as one, however, the margin of error was still quite high.[2] In these particular drills, there were only three defenders trying to prevent a goal from occurring, as opposed to the five who would be present during an actual game. Clearly, despite these efforts to make play mechanical and predictable, the realm of possibility in hockey is simply too vast for it to be fully perfected. It is this inability to ever truly master hockey that attracts both players and spectators to the sport, and it is for this reason that repetition in practice can never be fully exhausted.

What I have described as the "realm of possibility" needs further clarification if readers are to comprehend how the game of hockey defies pure structure. I am referring here to the insurmountable number of variables that present themselves in any playing situation and that simply cannot be foreseen in their totality. The variables in hockey – running from a rough ice surface that causes a pass to run errant, through human error, to a player simply seeing a better situation arising and making an alternative play – force players to make creative decisions on the ice. If these creative decisions cannot be made, the players will achieve limited to no success. An example of this was the short career of Reds forward Woody Stevenson in the NHL. As a player for the Reds, Stevenson had been an exceptional talent and highly exciting to watch. During the seven games he played in the NHL, however, he was virtually invisible on the ice and had no impact at all on the team. It was not surprising, then, that he was sent back down to the Reds after only a month with the parent organization.

Given the many factors that contribute to a player's success or lack of success in professional hockey, I was particularly interested in Stevenson's comments about his stint in the NHL. As Stevenson explained to the reporter in the *Reds' Magazine*, it "may be easier to play in the NHL because the game is more technical and everyone knows their job. There is less uncertainty, in a sense there is less mistakes" (1996–97b, 29).[3] The obvious irony here was that although the game was easier for Stevenson, he was demoted back down to the AHL because he did not provide a positive contribution to the NHL club. Moreover, on his return to the AHL, where he finds the game "more difficult," he is the Reds' leading scorer. Thus, where Stevenson is not confined to a system that entirely regulates his behaviour on the ice, he is creative and produces scoring opportunities. In the NHL, however, where Stevenson plays perfect systematic hockey, his behaviour is predictable and, ultimately, ineffectual. The paradox here is that the more technical and structured the game becomes, the more it forces higher levels of creativity on the ice; otherwise, a perfect game would be played, which would mean a zero-zero score (a highly uncommon result). Thus, despite claims made by critics of professional hockey that "the [creative] activity is subordinated to a set of highly regimented, restrictive practises in order to enhance team performance" (Beamish 1988, 155), these restrictive practices in fact guarantee creativity on the ice. The systems must be at once followed and subverted if players are to create chances for themselves and their team to achieve victory. How the players actually achieve creativity on the ice will be considered in the following chapters.

ON-ICE VOLATILITY

In more general terms, one might describe the practice as an intense physical ordeal largely motivated by the players' own competitive natures. As players perform their drills, they are genuinely trying to score on their shots and are often visibly upset when they do not. The goaltenders, in turn, are genuinely trying to stop the pucks from going into the net and they, too, will lose their temper when they perform poorly. It is common to hear expletives as players express their anger vocally, and sticks are smashed on the ice or against the glass as anger escalates. The intensity of the practices is demonstrated not only by expressions of anger, but also by the manner in which the drills are performed. In addition to the ferocious pace and physical contact of the drills, there is an element of cheating. In fact, the competitive nature of the players can at times actually undermine the purpose of the practice: instead of working on weaker areas of their game, they concentrate on success; they simply do whatever it takes to succeed. If cheating brings about success, cheating will occur.

I decided to record exchanges – both oral and physical – over approximately five-minute time spans so as to illustrate the intensity of the players and the ramifications of their highly competitive approach to practice. Although slightly cryptic, my field notes attempt to capture the players' responses to one another in this competitive environment. The notes remark on the players' comfort levels with one another, which seem to allow them to tell one another to "fuck-off" more frequently. Witness Steve Toll's to Peter Jackson, "Shoot the fucking thing!" or Proux's remark when Jackson scores on him: "Fuck off Jackson! You're fuck-all!" And Jackson only skates away shaking his head. Or note Bill Smith's and Chris Coles's later decision to go at each other's throats for cheating on drills. The danger here is that if the other player returns the aggressive pose they will both end up in a fight. Here, the upshot was a backing off on the part of both. I found that examples of temper tantrums were not infrequent, such as Pat Smith smashing his stick against the glass because he has screwed up in the drill or Jackson throwing his stick into the glass because he did not score on a play. (The glass is important to hit because it is loud and draws more attention.) Bill Smith's challenging of Jackson to a fight because of a perceived cheap shot brought a new set of surprises. Jackson, who is the weaker, tried to save face by responding to the challenge, but his response was so minor that it was not seen as an official acceptance of the challenge. Coach Murphy then waded in to reprimand Smith for picking on a small guy. Interestingly, Murphy, who is tough, can still embarrass someone who is trying to be tough. (Field Notes, 24 Oct. 1996) These brief notes attempt to display the aggressive behaviour evident during practice and the players' interactions with one another. There is one counterbalance, however, to this fierce and unforgiving attitude that is especially significant when considered in juxtaposition to these episodes.

Simultaneous with all of the aggression and frustration were jocular expressions. I found them most entertaining. Of the many examples of on-ice hilarity, two were most revealing, because of the way they intertwined with the anger detailed above. The first was actually, in its initial stage, exemplary of the unrestrained anger just discussed. It began with assistant coach Sam Dig screaming at the players in an apparent rage for consistently bungling the drills. When one player tried to explain to Dig why things were falling apart, his arguments were overridden by Dig's yell, "Wake the fuck up!" *Eight* times in a row, the player attempted to get his point across, but each time Dig repeated his command still louder. Finally, the player gave up and turned away, allowing Dig to punctuate his tirade by screaming "and get the shit out of your eyes!" However, less than two minutes later, when Dig's attempted pass to start off a drill went errant, not even coming close to the target, Bill Smith quickly seized the opportunity to say: "Digger! Get the shit out of your eyes!" Although three players close to where I was sitting burst into laughter, Dig did not laugh. I wrote in my field notes: "It is hard to tell if Dig is serious or not because behaviour which can seem so absurd can actually be serious. Yelling and screaming at the top of your lungs like a lunatic – "wake the fuck up" – so that the other person cannot continue to argue is one such example" (Field Notes, 24 Oct. 1996). As Smith returned to the corner near Dig, the two men exchanged chuckles. It was now apparent that they were making light of the situation. In this instance, one player's anger led to humour for another. This theme of capitalizing on anger or potential anger for the sake of humour is extended in the next example.

Keeping in mind previous passages that find players throwing their sticks in rage for either missing a shot or failing to execute a drill, examine the next incident. It is actually made up of two events, which, although identical in action, had drastically different results. In the first scene, one player skated to the net and attempted to take his shot on goal: he barely touched the puck, however, and it feebly rolled in the direction of the net. The players waiting in line for their turn broke into hysterics and began shouting verbal abuse at the player for his pitiful shot. In response, the player being mocked charged over to his antagonists and began playfully pummelling them. For about twenty seconds, the five players brawled with one another, harmlessly punching each other about the head. Laughing, they all continued to mock one another. The next occurrence was a product of this playful banter: one of the previously brawling players stepped up to shoot on net and another player, from his place in line, shot a puck that knocked the puck off the initial shooter's stick. When the shooter went to shoot he actually fell down onto the ice, because the puck was no longer there. Those watching found this quite hilarious, and I, too, was laughing at the slapstick nature of the scene. I was also amazed by the prankster's precision in knocking the puck off the other player's stick from about twenty-five feet away. All this for the sake of humour.

The contrast of humour and rage is interesting because of the apparent puerility of both forms of behaviour. Just as the frequent on-ice tantrums were difficult to comprehend, the levels of on-ice play were equally remarkable. From my perspective, these expressive acts demonstrated a lack of emotional restraint, yet apparently they were not perceived negatively by either the players or coaches. It is significant that the aggressive behaviour was predominant during formal practice times under the coaches' strict supervision, in contrast to the more prevalent jocular behaviour of "informal practice times." My discussion of game-day practice showed that the latter portion of the practice was an informal time; players were free to work on individual skills or to simply leave the ice altogether.[4] Indeed, such expressions of horseplay as the two just recounted were rarely seen during formal practice times; similarly, aggressive behaviour was virtually non-existent during informal periods. Thus, it was really during these informal practice times that the players were able to truly engage in unadulterated fun.

As I sat watching these grown men revel in their own fun and games at the conclusion of practice, I again tried to capture the essence of what was taking place. Although my translation of the experience pales in comparison to what was actually occurring, I have tried to stress not only the nature of the game, but also the players' performance. It goes something like this. "Okay. So it's me and Woody," says Peter Jackson to teammates Woody Stevenson, Mikel Zakov, and Lester Dell. Their game appears to be right out of road hockey. Jackson and Stevenson begin to play two-on-two against Zakov and Dell. As they play they hit and stick each other, muttering "ah, fuck-off!" When someone calls a person for cheating, or supposed cheating, the situation becomes mock confrontational.

The term "out" – a reference to a safe area or "home-free" status, which means out of bounds or out of the realm of play – is used often, as is the term "sieve" and the accompanying call of "fuck-off Dent!" to rookie goalie John Dent and the accusation of cheating when one team scores. The game culminates in football tackles, accusations, and much laughter, but not before Mikel Zakov and Lester Dell have tied the score up at three and Woody Stevenson has told them they scored a "cheesy goal." Meanwhile, one team has taken advantage of the rules, to which Peter Jackson says "aw come on!" His team has been duped, which bothers them. Another incident has Zakov landing on Stevenson; they lie there laughing and when Zakov gets up, Stevenson knocks his stick to the corner. Finally, Stevenson and Jackson score and win. Zakov, though, denies the goal, saying "You are a cheater you fuck!" (Field Notes, 24 Oct 1996). There must always be a winner and a loser, and the losers pick up the extra pucks while the others leave the ice. Nothing unusual took place here. The last players finally skate off to join the rest of their teammates in the dressing room.

MAINTAINING DISTANCE

The role of the ethnographer is one of selection, in that decisions are constantly being made to privilege one component of observation over others and to insert it into the actual written ethnography. In short, ethnography is a process of editing human experience. Decisions to incorporate certain aspects of behaviour and deny others are often difficult. None, though, has been as difficult as the decision to include the following. In part, I am including these observations because they provide further commentary on the perceived farcical behaviour on the ice. As well, the behaviour is consistent with the natural chronology of events. I hesitated to include it, however, for two reasons. First, it is removed from the actual performance of professional hockey (both formally and informally). Second I am concerned that my personal reaction to it may be the prime motivating factor for its inclusion. Perhaps my only recourse, therefore, is to preface the observation with this brief reflexive commentary, thereby allowing the reader access to my imaginative process and, in turn, the process of editing.

   I am referring to the manner in which the players leave the ice. Considering that the players have just been involved in a form of

interactive play that is rarely, if ever, paralleled in an adult occupational sphere, it is difficult to fathom the "cold" exit they make
as they head to the dressing room. I have referred, on occasion, to
Ted Right, the loyal Reds follower who, whenever physically able,
attends every Reds game and practice. Right appears to be in his
mid-sixties, he wears his Reds hockey jacket every day (unless it
storms, when he wears a jacket with a hood) and his countenance
is always cheerful. He is usually at the stadium fifteen minutes
before the players are on the ice, and does not leave until all the
players have left. As the players step onto the ice in staggered
fashion, he calls out to each one by name, either commenting on
a previous night's game or wishing them a good practice. At the
conclusion of practice, his involvement is greater, as he himself
opens and closes the door for the players as they exit the ice, also
in staggered fashion. In order for the players and coaches to exit,
then, they are forced to walk directly past Right, who says such
things as, "How ya doing Wally?", "You're starting to come
around Vesty?", or "The team's starting to look good, Dennis."
The players and coaches, however, avoid eye contact and usually
walk past Right saying nothing, although at times a barely audible
"good" escapes. Veteran goaltender Paul Proux was the only
member of the Reds who thanked Right for opening the door and
responded by asking how Right was doing. As Right's face lit up,
he replied, "Good Paulie! Have a good one." And Proux walked
on to the dressing room.

The aloof manner of the players towards Right was difficult to
comprehend after I had just witnessed them rolling around on the
ice, laughing with one another and hollering playful accusations.
But on further inspection, the behaviour seemed typical of this
banter: team interaction is accessible to members only. Intentionally exclusive, the player's behaviour maintained Right's spectator
status and his position outside of the community. Right's attempt
to work himself into the team dynamic illustrates the striking
division between members and non-members; it also reflects the
distinctiveness of this occupational community. Yet although I do
not wish to deny my critical response to the players' and coaches'
reaction towards Right, there are academic implications of this
expressive behaviour. I hazard a guess that the otherworldliness of
the players' occupational environment is perpetuated through their
exclusive behaviour and shunning of outside intervention. The

ramifications of this solipsistic existence will be considered in the following chapters; it is necessary, though, to recognize that the division is substantial and expressed in the most mundane of the players' daily routines.

Now that the practice had officially ended, the players moved to the dressing room, where they were required to view game videos for approximately an hour. Once the viewing was over, they were free to do as they pleased until the next day. Thus, although they practised every day for a maximum of two hours, the practices usually ran for only an hour to an hour and a half. If things were going well for the team they might occasionally have an optional practice; rarely, however, would there be an outright day off. Practices ended by noon, at the latest, and the players not needing therapeutic treatment from Jones would generally go out for lunch in various groups. The rest of the day was spent either doing errands or simply relaxing with one another. As rookie forward Dell explains: "So, there's a lot of free time here. There's so much free time on your hands after practice. [You] go out, go home and then you have something to eat. And then you have the rest of the day to do chores or just relax there, just do whatever you have to do" (Dell 1997a). On off-days, then, the players' workday began at around nine in the morning and concluded at around one in the afternoon. On game days, the morning schedule was structured similarly, but the players had to show up in the evening an hour and a half before game time and would leave the rink at about 11:30. This work routine was followed throughout the entire season for the games played in Troy. The team's schedule was set up to encompass between two and three weeks at home, followed by road trips for about a week or two throughout eastern Canada and the United States. They travelled by bus primarily, as do all AHL teams.

THE DRESSING ROOM

It is important to consider one more aspect of the professional hockey environment: the place in which the players actually spend most of their workday. This is the dressing room, which serves as a recreational site, an exercise area, and a therapeutic, rehabilitation treatment locale. I decided to approach Jones after practice to see if I could get a tour of these facilities in order to document the

players' so-called sacred space. Jones said he would happily provide
a tour and suggested that I visit on Sunday after practice, at around
two o'clock. The term "sacred" is an esoteric term that I have heard
used on numerous occasions. In an interview conducted with a
former professional hockey player the year previous to my ethnography project with the Reds, John Doe expressed these sentiments
about the dressing room: "I know all the dressing rooms that we,
that I, played in had TV's and stereo systems. I know one thing:
after a lot of practices, we used to watch *Cheers* in the dressing
room. And we looked forward to it, watching it all the time as a
whole team. And we had a fun time doing that. So the dressing
room was kind of sacred to us as a team" (Doe 1996). The comfort
that Doe was describing was the first thing I looked for as I began
my tour of the dressing room with Jones that Sunday. In order to
get to the dressing room, one must walk through royal blue drapes
that serve as a partition between the public space of the arena and
the private space of the Reds. Once past the curtain partition, I
came upon a hallway identical to all the other hallways within the
stadium. The only difference was that there were three red doors
in this hallway: the first door on the right, immediately past the
curtain, announced "Reds' Dressing Room" and had the Reds' logo
situated underneath; the next two doors, also red, were smaller and
had nothing written on them.

As we walked through the first door, the main entrance to the
Reds' dressing room, we were hit immediately by the stale air and
pungent odour of the drying leather and canvas of hockey gear.
The stale air should not have been a surprise since approximately
twenty players had left the room just half an hour prior to my visit,
leaving their sweaty equipment and garments to be washed or
simply hung to dry in a windowless room. Overhead was the sound
of a ventilation system, whirring loudly in an attempt to rid the
room of odour and damp air; the room was kept as dry and warm
as possible to allow the equipment to dry quickly. My reaction to
the smell of the room was immediately qualified by the impeccable
cleanliness of the room. Almost entirely red, the room was tidy and
compartmentalized. The floor, covered with red and white carpet,
was also spotless. The players' equipment was neatly hung up in
individual stalls; each stall featured a name plate, demarcating a
particular player's place. The room was smaller than I had imagined, but impressive nonetheless.

As Jones walked me through the room and its adjoining spaces, he provided information about the respective rooms' contents and uses. As he told me of the various rules that the players must follow while in the dressing room, it was apparent that he was very proud of this area. He equated the dressing room to a living room and expected the players to treat it as they would their living rooms at home. In fact, the room did have a living-room feel to it: a fine-sounding stereo system was playing rock music, while above the east portion of the stalls sat a large television with a cable hookup airing NFL football. And the players' benches were carpeted for added comfort.

Jones took me into the shower area, which contained several showers, sinks, toilets, and a whirlpool bath for therapeutic use. Adjacent to the bathroom was another section of the room that had a refrigerator and sink, and a counter area that appeared to be used for making coffee and storing other beverages. Jones then took me into the exercise room, comparable in size to the dressing room. It too was carpeted and equipped with a sound system. Another member of the training staff was in the room, engaged in a workout. The room contained a row of stationary bikes and an assortment of free weights and exercise equipment. It also contained a coat-rack area and a series of small compartments that served as the players' mailboxes. The last room was Jones's office, which he shared with the other three training staff members. Set up with a desk and typical office supplies, it also housed Jones's therapy table – the one on which I had seen a player being treated the night of the Reds' game. Jones proceeded to go over his duties with me, as well as his responsibilities as an athletic therapist. The only room he did not show me was the coach's office, accessible as well through the main dressing room area. This room was private and Jones simply told me about it.

Once the tour was over, I asked Jones if I could wander about on my own; I wanted to draw up a floor plan and make some observations. He complied, occupying himself with paperwork while I noted dressing room specifics. On the wall above the television was a message painted in large red letters that called for excellence from the players. Underneath this was the Reds' logo. Everything about the room expressed efficiency and order, from the stark red-and-white patterning of the carpeting, to the easy-access garbage bins built directly into the benches at every corner of the room. Each player's gear was stored in exactly the same manner: specific equipment sat on the two top shelves of the individual's stall, undergarments in a mesh bag that hung from a hook in the stall, and remaining gear packed into compartments built into the player's bench. There was nothing sitting on the floor or on the benches except for the traditional two sticks of Wrigley's Spearmint Gum, placed there for the players before and after every practice and game.

The entire room was colour coded to match the Reds' uniforms, and everything was labelled clearly, again reinforcing the efficiency of the room. For example, by the main entrance of the dressing room stood a rack holding all the players' hockey sticks. Each rack was labelled with a number, indicating where each player was to place his sticks. Each rack had a minimum of four sticks, and the sticks were all numbered – with the numbers facing outwards. In addition to the clear numbers inscribed with magic marker on the taped butt-ends of the sticks, the players' names were printed into the upper end of the stick by the specific manufacturing company. I was amazed at how ordered everything was in the room. And the more I observed, the less the room felt like a living room; an institution was more to the point. In fact, the slogan painted on the wall took on an ominous feel and the room began to feel oppressive. When I played hockey I had loved being in the dressing room – it was one of my favourite aspects of the game. Yet as I stood there taking notes, this dressing room disturbed me. I began to wonder if, ironically, it was the room's very efficiency and order that restricted the players' behaviour and individuality and made the room sacred.

CONCLUSION

Over the course of the ethnography, the distinctive essence of professional hockey became increasingly apparent. To begin, there was the actual working environment – the arena – which was deliberately removed from reality and/or anything natural (in an environmental sense). It was a sphere – or as John Bale designates it, a "sportscape" – that defies its natural surroundings. Bale explains that "the landscape of sport became increasingly artificial" (1994, 39), which he attributes to "sport's fixation with neutralising or altering the effects of the physical environment, and producing a landscape given over solely to sport" (1994, 40). The climate-controlled stadium with its painted, artificial ice surface glowing brightly exemplifies the artificiality of the sport domain; it immediately tells those inside the building that they have entered a space outside everyday experience. The behaviour within this constructed space extends still further the distinctive nature of the hockey occupational community, the very framework of the game being situated outside of the natural order. As Wagner puts it: "There is nothing natural about a sports event" (1981, 94).

As both product and architect of this constructed universe, the players themselves both consciously and unconsciously express themselves as members within it. The participant/spectator division is highly apparent during the actual sporting contest, with fans revelling in the carnivalesque atmosphere of the stands, while the players thrive and struggle in the intensity of skilled competition on the ice. But the division does not end there. As players skate from the ice after games, adoring fans call out to them and ask for their autographs. The players, however, generally ignore them or respond minimally.[5] The players return to their partitioned-off dressing room, into which those outside the community attempt to look to catch a glimpse of an exiting player. But the players leave through a back door and, helped by securities' maintenance of a public-free zone, avoid the mass of people.

When I talked to the players, they expressed this division of worlds clearly. They used such typical phrasing as "you feel apart from the *everyday world*" (Hammer 1996); or "if you compared it to *real life*" (Feld 1997); and "I think that hockey, first of all, is sort of within a *cocoon* that shields [the player] from the *world's realities*" (Pack 1996). The players were aware, then, of the constructed universe in which they existed and, willingly or not, had limited contact with the outside universe. The task at hand is to consider what makes up this universe and what is being produced as a result. The next chapter will focus on the various initiation or hazing rituals that function as a means of incorporating players into this community. An attempt is made not only to describe the rituals, but also to explore what these rituals tell us about the group and how we may begin to critically consider the occupational community of professional hockey.

CHAPTER SIX

Entering into the Trade of Professional Hockey

Professional hockey is an intricately constructed, firmly bounded universe to which the players are totally dedicated. Aside from being required to spend the majority of their time within a hockey framework, players are separated from mainstream society. The privacy of the enclosed hockey world naturally encourages players to live according to the team's traditional standards of behaviour and the larger principles of the hockey industry. It is therefore important for us to approach this community as a culture in and of itself, one which younger players must learn in order to become culturally competent. One way of approaching any cultural group is to explore the means by which individuals gain access to the community: to consider not only *what* is learned in order to become culturally competent, but also *how* it is learned. In the case of hockey we are somewhat fortunate: in place are clearly marked behaviours that inform players (and subsequently us) of this transitional process and the desired end of the transformation. The focus of this chapter will be to explore and interpret these behaviours in the hope of acquiring sufficient understanding to enable us to discuss this segregated world of professional hockey.

One gains entrance into the realm of professional hockey by abandoning one form of existence in order to assume another or, in symbolic terms, by experiencing a rebirth. The players have established rituals to celebrate this rebirth that help signify the transition from one status to the next. These rituals, which can be understood as communicative acts that serve to "dramatize, enact, materialize, or perform a system of symbols" (Bell 1992, 30) are not especially elaborate or complex, but they are nonetheless rich in meaning. The difficulty for the researcher is how to interpret the symbolic behaviour so as to make sense of what appears to be barely understood by the actors themselves. Not only are the rituals encountered in hockey especially problematic in that they are an overt rejection of sociocultural norms, but the researchers must approach, decode, and interpret these acts from a vantage point outside of hockey. Clearly, an authoritative reading is somewhat elusive. This chapter therefore considers various hockey initiation rituals, approaching them as cultural texts.[1] From a methodological standpoint, this means positing that behaviour is made up of a multiplicity of texts and readings that we can eventually decipher and interpret (Jameson 1975–6, 205). Acknowledging that behaviour is multivalent does not reduce it to an imagining; rather, it liberates action from any one specific meaning. If ritual is expression through symbolic behaviour, the actions are mere representations of what is signified. Thus, the onus is placed on the readers/ participants/audiences/scholars to impose their own gestalt of what has been performed.

THE INITIATION

All rookies on the Troy Reds must undergo one set ritual early in the season to indicate their new status as professional hockey players. I use the term "professional hockey players" as opposed to "Reds," because the initiation is only performed by players who have not previously played in the AHL. In other words, if a player played the previous year with another AHL team and is now playing with the Reds, he would not be initiated.[2] The initiation is quite basic in its structure and performance. It involves a team dinner in a specific dining establishment rented out exclusively to the team. The rookies must pay for their meals as well as for those of the veterans and team officials. Athletic therapist Al Jones explains:

For the most part the rookie night is a big dinner for the team and for the players, and the training staff are invited. And what happens is there are a number of rookies – this year we had, I don't know, seven or eight – we had a lot of rookies. They have to all give in a sum of money to pay for everyone's meal. And it gets quite expensive some times, but the last few years they've been keeping the menu to a reasonable amount so the guys aren't paying thousands of dollars like they do in the NHL. What happens is each rookie has to give to whoever is the organizing guy, say it's the captain. It's so many hundred dollars and they collect it all and they've got so much money. In the past we've been going to a certain restaurant in town and we rent the upstairs. It's blocked off just for us. We'll have a bar there and there will be basically eating and drinking for the evening on the rookies. There isn't really a lot of crazy pranks. At the very worse, it's chug a beer, a couple of shots. It's fairly harmless fun. For our organization anyway. I'm not sure how it goes with the [parent organization]. I know they have higher salaries and so on. But I don't think they try to hurt anybody or anything like that. So basically it's a fun evening. Some of the rookies get quite drunk because some of the veterans make them do a few extra shots or something like that. It's fairly harmless and the guys are good about it; they make sure the guys get home. (Jones 1997)

I later learned from rookie Lester Dell that the rookies were required to pay one thousand dollars and, despite the fun experienced by some, it is not necessarily an enjoyable experience. As Dell remarked, "Well, I don't know what's worse: paying a thousand dollars or pay[ing] nothing and do[ing] a humiliating thing. I don't know, it's kind of your choice – well, it's not whatever you like. There's no real choice; the standard is a thousand dollars for the meal. And you're making pretty good money. It is a lot of money obviously, but a thousand dollars and that's it – you're done" (Dell 1997b). Throughout the dinner, the rookies are introduced to rare and expensive treats that were previously, in general, beyond their financial means. The veterans flaunt their knowledge of fine things and revel in the evening's excesses. "Guys will say, 'give me a hundred dollars and I'll go out and get some cigars.' And they'll come back and all the veterans will be smoking cigars and stuff like that" (Jones 1997). It is not a particularly late evening. Typically, it ends around midnight, because the players have practice the next morning.

There is much to be learned from this particular behaviour if we consider the communicative value of ritual. As has been stated, ritual consists of symbolic behaviour and, like all communicative acts, it is the physical manifestation of encoded messages. It is unlikely – especially considering the responses of the players and team staff – that these codes are deciphered at the intellectual level by the participants; thus the meaning would potentially be left unrealized. In fact, when I asked Dell why they did these things, his response was, "I really don't know why we do it … It's just like [pause] I don't know ... it's been going on every year. It's kind of this thing that started. If at the beginning it was to put on a million pairs of clothes, that's what we would do" (Dell 1997b). It is uncanny how similar his response is to Catherine Bell's discussion of the ritual process, when she argues that ritual participants "do not see themselves as projecting schemes; they see themselves only acting in a socially instinctive response to how things are," which "tends to be experienced as deriving from powers or realities beyond the community and its activities, such as God or tradition" (1992, 206). The lack of critical introspection, however, does not mean that the ritual's significance is lost on Lester; indeed, a later response he provides – "it's kind of just a dumb thing we do" – indicates an unarticulated understanding, which Stuart Hall would call "consumption" (Dell 1997b).

In Hall's general discussion of the meaning-making process, he explains that in order for a message to be decoded, it must be physically manifested; otherwise, the message, or in this case the ritual, is completely ineffectual. He states that "discourse then must be translated – transformed, again – into social practices if the circuit is to be both completed and effective. If no 'meaning' is taken, there can be no 'consumption.' If the meaning is not articulated in practice, it has no effect" (1993, 90). In other words, for the symbolic value of the ritual to be realized, it must be acted out; this, in turn, means that it is the performance of the ritual that achieves meaning; or better still, it is performance that sets meaning into action. It is unnecessary, then, for Dell to know *why* the ritual is done, as long as he consciously participates in its performance. Ritual is essentially a learning process, the performance of which brings about a "learned identity." In a discussion of male fraternity rituals in American colleges and universities, Peggy Reeves Sanday argues that the young pledge, by "yielding himself to the group in this way," "gains a new self, complete with a set of goals, values, concerns, visions, and ready-made discourses that are designed to help him negotiate" the complexities and contradictions of the group (1990, 135–6). The same premise holds true in the context of hockey initiations: the rituals provide ready-made discourses that enable rookies to function within the social/cultural framework of the team. What, then, makes up these discourses?

While there are likely many responses to this question, we can ultimately understand much of what is taking place here in terms of engaging in the negotiation of power relationships. First, and most obviously, the veteran players are celebrating their power over the rookies and, in turn, the rookies are voluntarily succumbing to this power by complying with the demands placed upon them. The rookies do not challenge the tradition – "I mean there's no real way around it" (Dell 1997b) – which means that they acknowledge and accept the hierarchy already in place. At the same time, the rookies are empowered by the situation: they achieve communion with the group and its practices/beliefs. It is through this communion, however, that the players also become resistive agents; the rookies are required to shun their past experience in order to be born again into a new one. But if we are to truly grasp this rebirth, this relationship of power and resistance, a step backward must be taken to explore a far more crucial transformation that occurs earlier in the career of a hockey player. The Reds' initiation, as described by Jones and Dell, does not appear to embody all that is necessary to represent the transformation of self. The overindulgence and excess evidenced in this ritual seems to be more emblematic of a change in economic status, as opposed to an actual rebirth. Therefore, if we are to gain a deeper understanding of the standard AHL ritual, it is crucial to acknowledge where the transformation from *non-player* to *player* originally takes place. Dell claims that it occurs as players enter Junior hockey.[3] When I asked Dell about the difference between Junior and AHL rituals, he said that in the AHL "they push to the side ... the little games and stuff ... because everyone's been through it" already, in Junior hockey. It is necessary, then, to make a brief descent into the world of Junior hockey.

GAINING ENTRANCE INTO LIFE AS A HOCKEY PLAYER

The attempt to explore ritual behaviour in Junior hockey presented an obvious problem, inasmuch as the fieldwork for this project was done exclusively in a professional context. It meant I had to rely on players' memories and interpretations of their Junior experience, rather than observe and record initiations. First, I asked Reds rookie Dell about initiation practices in Junior hockey and his own initiation experience. I had my own initiation experience from which to work as well. A comparison of our experiences showed that Junior teams followed two standard initiation rituals. Reports of the exact same rituals were later aired on what turned out to be a timely CBC broadcast of *The Fifth Estate* (1996), and later printed in Laura Robinson's book *Crossing the Line* (1998), which documented initiation practices in Junior hockey. The program, entitled "Thin Ice," depicted various Junior hockey players discussing initiations in their respective leagues. I base my observations of Junior initiations on this testimony, as well as on the experiences of Dell and myself.

The importance of the Junior initiation ritual is that the players actually gain entrance into the realm of hockey during this period of their careers; it is here that the initial transition from civilian to hockey player occurs. Although in theory Junior hockey fits under the rubric of amateur hockey, researchers have stated that "Junior hockey is amateur in name only" (Cruise and Griffiths 1991, 346). John Barnes, too, explains that Junior leagues "operate in professional form: member teams obtain players through territorial rights and by drafting boys of 'midget' age [15 to 17 years old]. The players then serve under a standard league contract; they are paid for their expenses and receive small weekly salaries" (1988, 33–4). Reds Athletic Therapist Jones equates Junior hockey with professional hockey as well. As he put it: "I'll see the guys that come to us straight out of Junior, and these guys for the most part are already professional hockey players. You've played junior, and you understand that they're practising and playing almost every day" (Jones 1997). Thus Junior hockey has become the logical place to initiate hockey players. We must give these initiations our full consideration.

In *The Fifth Estate* broadcast, Judd Richards, formerly of the Sault Ste. Marie Greyhounds, talked about initiation rituals in the Ontario Hockey League. In his interview with host Linden MacIntyre, he attempts to explain the generic initiation ceremonies experienced by most hockey players at some point in their career. He narrates the first experience as follows:

RICHARDS: It was a hotel that we booked, and we go there and the veterans are already waiting for us. You know, we basically … took off all our clothes because they would get pretty well messy with the activities we were doing. And basically, we just drank.
MACINTYRE: Drank naked!?
RICHARDS: Yeah, basically.
MACINTYRE: What were you drinking? There was a big bowl going around there.

RICHARDS: [Laughs] Uhm, well there was a bowl that went around and it was – there was a number of stuff in it ... different alcohols, different substances. I'm not totally sure.

MACINTYRE: *What* kind of substances?

RICHARDS: I have no idea. I'd imagine things like – gross things – I'm not exactly sure what. Possibly spit and maybe urine; I'm not sure. (*The Fifth Estate* 1996)

Richards explains the second ritual, entitled "the sweat-box," as follows:

On every team I think in the OHL [Ontario Hockey League], or anywhere, there's one basically set initiation. I mean basically it's when everyone's naked and they pile you into the bathroom at the back of the bus. And we ended up getting, I think, about eight people in there. Basically every-one was just in there; we were sweating buckets. And there was one particular player on my team that was claustrophobic. And we didn't know that until we got in there and we were trying to make room for him because he told us. But I guess he just felt sort of sick and ended up puking all over me. So that was one of my more negative experiences with initiation. (*The Fifth Estate* 1996)

Both accounts by Richards were told with a certain amount of apprehension and subsequently received by MacIntyre with a mix-ture of condescension and disbelief. The interview, however, won-derfully captures the disparate worldviews of the two men.

The two rituals Richards describes have been experienced by virtually every player who plays Junior hockey. In my interview with Dell, who played four seasons in the same Junior league as Richards, I asked him about the initiations he experienced in Junior hockey. His response was identical to that of Richards: "Well in Junior it wasn't really too bad. In Junior we had to do the thing called [he laughs uncomfortably] 'the sweat-box.' You know what that is [he knew that I had experienced the same ritual]. And then we had a rookie party, and there was drinking involved. There wasn't, it wasn't as bad as other stories I've heard. It was just kind of at your own pace. And the guys were pretty good. And it was just the guys: no one else, no *off-ice* guys or girls or anything like that. So, [we] just sat around and drank. It wasn't too bad" (Dell 1997b). Dell made it clear to me that he did not want to talk about any of the rituals in detail because some of "it was bad, it was gross stuff." I therefore began providing details, to which he could simply provide yes or no answers, as follows:

ROBIDOUX: When you guys did the "sweat-box" – we were in Peterborough when we did the "sweat-box," they would tie up our clothes in knots ...
DELL: Yeah.
ROBIDOUX: And then we had to untie our clothes. Is that what you guys had to do?
DELL: Yeah exactly. Yeah, you come out when you're dressed.
ROBIDOUX: Right, one at a time, basically.
DELL: Yeah, it took pretty much three or four hours. (Dell 1997b)

I then asked if many of the rituals involved nudity, and again Dell responded in the affirmative: "Yeah, it seems like a lot of times it does: right." Although he was clearly uncomfortable talking to me – "an off-ice guy" – about these behaviours, I decided to ask one final question: "Have you seen or heard of various forms of masturbation, you know contests and stuff like that?" to which he responded, "Yeah." I did not pursue matters further because, as stated earlier, the events being described are consistent with my own and others' experiences. Clearly, these two rituals are seen as the predominant initiation practices.

Presumably, rituals that are less commonly performed, which neither Dell nor myself have experienced but may only have heard of, are out there. It is arguable that many of these rituals function more as a threat than an actuality for the rookies apprehensively awaiting their initiation, thereby acquiring legendary status. One player from *The Fifth Estate* broadcast stated that he was "told to bring condoms" to his rookie initiation party; this request forced him to grapple with a well-fed imagination: "Who knows what to expect, whether it be a girl – I heard stories of it being a cat, a cat being there." As it turned out, no girls or cats were present. But according to fifteen-year-old Scott Macleod – he also appeared on the *Fifth Estate* broadcast – there are places where these rituals apparently do exist:

Well they brought two boys in at once and made them strip. And all the coaches and managers and that were there, and a lot of the veterans. And there were two beer cups lying there about ten, fifteen feet away from them. And they told us to do push-ups with our genitals to go in the beer cup.

The Captain took a marshmallow – I remember he had rubber gloves on. And he would insert it into the players rectum and the players would have to, well, squat over a cup and get it into that cup. And if the players missed, he'd have to eat it.

The worst part, like what I saw, was the trainer sitting on one of the other rookie's face ... with nothing on. (*The Fifth Estate* 1996)

I have never witnessed any of these behaviours or talked to anyone who had these things done to them. However, a former teammate of mine,[4] while playing in the OHL, once told me about an even more violent act. He explained that during the initiation evening for his rookie year – which was taking place in the team's dressing room – a particular player who was disliked by the veterans resisted being initiated. A few of the veterans responded by grabbing the rookie and taping him up to a squat rack[5] in the exercise room. One of the veterans applied A5–35 heat ointment to his finger and then inserted his finger up the rectum of the rookie, suspended helplessly from the rack. The player was left there, screaming in agony, as the balm quickly began to burn the sensitive skin.

As far as I know, the extreme nature of this last episode is exceptional in hockey initiation rituals. It is uncommon for players to inflict physical pain upon the initiates, for the simple reason that if a player gets hurt, it prevents him from playing, which is a risk coaches and management will not tolerate. Reds veteran defence-man Jim Falk makes it clear that when a player is injured, he is perceived as damaged goods: "You know a team is going to shy away from guys that come up in their first couple of years who are injury prone. They don't want to take the chance and put up the money – and you know the kind of money they put up these days – and have the player only play forty or thirty-five games. So it's a big gamble for teams" (Falk 1997). Another aspect of ritual that was once predominant in hockey was to shave the head and various body parts of the initiates. But after seeing games played in Canadian Junior leagues, the AHL, and the NHL, I concluded that not one player had had his head shaved and that this practice appears to be virtually non-existent in the leagues specified. One reason for the termination of these behaviours is the recent bad press received by hockey initiations (including *The Fifth Estate* documentary and Robinson's *Crossing the Line*), which provoked league officials to look critically at more dubious practices. Dell explained that "since the shows on TV and stuff – there was a couple of instances in Junior B where guys got charged, I think – I know the OHL has really cracked down on initiation" (Dell 1997b). Therefore, if rituals persist – which they do – they must be taking place behind closed doors. Bodily shaving would expose the act, not only to coaches and management but to the general public, thereby endangering all initiation practices. My conclusion is that initiation rituals in hockey have largely been reduced to the "sweat-box" and a night of heavy drinking, during which rookies are often forced into performing humiliating and degrading acts.

Certain themes undergird these two rudimentary performative situations. The first is the emphasis on nudity: the players are forced to endure rituals while wearing no clothes. The second is the emphasis on group unity; that is, players engage in activities collectively.[6] It is noteworthy, too, that while the players do not look forward to the initiation, they approach it in a somewhat pragmatic fashion: "Well at first you're not laughing, but then when you look back, you just say this is once, hopefully you only do it once, so let's have fun with it. At least you can say I've done this, or whatever. It's kind of the approach you take. You have to take it or otherwise, it would be a bad experience" (Dell 1997b). The general tolerance expressed by players should not be interpreted as passivity, however. Even though the players do not often analyze their performance within these rituals, there does appear to be a general understanding of the event as a means of group "bonding." As a result, the experience is not usually seen as negative, but rather as a necessary procedure in the process of achieving group solidarity. To push this still further, rookie participation in these events can be interpreted as an example of sacrificing oneself for the sake of the team. The group dynamic takes precedence over individual identity. Moreover, team cohesion benefits the team or franchise, which explains why officials monitor, but do not abolish, initiation rituals. Let us look then at the unifying characteristics of these initiation ceremonies which, in most other contexts, would be deemed unacceptable. Such an analysis sheds light on a community that not only tolerates this behaviour but actually celebrates itself through these annual rituals.

COMING TOGETHER

The players' recognition of the initiation process as a bonding experience is fundamental to their understanding of their new group membership. Those who go through the ritual claim to be closer to one another; they feel part of what is commonly referred to as a family. As Dell says: "It's kind of your dues, you know. Just breaking in [stutters] I find after, after the party it brings you closer together. Because it's kind of a little thing that we do and then afterwards, assuming there's no real big problems, we're kind of closer knit. And in hockey, any team, that's what you want. Guys are like a family, like a big family. So it's just a little initiation to bring the guys on the team closer together" (1997b). Judd Richards provides commentary that supports the notion of unique bonds being formed through initiation: "Your teammates are all that you have. I mean you don't have anything else. And what it does is gets you bonded with one another quicker than any other method. You're there for six, seven months of the year – I mean you have to start off, you have to be gelled into one" (*The Fifth Estate* 1996). The process of "gelling into one" suggests that a transformation occurs whereby players abandon one form of being in favour of a new collective existence. This unifying power of ritual makes it a useful tool for achieving a shared identity. For this reason, ritual has been universally used, and for identical purposes, throughout history. Anthropologist L.L. Langness's discussion of the initiation tradition of the nama cult of the Bena Bena of the New Guinea Highlands applies equally well to hockey culture: "[It] links the members of the dzuha with their ancestral past. It symbolizes, on the one hand, the solidarity of males, and, on the other, the common origin and continuity of a particular group of men" (1974, 200). These ritual contexts are not restricted to more tribal societies, as James Diego Vigil discovered in his research on Chicano gang initiations in a North American urban center. It is noteworthy, too, that these initiation rituals share a similar unifying function. As Vigil indicates: "Gang baptism jointly marks passage to a new status, enhances social cohesiveness, creates a ceremonial atmosphere, encourages ritualistic behaviour, and serves practical gang goals" (1996, 151).

All these sentiments describing the unifying capabilities of initiation rituals are in fact rearticulating, directly and indirectly, what Arnold van Gennep has designated a "rite of passage." The unity described in each scenario is essentially a rebirth, or a change of status made possible through initiation. Through ceremonies, participants engage in "a direct rite of passage by means of which a person leaves one world behind him and enters a new one" (van Gennep 1960, 19). The ritualistic journey does not merely position the participant in this other world, but serves to unify him or her with the new environment. As van Gennep explains, "To cross the threshold, is to unite oneself with a new world" (1960, 20). The process is invaluable, then, in an occupation such as hockey, where group cohesion is critical for team success. And from my own experiences and from comments made by other players, the rituals are generally successful in achieving this end.[7] But having said this, why do the symbolic expressions take the shape they do? Why do the players express themselves through unconventional acts of nudity and sexual posturing? Alan Morinis asks similar questions about initiation rituals. But instead of focusing on nudity and sexuality, he asks, "Why has the painful ordeal been the preferred vehicle to this goal" when pain is "surely not the only stimulus to bonding?" (1985, 155).

Although hockey rituals rarely incorporate physical pain, parallels exist with those that do. In effect, Morinis is arguing that many initiation rituals have been discussed for their "social-psychological functions" (1985, 155), but that the extreme nature of the behaviour manifested is rarely, itself, a concern. The fact that in one particular tribal initiation ceremony the initiate is "beaten with more or less heavy sticks," and his "screams are answered from afar by the lamentations of his mother and other relatives," is not an issue for van Gennep. He simply understands this behaviour as a means for "the novice to recognize that he is a man" (van Gennep 1960, 82). But again, it needs asking, why is a ferocious beating seen as an appropriate way to signify the transition from youth to adulthood – especially considering that the acts are merely *representations* of the signified, and thus can be represented in any way imaginable? To return to a hockey context, squirming together naked in the back of the bus washroom may bring the players closer together, but why achieve this end through such compromising behaviour?

The tendency for scholars is to discuss such behaviours – those exceeding the restraint and regulatory measure of their social surroundings – as characteristic of "transitional rites," or "liminal rites" (van Gennep 1960, 11). I, too, initially found van Gennep's, and later Victor Turner's (1969), theoretical construction of liminality highly useful for discussing expressive behaviour within hockey rituals. I felt the concept of liminality perfectly described the "other worldliness" of the players' accounts and shed light on the behaviours themselves. Indeed, van Gennep argues that while participants are in this liminal stage they find themselves "physically and magico-religiously in a special situation for a certain length of time: [they] waver between two worlds" (1960, 18). From this stance, Turner developed a fuller definition of liminality: "Liminal entities are neither here nor there; they are betwixt and between the positions assigned and arrayed by law, custom, convention, and ceremonial"; thus, "liminality is frequently likened to death, to being in the womb, to invisibility, to darkness, to bisexuality, to the wilderness, and to an eclipse of the sun or moon" (1969, 95).

The nudity, the "anal and genital games," the excessive drinking, and the humiliation and degradation that exist in the narratives provided by the players are all consistent with liminality in theory. But are these, in fact, liminal behaviours? To answer this question, we need to address an inherent shortcoming of any structuralist argument – in this case, ritual structure – which is, the natural assumption of a centre. Jacques Derrida explains that structure "has always been neutralized or reduced, and this by a process of giving it a center or referring it to a point of presence, a fixed origin" (1989, 231). He later argues "that the center had no natural locus, that it was not a fixed locus but a function, a sort of non-locus in which an infinite number of sign-substitutions came into play" (1989, 232). If we consider Derrida's arguments in terms of Turner's discussion of liminality, Turner appears to be limited by ethnocentrism – a danger each ethnographer faces. Accordingly, in order for behaviour to be deemed liminal, there must be an assumed normalcy, which functions as the centre. More specifically, behaviours that are considered either inverted or extreme are defined in terms of some pre-set standard of behaviour; conveniently, the standard here is a western, industrialized, heterosexual construct. Therefore, one might ask if the content of the rituals described by such players as Judd Richards of the Sault Ste. Marie Greyhounds and Scott Macleod are, in fact, liminal. The answer, at least initially, is no. Although these behaviours likely appear to those outside the hockey world as liminal, they are not atypical of the hockey community as a whole. What seems to be a more accurate assessment is that for the players, larger society is "neither here nor there" and is "betwixt and between the positions assigned and arrayed by law, custom and convention" (Turner 1969, 95). Thus, our assumption of a centre needs to be reevaluated.

The seemingly disturbing testimony provided by the players regarding their initiation into Junior hockey may seem unacceptable to everyone, hockey player or not. Even Dell says he would find it hard to understand, if he were not a hockey player: "I really don't know why we do it like that. Because yeah, if I look at it – if I wasn't a hockey player, I'd say, well that's ridiculous" (Dell 1997b). But because he is a hockey player he not only understands the behaviour but accepts it. Moreover, if we apply aspects of Richards's testimony, along with what is narrated by *Fifth Estate* host Mac-Intyre, to the everyday behaviour of the players, certain insights emerge. At two different points in the interview, Richards says that the rookies were nude, either drinking together or "squished" together in the back of a bus. Despite MacIntyre's contemptuous response to this information, if we listen to Richards's narrative, the only difficulty *he* has with either of these situations is that he was forced to sit in vomit; he is unconcerned that he and his teammates were not wearing clothes. From my own experience studying the Reds, it is clear that nudity has a very different significance for the players than for society at large.

In the dressing room – which is not merely a dressing room, but a lounge and exercise area where the players spend the majority of their working day – players can be found completely naked, standing or sitting, simply interacting with one another. On two separate occasions I conducted interviews with players who were nude at the time and, despite my extensive background as a hockey player, the thing that kept going through my mind was "keep eye contact, Michael!" I quickly learned that, now that most of my time is no longer spent in dressing rooms, I had grown unaccustomed to, and was ill at ease with, such overt nudity. Throughout the interview, I attempted to appear casual, to not let it bother me that I was holding a tape recorder toward a nude man. At the same time I remembered that on one occasion, when playing hockey in Owen Sound, Ontario, I too had been interviewed, nude, by the local sports reporter. In fact, convenience had dictated that particular situation, for the reporter had needed the interview just as I was getting into the shower and I had complied by making a right turn into the interview area instead of a left turn into the shower. At the time, the fact that I was nude had not been an issue for me or my teammates. But I was bothered now. I do not wish to imply that the players' nudity signifies some unconsciously pure, esoteric perception of the body. Rather nudity is an expressive act that holds a different significance for the players than for those outside the community. Exactly what is being expressed will be considered later.

Another crucial aspect of the interview is Judd Richards's description of the contents of the so-called punch that he and his teammates drank on the night of initiation. He states that the contents contained – in addition to alcohol – a whole "bunch of gross stuff." While we can term consuming bodily fluids and performing various other humiliating acts as simply repugnant, we need additional context to discuss these behaviours further. Although I have never met Richards, nor spoken to him about this event, different players have told me about drinking similar concoctions. Incidentally, it should be noted that the rookies are unaware that the veterans are "fixing" the punch. It is very common to have parties where each individual pours his alcohol of choice into some kind of container containing juice or another form of mix, creating one large and highly potent beverage. The result is almost immediate intoxication, making those who are most vulnerable susceptible to the worst pranks. Urinating or spitting into the vat is easy, and it serves to humiliate those who learn (more often than not, the next day) that they have just consumed such substances. But once again, if we were to discuss this behaviour as liminal – exclusive to initiation rituals – it would be an exoteric assumption using larger social norms as a natural centre or locus.

Although drinking bodily fluids may not be a typical practice in the realm of hockey, it is also not completely unknown. Nor does it constitute highly exceptional or "liminal" behaviour. To pursue this still further, Dryden, in *The Game*, describes a humorous event with a similar outcome: "Suddenly Shutt goes to the skate room, picks up a plastic cup, fills it with ice, and returns to the room. Then, as we watch with squeamish, open-mouthed glee, he urinates in the cup until it's almost full, tops it with Coke for color, puts it down beside him, and walks to the shower ... Moments later, water dripping from his body ... Tremblay reappears and sits down. He looks around for Shutt, then, sharing smiles with those around him, grabs the Coke and sips from it – no laugh, no wink, no devil-may-care leap this time" (1983, 152). In both Richards's and Dryden's narratives, the prank involves getting dupes to drink urine. Yet the latter is not part of a ritual; it is a practical joke no different from loosening the top of a salt shaker before someone uses it. Within the specific context of hockey, such behaviours are not only tolerable but a means of entertaining one another. On a similar note, when host MacIntyre refers to the "degrading" ... "anal and genital" rituals, he does not take into account a particular sensibility that permits certain physical gestures among the players. For example, I recorded in my field notes: "A guy falls on the ice and another guy skates by and gooses him with his stick. There is no reaction from the guy who was jabbed; the gesture is as natural as patting a guy on the back." The act of jabbing someone (either with a stick or with a hand) in a vulnerable area is common and has multiple significations. In this particular case, the player was basically greeting the other player with a gentle poke. Other harsher gestures of this kind, though, are used to tease, or maliciously play with, one another.

Another example of "rectal play" commonly found in North American dressing rooms illustrates still further the general acceptance of such unconventional behaviour. I am referring to a joke that is executed with regularity, and which I have witnessed repeatedly, at all four Junior teams on which I have played. For lack of a better term, the joke can basically be described as the "where's the soap?" routine. The joke takes place in the shower and involves a player taking a bar of soap and secretly inserting it into his rectum. He then asks those in the shower area with him, "Where's the soap?" Again, each time I saw the joke performed, all members of the team had heard it many times before and knew exactly where the soap was located. The humour generated by this prank (at least esoterically speaking) resides not in the fact that a player has soap up his rectum, but rather that he has decided to perform a stupid joke that has been performed far too often already. It is important to note, once again, that these behaviours rarely generate any kind of response from the victim. Typically, laughter or a brief and benign verbal quip follows.

What I have tried to demonstrate through these examples is that the behaviour associated with rituals is not unique to them, but rather is consistently experienced by the players throughout their careers in hockey. Therefore, describing the behaviour that transpires within the rituals as liminal is ultimately calling the entire hockey experience liminal – which from an outsider's perspective is likely a reasonable assessment. In fact, because liminality is a *temporary* phase, one can argue that the "other worldliness" of life as a hockey player is a liminal phase in an individual's life (because this period obviously terminates with the conclusion of the player's career). This assessment suggests that life as a hockey player is a separate existence, and that at one point in the players' lives they undergo a transition that sees them moving from one state of being into another. In other words, a rite of passage must have occurred. Moreover, if Junior initiation rituals signal that transformation, van Gennep's theoretical position is validated, and there *is* a transitional period where liminality is evidenced.

The failure to recognize liminality within these rituals derives from relying heavily on Turner's usage of the term. Unlike van Gennep, Turner provides descriptive information about what liminal behaviour often entails, such as being "likened to death, to being in the womb, to invisibility, to darkness, to bisexuality" (1969, 95). Van Gennep limits his discussion of the term to a period of transition in which the person is wavering between two worlds (1960, 18). In other words, assessing certain behaviours to be liminal – as Turner, and now I, have attempted to do – becomes an exercise in ethnocentrism. It assigns value to behaviour that falls outside a suggested norm, which makes my assessment of these behaviours as non-liminal just as ethnocentric as the claim that they are liminal. In order to recognize what is liminal about these rituals, it is necessary to move beyond the content to begin considering the performance itself.

Let us first accept that the examples of nudity and the players' various degrading and humiliating acts within the rituals *are* noticeably different from the examples of nudity provided in everyday contexts. As already illustrated, the difference lies not in the acts themselves (the content), but rather in the manner in which they are performed, which changes the entire dynamic of the situation. The sense of expectancy and apprehension that rookies feel prior to the ritual makes the performance context particularly significant. For example, the sweat-box ritual is not explained before it occurs, yet the rookies are told that something will take place on the bus ride home. Once the players are all on the bus, a selected veteran will begin shouting orders and the rookies (usually) comply without knowing what lies ahead. "I guess both times you're kind of nervous and anxious. You don't really know what to expect" (Dell 1997b). The apprehension and imposed vulnerability establishes a heightened sense of performance absent in the everyday examples of nudity. Suddenly, the nudity within the rituals carries with it additional significance: it is the focus of the players' actions as opposed to being a routine occurrence.

The removal of the rookies' clothing is a symbolic act of rejecting one's previous life in order to become a hockey player; in other words, the players are being stripped of their past lives and invested with qualities necessary for existence as a hockey player. By performing compromising acts without clothes, the ritual "create[s] a status and a position outside, or in opposition to, existing social forms" (Morinis 1985, 157). As the younger players are exposed to these behaviours they are truly vulnerable – forced into making a decision to become one with the team or be rejected and ostracized for not conforming (as was the case with Sean Pack's teammate who was physically tortured). It is this vulnerability that further removes the performance of these rituals from the seemingly perverse acts that occur within the hockey framework, and that qualifies the rituals as a liminal experience. In addition, it is within this liminal state that the players willingly reject their lives outside hockey, embracing the at times abhorrent behaviour of the group for the sake of union with the team.

But once again, why do the behaviours take the shape they do? How does "the symbolism of nakedness, purification ... serve equally well to make the point about divestiture of status" (Morinis 1985, 157)? Why force the rookies into performing compromising and degrading acts – whether that entails cramming them naked into a tiny space for hours on end, or making them drink saliva or urine? If, as Dell claims, in the "beginning when it started, if it was [to] put on a million pairs of clothes, that's what we would do" (Dell 1997b), would the rituals serve the same purpose as they do today? The answer is no, and for two important reasons. First, the degrading behaviours are not empty signifiers, but rather physical articulations of rejected social standards. This collective rejection allows for the divestiture of certain characteristics. Second, the rituals also invest the rookies with the characteristics necessary for coexisting in this new sphere.

A fascinating parallel can be made here with A.E. Green's discussion of initiation rituals within a coal-mining community. Green argues that by breaching the "initiate's sexual privacy," a need arises for him to "accept a corporate definition of his humanity and he is prepared – necessarily abruptly because this community cannot afford a lack of consensus – for a life of rough treatment among his workmates" (1981, 63). Much like in hockey, the coal miner quickly learns "that the values of the surface-world, which involves women, are not the values of the pit, which is exclusively male. Above ground, reticence, delicacy, and tenderness are valued responses; below ground they are dysfunctional" (Green 1981, 63). The actual content of these behaviours make up the "ready-made discourses" necessary for workers or players to become successfully incorporated into the group. It becomes necessary to explore how particular behaviours found within a hockey context provide younger players with in-group competence and a basic understanding of life within the hockey world. The actions will be discussed as a means of legitimizing power as it is perceived within the hockey environment, and as a means of liberating the players from the restraining forces of the greater community.

LEGITIMIZATION THROUGH RITUAL

It needs emphasizing that the rite of passage young men undergo in Junior hockey is a substantial life-changing experience, not simply a symbolic or figurative transformation. Signs of this alteration become visible as younger players take on characteristics that they did not possess on first entering the league. One young woman on *The Fifth Estate* television program who befriended many of the players on the Peterborough Petes[8] discusses the transformation: "The rookies always come in really shy, really quiet. And then once the veterans get a hold of them, and they have their initiations – that's it! It's a totally different person. It's not the same one" (*The Fifth Estate* 1996). Ritual facilitates this transformation through a legitimization of experience. The ritual enacts symbolically what is fundamental to the group and, by its execution, becomes accepted by those wishing to access the community; it serves, then, as an expression of power.

The ability to transform is an exercise of power; at the same time, however, ritual allows power to be wielded without overt force or coercion. I say "overt force" because those wishing to gain entrance into the group willingly place themselves in a position to be initiated. Without undergoing these practices, they do not become part of the desired community. Therefore, ritual expresses power in its truest sense, inasmuch as there is a voluntary submission of will to a predetermined standard of knowledge. The fact that submission is voluntary is crucial here; as Michel Foucault explains, power requires "essential obstinacy on the part of the principles of freedom," meaning "no relationship of power" is possible "without the means of escape or possible flight" (1983, 225). Ritual for Foucault is a perfect expression of power because it is a performance of strategies necessary to exist within the system at hand. In *Discipline and Punish*, he explains how ritual executions were public displays of power relations, which had "the effect, in the rites of punishment, of a certain mechanism of power: of a power that not only did not hesitate to exert itself directly on bodies, but was exalted and strengthened by its visible manifestations ... of a power that was recharged in the ritual display of its reality as 'super-power'" (1977, 57). In other words, rituals enact and subsequently suggest a continuous course of action, which is symbolically embraced by the participants through their own enactment. Ritual, then, does not magically transform the young hockey players into something other than what they once were; it does, however, shape identities through actions learned through their performance.

The boys leave their families and friends at roughly sixteen years of age and enter into something beyond their previous experience. But the question remains, what makes up this new experience? The task at hand is to consider what is actually being learned through what may appear to be nothing more than pubescent acts of perversity. Two works have helped me come to terms with the unconventional behaviours of hockey: Friedrich Nietzsche's *The Birth of Tragedy* (1967) and Freud's *Civilization and Its Discontents* (1961). In both works, the authors present arguments that discuss existence in terms of tenuous binaries: whereas Nietzsche discusses the deities of Apollo and Dionysus, Freud examines the states of pleasure and unpleasure. According to Freud, while unpleasure is not in true opposition to pleasure, the apathy that arises out of unpleasure ultimately leads to discontent, and finally to misery (1961, 33). Significant to us here is the opposition that both authors are exploring: the illusory world of Apollo/civilization versus the instinctual reality of the pleasure-driven Dionysian. Although Freud does not use the Apollonian/Dionysian construct, his argument echoes the very nature of that relationship. He argues that "civilization is built upon a renunciation of instinct ... it presupposes precisely the non-satisfaction (by suppression, repression or some other means?) of powerful instincts" (1961, 44). Nietzsche, on the other hand, explains "that measured restraint, that freedom from the wilder emotions, that calm" is only made possible through Apollo (1967, 35). More important still, both Nietzsche and Freud recognize that the calm provided through Apollo/civilization is an illusion, and that in this imposed dreamlike state the "poor wretches have no idea how corpselike and ghostly their so-called 'healthy-mindedness' looks when the glowing life of the Dionysian revelers roars past them" (Nietzsche 1967, 37).

It is precisely this Dionysian movement that applies here, as Nietzsche describes a community of individuals who exist outside the illusory world of Apollo, of civilization, and thrive in the revelry of "festivals centered in extravagant sexual licentiousness, whose waves overwhelmed all family life and its venerable traditions; the most savage natural instincts were unleashed, including even that horrible mixture of sensuality and cruelty" (1967, 39). In Freudian terms, the Dionysian experiences "happiness derived from the satisfaction of a wild instinctual impulse untamed by the ego" which "is incomparably more intense than that derived from sating an instinct that was tamed" (Freud 1961, 26). Although Apollo/civilization serves to protect us from the dangers of reality and the potential chaos of unbridled passions, it simultaneously deprives individuals from experiencing the joy of instinctual satisfaction, or as Freud designates it, "pleasure." In order to satisfy these instinctual desires, we must either break the laws civilization imposes upon us, or function outside the restraints of civilization. The world of professional hockey, as has already been stated, clearly functions outside these restraints.

What I am arguing is that the professional hockey community is motivated by these same instinctual desires that Nietzsche and

Freud describe, and, unlike members of larger society, they are able
to fulfill these desires without the consequences of civilizing forces.
But if one is to give oneself up to the passions of pleasure, one
must also concede to the passions of pain, terror, sorrow, or, indeed,
of any other passion that situates the hockey player in a vulnerable
position. The hockey player is left to contend with a reality that
"is subject to the arbitrary will of the individual: that is to say, the
physically stronger man would decide ... in the sense of his own
interests and instinctual impulses" (Freud 1961, 42). It is not
surprising, then, to hear players talk about their interaction with
one another in the same instinctual fashion. Reds veteran Darren
Feld explains:

FELD: One thing I find about hockey players is, if I've got something
wrong with somebody, I'll tell him right to his face. And we'll go from
there. I don't know how it works in real life. I don't think there's so much
of that in real life.
ROBIDOUX: Yeah, that's what I've been noticing. If someone gets pissed
off in practice, they'll turn around and tell the person.
FELD: That's right. Right in his face and if you want to drop the gloves,
then drop the gloves and get it over with. And after the game, or after
the practice they're having a Gatorade together. I think that's really good
too. (Feld 1997)

Just as quickly as the players drop the gloves and fight one another,
they are also found laughing and sharing in each other's banter.
    The players discuss the pleasures they receive as hockey players
in terms of their playful framework of existence, and of a life
without having to face the concerns of adulthood. In my discussion
with Reds defenceman Steve Toll, he explained to me that the
players are "always acting like kids too. So you have to be grown
up and you have to be mature, at certain levels. But other times,
you're mostly having fun. And you're mostly still being a kid. And
the job is just fun, right now. And that's the way I think everyone
tries to look at it. I mean I'm not in a hurry to grow up and get
married or whatever" (Toll 1996). However, in a perpetual state
of childishness, the players are equally as vulnerable to tantrums
and unrestrained anger as they are to the laughter and games that
arise out of this explosive occupational atmosphere. It is difficult
for an outsider to imagine existing in an environment where, on a

regular basis, one might encounter what is related to us by Reds' sophomore Jerry Wall:

Yeah, I think – you know the times I did see him fight, he certainly didn't, you know, face the guy, "face-to-face." He would – he always wants to get a jump on the guy, like he did on me the other night. He jumped me totally from behind. And, you know, obviously caught me by surprise. I didn't even see the guy coming. I heard he did it a lot in Junior, so it is something you have to be aware of on the ice. And we certainly have the guys that can stand up to him on this team. And we face him face-to-face because, if he wants to get that kind of game going, it could be a long night. (Wall 1996a)

But this volatile environment would not be possible without group members completely surrendering themselves to its uninhibited nature. Players are therefore forced to contend with the essence of the Dionysian philosophy: "pain begets joy, that ecstasy may wring sounds of agony from us" (Nietzsche 1967, 40) – or in the contemporary vernacular, "no pain, no gain."

With this said, let us focus again on the initiation rituals of hockey. As has already been pointed out, the initiation rituals in Junior hockey formally incorporate boys into the world of hockey, but it is not until they reach the official status of professional that they are incorporated officially into *professional* hockey. The ritual of dining lavishly at the expense of the rookies may not produce the change of status evidenced from Junior rituals; nonetheless, it does represent a change. Similarly, the ritual does not involve celebrating nudity and/or sexual excess and lasciviousness, but it does introduce the notion of money in (perceived) large quantities, something to which the Junior players have not yet had access. I say "perceived" because even if players are making only an average American Hockey League salary of $55,000 per season, the two-way contract[9] they sign indicates the possibility of earning enormous salaries (see Appendix B for a list of 1999–2000 NHL salaries). Moreover, the majority of players will receive a signing bonus when they first sign with the organization, which gives them a large sum of money whether they make the team or not. These contracts are made public and ultimately serve as a price tag for the players, defining their worth by categorizing them in terms of monetary value. Money is therefore central to the professional hockey experience (as is the case for paid labour in general) and, not surprisingly, becomes the focus of the professional hockey initiation ritual.

The initiation, as in all initiation rituals, is as an expression of power whereby one particular frame of being is legitimized through its performance. For the first time in their lives, these young athletes are exposed to a certain level of fame and notoriety, in addition to large sums of money. The initiation celebrates this privileged status, disclosing a way of life to the rookies; its very performance validates the experience. How this "way of life" is introduced to the players is significant in that it illustrates the paradox of satisfying desire; that is, all of it comes at a price. The players learn that they are able to experience the pleasures that money can buy, but that they must suffer the consequences of doing so. The entire ritual consists of costly indulgence and its execution legitimizes the behaviour. No pedantic overtones instruct the younger players to be careful with their new-found wealth; it is an expression of excess and the price one must pay to have it realized.

It is therefore reasonable to conclude that the AHL ritual, like the two Junior hockey initiation rituals, is a manifestation of this same philosophy, whereby these tenuous binaries are exploited and ultimately deconstructed. Satisfying what is denied by civilizing forces means giving oneself up to passion and instinct. The individual is vulnerable to these same instinctual drives, which may be as ferocious as they are blissful. Following Freud's lead, many of the behaviours found within the Junior rituals can also be considered as "the irresistibility of perverse instincts, and perhaps the attraction in general of forbidden things" (1961, 26). While I do not want to insist on particular readings of these cultural texts, I do feel that interpreting the realm of professional hockey in these terms allows researchers to better read particular behaviours, such as displays of nudity. Surely Richards's testimony about sitting naked together, drinking, can be appreciated for its symbolic value if we acknowledge that the players are, in fact, being reborn into the world of the Dionysian: a world of excess and instinctual desire. Nudity becomes a means of establishing a way of life that is quite removed from the larger society, which is why nudity is not only found in ritual. By consistently being nude, the players force each other into accepting the vulnerability that nudity entails. Only when they become naked to one another are they able to experience the pleasures of an uninhibited existence and, ultimately, what Nietzsche labels "the fantastic excess of life" (1967, 41).

While this explanation does not make this behaviour any easier to accept for those outside the community, it does provide the scholar with a means for discussing hockey culture. Drinking saliva or urine is no easier to accept if we recognize the layers of meaning present in this expressive act; perhaps, though, we can move beyond simple repulsion and/or condemnation. Perhaps drinking another player's spit or urine can be seen as one player taking advantage of another player's vulnerability; perhaps, too, to experience this humiliation and degradation is the cost of weakness, or the cost of letting down one's guard. It forces rookies – or anyone willing to be duped – to recognize their tenuous position within the world of hockey and, ultimately, forces them to respond accordingly.

Certainly, though, arguing that the perceived perversity and offensive nature of the behaviour is largely an ethnocentric perception – and not understood as such esoterically – will not likely alter the disdain with which many Canadians view these actions. Nevertheless, the Dionysian/Apollonian construct and Freud's pleasure principle can provide insights into this ethnocentric response. Consider for a moment an arena housed with upwards of twenty thousand fans, screaming as "their" team wins the crucial game or scores the winning goal. Now imagine the same twenty thousand fans going into a state of frenzy as they witness two or more brawling hockey players severely beating one another in a fight. Can we not see this audience in terms of Apollonian culture responding to the Dionysian revellers? As Nietzsche describes it: "We hear nothing but the accents of an exuberant, triumphant life in which all things, whether good or evil, are deified. And so the spectator may stand quite bewildered before this fantastic excess of life, asking himself by virtue of what magic potion these high-spirited men could have found life so enjoyable that, wherever they turned, their eyes beheld the smile of Helen, the ideal picture of their own existence" (1967, 41). The multimillion dollar industry of professional hockey, made possible by these "high-spirited men," clearly reinforces the voyeuristic role of the masses revelling in the security of their role as spectators, as opposed to participating in life's excesses. Therefore, from the safety of their seats, fans vicariously celebrate the joys, the pains, and the sorrows experienced by the players in the flesh, without actually paying the price of allowing themselves to become vulnerable to the horrors of unbridled existence.

The question that subsequently arises then is, does this voyeurism remain in the domain of the arena? In other words, while spectators virtually deify the instinctual play on the ice, are not the forbidden pleasures equally appealing off the ice? Is it not possible that the institutionalization of hockey in Canada makes it culturally acceptable to celebrate the physical beating of an individual? One might argue that without a culturally viable vehicle for other more licentious behaviours, the opportunity is missed to celebrate similar voyeuristic tendencies – such as the behaviour described in "Thin Ice" and, occasionally, through the everyday practices made evident to me as player and, now, as ethnographer. Freud observes that within the "civilized" world "most extra-genital satisfactions are forbidden as perversions" (1961, 51), yet these forces have left so-called civilized peoples sexually "impaired" and "frustrated" (1961, 52, 55). Like the Greeks gazing at the beauty and the horror of the Dionysian revellers, are contemporary spectators also recognizing their own forbidden desires within hockey culture, both on and off the ice? Does the base behaviour described by Richards and Macleod offend and disturb because it also reflects the "irresistibility of perverse instincts" and "of forbidden things" (Freud 1961, 26)? And thus are spectators simply applauding one form of instinctual desire and condemning another?

I must concede that at this point I am pursuing matters that exceed this particular study. Certainly, I cannot venture further than mere speculation in regard to the queries I have raised. What is clear, however, is that as spectators we are able to exercise the power that comes from being removed from actual events – the ability to shut our eyes and to dismiss or shun things too horrible to consider. As spectators we can celebrate instinctual drives in the framed (make-believe) context of the game, while considering them ugly and intolerable outside these boundaries. Yet for the players, the game is no more made up than an operating room is for a surgeon, or a shop floor is for the industrial worker. The "game" is the hockey player's occupation, his livelihood, his life. The game, then, is one of the few windows through which those of us on the outside can view the world of the hockey player. However, as more windows are opened by such media productions as "Thin Ice," it is apparent that few of us wish to look in.

The process of initiation, then, however ugly, formally symbolizes a transference of status, as young players embrace a way of life outside their previous experience. Through the players' participation in the rituals, they perpetuate and legitimize an existing body of knowledge that serves to inform and ultimately socialize the novices to their new environment. But these rituals are much more. Ritual is also a homogenizing process that diminishes certain individual characteristics in order to invest the initiate with qualities that will allow him to become part of the group. Those who resist these homogenizing forces suffer the consequences, as did the one player who was taped up to the squat rack and physically tortured. One player from *The Fifth Estate* broadcast who had refused to participate in a particular initiation ritual was ultimately forced off the team by the players. He explains that "the upside of taking part in this kind of hazing is that the veterans will love you as a rookie. The downside is if you don't take part in what they tell you to do, it can result in getting into fights with the veterans, and basically just quitting hockey" (*The Fifth Estate* 1996). Once again, the power that lies within ritual stems from the voluntary submission of will; without this submission, the ritual proves ineffective. Players who do not comply with the initiations challenge what the world of hockey entails and are seen as resistant to making the transition. Those individuals who refuse to make the transition often suffer serious repercussions. As was the case with the player from "Thin Ice," it is a task not worth the effort.

The young men who have dedicated their lives to becoming hockey players are vulnerable to the pressures imposed upon them. The younger players generally look up to the older ones. Knowing that the older players once went through these same experiences makes the rituals that much more endurable, even welcome. There are, however, serious ramifications of conforming to a pre-set standard of behaviour that tends to function outside perceived social norms and conventions. The rituals can strip players of their individuality and immerse them in a collective whole with a belief system, world view, and values that are often counterproductive to personal development. Ironically, players find strength and solace in this environment, since it is within this sphere that they are socialized and validated for acting within these so-called norms. However, serious problems can present themselves. These will be explored in the next two chapters, as I consider the extent to which this occupational group functions as a closed society and the consequences of living within this collective identity.

CHAPTER SEVEN

Homogenizing Men in Professional Hockey

In a discussion with Reds rookie Lester Dell concerning his initiation into hockey, I suggested that initiations are a process of transforming individuals into something other than what they once were. Could Dell, I asked, tell me what one became after going through the standard hockey initiation rituals. After suggesting, "It's kind of your dues, maybe," he reflected further. He then elaborated on what has already been discussed as a process of coming together "like a big family," saying that the players were "knit" or "gelled" into one (Dell 1997b). Although the description provided by Dell and, earlier, by Judd Richards, has become a cliché in sport discourse, its significance has not diminished. To all the young players entering into the professional hockey community, the notion of becoming "one" does not end with sharing team goals and commitments; it also includes adopting a collective worldview that is both narrow and restrictive. The result is a shared identity, one informed by a physically dominant, white, heterosexual male model that has been validated through annual rituals and everyday behaviour. It is this model that is privileged within the community as ultimately the only legitimate masculinity.

The identity continuously reaffirmed and rearticulated with each new generation of hockey player provides team members with a means of measuring their worth as professionals and as "men"; in fact, players generally appear to draw solace from the security provided by this rigid structure. One player from the Reds, veteran defenceman Darren Feld, associates his job with what it means to be male: "It's a contact sport, and it's ... a male thing – maybe a little macho" (Feld 1997). On closer inspection, however, the comfort that the players draw from these pre-existing boundaries is potentially detrimental to their personal development. First, this construction of masculinity privileges only one male experience, denying, in turn, other expressions of masculinity. Second, the constructed image of manliness stems from a patriarchal tradition that already privileges what is male; thus, the players largely understand it as the only legitimate experience. In other words, repeated celebration of what it means to be a man through the execution of the trade and through an exclusively male environment creates a process of "inferiorising femaleness and female activity" (Bryson 1983, 422). Finally, the constructed image discriminates not only in terms of gender, but also in terms of ethnicity, belief, and skill. The effect is a homogenized workforce achieved at the expense of the individual. But how can such a restrictive existence be – as many players claim – the most desired aspect of the trade?

EXPRESSIONS OF MASCULINITY

It is undeniable that hockey is a sport that involves intense physical competition. Bodies undergo enormous physical punishment for the common goal of winning: players consistently receive bone-crushing bodychecks; they regularly put their bodies in front of pucks moving at speeds exceeding a hundred miles an hour; and they often fight to establish a solid physical presence. Like so many aspects of the game, the sheer brutality of the sport evidenced in both games and practices has become ingrained in the players. Violence is expected and must be responded to in kind. I asked Reds player Steve Toll if it bothered him to see one of his teammates receive an injury on the ice. His response is noteworthy because of the way he rationalizes the experience:

Yeah, definitely. I mean – it depends. If a guy gets hit, no. I mean, just a regular hit, and he gets hurt, and it wasn't that big a deal, like where a guy was running him and he intentionally tried to hurt him, you don't feel bad for the guy. You suck it up, and you keep going. But if it was an attempt to injure or whatever, yeah, you feel for the guy, but you also get angry at the guy that did it. And you've got twenty guys on your side, and they're getting pissed off at the one guy that did that to your player. So there's all kind of things like that: revenge and whatever else. I mean

you take it – you don't take it that far, but you take it to where you need
to stick up for your players, and stick together. (Toll 1996)

These intensely physical aspects of the game require the players to
assume a certain bravado that is unnecessary in most contexts other
than sport. Thus, the very existence of sport provides what Ray
Raphael calls a "public arena, a ready-made structure, in which we
hope to validate our worth" (1988, 110). As superficial as these
structures appear to be to those on the outside, for the group members who exist in what one player refers to as a "cocoon" (Pack
1996), the sense of validation is quite real. Every day the players
engage in a highly demanding physical competition; thousands of
screaming fans celebrate that competition, reinforcing the players'
successes and failures and, hence, publicly validating their performances as men. By simply fulfilling their occupational demands, the
players are embodying specific qualities of one form of masculinity
and establishing, at least esoterically, their male worth.

The traditional behaviour inherited by each new generation of
hockey players is structured around ideals of physical superiority
and dominance that have "played a key role in the construction
and stabilization of a male-dominant, heterosexist system of gender
relations" (Messner 1992, 16). This stabilization of gender relations
can be achieved in a variety of ways, but it is through language
that Reds players most distinctly stabilize their masculine power.
The language is one of violence, which threatens anything not part
of this hegemonic paradigm. Masculine power is expressed through
the everyday language of the group, now become mundane through
its perfunctory performances. Whereas the words themselves are
overt expressions of misogyny and homophobia, the meaning
behind their usage is often more subtle. This apparent contradiction
emerges because players usually do not assume misogynistic or
homophobic positions, at least publicly, although their informal
speech plainly illustrates the contrary. (Misogyny and homophobia
were actually downplayed in my discussions with the players.[1]) The
players' language is riddled with derogatory comments about
women and homosexuals. Although used in playful and serious
contexts – such as the constant referral to one another as a "cocksucker" or "faggot," which will be considered later – these epithets
are not seen by the players as referents to either group. However,

while these comments are often described as "just words," they are, in fact, violent acts injurious at a political/ideological level: once expressed, they become physical manifestations of violence and power. Before examining the locutions themselves, we must first consider the performative value of the word.

In J.L. Austin's *How to Do Things With Words*, he explores the performative quality of "the word" by considering a seemingly basic premise: "Can saying it make it so?" (1962, 7). Austin pursues this adventurous theoretical premise by offering three fundamental principles that locate speech as being inherently active: "to say something *is* to do something, or *in* saying something we do something, and even *by* saying something we do something" (1962, 94). Not all speech acts, he concedes, carry with them the same action. Thus, he breaks down utterances into three relatively unstable, but still effective, categories of action: locutionary ("He said to me 'Shoot her!'"); illocutionary ("He urged me to shoot her"); and perlocutionary ("He persuaded me to shoot her") (Austin 1962, 101). He defines these three separate speech acts further as follows: the locutionary utterance has a definite and identifiable "*meaning*"; the illocutionary utterance has a "certain *force*"; and the perlocutionary act is "*the achieving* of certain effects by saying something" (1962, 120). Notice that what Austin defines as perlocutionary is essentially the result, product, or consequence of an illocutionary act. For our purposes we shall focus on the illocutionary force, because of *what it can do*.

The ability of a word to "do a thing" is a powerful suggestion; it takes into account not only the act of saying, but also the literal performing function of the word itself. Judith Butler considers the performative value of the word by postulating that "if a word in this sense might be said to 'do' a thing, then it appears that the word not only signifies a thing, but that this signification will also be an enactment of the thing. It seems here that the meaning of a performative act is to be found in this apparent coincidence of signifying and enacting" (1995, 198). However, this description of the illocutionary act does not reveal to us *how* the word actually performs the action it articulates. The statement "He urged me to shoot her" is quite separate from the act of shooting; similarly, it will not necessarily produce such an effect simply by its utterance. More specifically, if we are considering injurious speech, we need to ask the question, "how are we to understand the relation between the word and the wound?" (Butler 1995, 201). When racial slurs are directed towards another individual through language, does the word shape, or effect violence upon, the individual? Or is the speaker even responsible for such violence? In other words, does the victim of the abuse receive injury from the actual word itself or from the malicious motivations of the speaker? These queries lead us in the direction of intention, which, however significant to Austin, misrepresents the speech act, since "intention cannot serve as the decisive determinant or the ultimate foundation of a theory of speech acts" (Culler 1989, 223). For example, is the illocutionary force of the word "nigger" any less injurious if the speaker does not intend harm – as is perhaps the case when a child referring to a person of African descent has not the wherewithal to do otherwise?[2]

To understand the power of the word, we must, at least temporarily, remove the word from the speaker and consider its associated network of meanings. The illocutionary force of the speech act must be placed in a larger historical context rather than viewed merely as the product of the will of the speaker. Jacques Derrida asks if a performative utterance could "succeed if its formulation did not repeat a 'coded' or iterable utterance, or in other words, if the formula I pronounce in order to open a meeting, launch a ship or a marriage were not identifiable in some way as conforming with an iterable model, if it were not then identifiable in some way as a 'citation'?" (1977, 18). The effectiveness, or performative value, of the speech act draws from the possible significations of the word itself; that is, without the recognizable meanings associated with a word, the utterance becomes ineffectual. We can conclude, then, that what is spoken will not necessarily correspond to what was intended; in effect, the historicity of the word exceeds that of the speaker's appropriation of it. The unwitting child uttering racial epithets injures not by will, but by succumbing to the word and its associated meanings. The violence imposed by uttering the word "nigger" is made possible "because that action echoes prior actions, and *accumulates the force of authority through the repetition or citation of a prior and authoritative set of practices*" (Butler 1995, 205). Recognizing the illocutionary force of the word does not alleviate the responsibility of the speaker, however; "the category of intention will not disappear; it will have its place, but from that place it will no longer be able to govern the entire scene and system of utterance" (Derrida 1977, 18). From here, then, we can begin looking at the violence of the word in professional hockey.

Examples of violence committed through speech acts are numerous in hockey. A particular expression stands out, however, because of its frequent usage and menacing signification. I was first introduced to the terminology while concluding my first interview with athletic therapist Jones. As I thanked Jones for his time, team captain Darren Feld walked into the trainers' room with a bag of fast food in his hand. Feld, who was about to receive therapeutic attention for a pulled muscle in his leg, had brought some lunch for Jones. As Feld deposited the food in front of Jones, the latter responded, "Thanks bitch." The remark did not appear to offend Darren, nor did it draw a response from him. Evidently, the word held regular currency among the team members. Indeed, the term was employed consistently throughout the season, and it soon became apparent how and to what purposes it was used. Although deployed exclusively in playful contexts, the use of the word "bitch" signifies power or advantage over another person.

Another example illustrating the performative value of the word "bitch" comes from an instance at practice during which Ted Simms prevented the offensive forward Jason Dodd from scoring. Simms asserted his defensive dominance by yelling at the unsuccessful shooter, Dodd, "Not here bitch!" In this example, and in the one previous, those who employed the term bitch are in a position of privilege over the other, and they accentuate this position by labelling the other as "disadvantaged." In the first example, Feld makes himself vulnerable by performing a voluntary act for Jones – he puts himself in the service of the other by buying him food. Because of this submissive posture, he receives a name that "not only names a social subject, but constructs that subject in the naming" (Butler 1995, 202). Similarly in the second example, one player asserts his physical dominance over the other by proving victorious on an individual scoring play. Simms's temporary victory allows him to impose himself over the other, by defining the player's temporary subordination with a name. The illocutionary force of the name is made possible through its greater historical context and the meanings it carries along with it. It is important to briefly consider this larger framework.

The term "bitch" is highly significant because of its network of associated meanings. Literally, it is a noun, meaning a female dog;

in a more vernacular tradition, however, the term has been anthropomorphized. A bitch is "a spiteful woman," and one who "bitches" is someone who takes on a bitch's characteristics: "to speak spitefully" (Hawkins 1988, 78). Although "woman" and "negativity" are meanings associated with the term, even more vernacular associations are pertinent here. Referring to someone as a bitch is an act of condemnation – "I hereby claim you to be a bitch" – and in its traditional patriarchal context it is an act of empowerment; that is, by debasing the other with the slanderous signification, the speaker is raised above the baseness of the referent. These associations have been subsequently appropriated into other forms of patriarchal and misogynistic discourse and have come to mean one who assumes (voluntarily or involuntarily) the submissive and tainted role of the traditional bitch female model. For example, the term "bitch" is used to describe a male inmate within a penitentiary who is sexually submissive to another male prisoner. Thus although the term is part of a male tradition, the associated meanings are still derivative of the illustrated female model.

When players refer to one another as bitch, they are iterating these formulas of signification and contributing to what needs to be understood as a network of violence. For the players, a term such as bitch is "just terminology" (Murphy 1996) found within hockey, devoid of significance, and likely not expressed in order to injure. Moreover, the fact that players who receive the injurious name do not seem harmed by the act prevents the players from seeing the danger in "a word." What needs to be understood, however, is that the act – in this case calling the person bitch – is a means of "making linguistic community with a history of speakers" (Butler 1995, 206); whether intended or not, it perpetuates this imposition of violence. It is an act of defining woman or womanly characteristics in terms that are seen as subordinate, conquerable, weak, and/or contemptible. It simultaneously serves as an act of privilege, in that it removes the speaker from what has been reduced to mean bitch. It is an act of separating oneself from what is perceived as female, while legitimizing one specific form of masculinity. The expression is part of a reductive process that subordinates all experience that does not fit within this physically dominant, white, heterosexual male construct.

The word "bitch" is, in fact, only one term of many within a larger system of meaning that injures through collective condemnation and subordination of experience. The use of verbal quips and verbal attacks are frequent on the ice and play an important role in the intimidation and distraction of opponents, the hope being to throw opposing players off their games. These illocutionary acts (which these expressions clearly are) are thematically consistent; like the use of the term "bitch," the violence of these expressive acts exceeds the immediate perlocutionary injury, if that injury is even realized at all. For example, during a game the Reds were losing, Steve Toll was punched in the face. The referee either did not witness the assault or did not feel it deserved a penalty. I recorded in my field notes that Toll screamed "You fucking faggot!" It was unclear, however, if this was directed to the referee or to the player that punched him. The next day, during a Reds practice, Sid Zeal attempted to draw teammate Mikel Zakov into a fight by yelling "Fuck off you cocksucker!" In a more playful context in a practice two days earlier, Colin Best had goaded Toll into action by yelling "Come on you cocksucker!" In effect, the players attempt to accost and mock one another by consistently using epithets that use homosexual images as the frame of reference; this consistency collectively condemns male homosexuality.

Feld's comments on the Graham James incident and the repeated molestation of fifteen-year-old hockey player Sheldon Kennedy confirm the prevalent nature of these expressions. The James incident was publicized in the autumn of 1996, when Kennedy, a professional hockey player with the Boston Bruins, revealed that he had been sexually molested over 300 times in a span of six years by his former Junior coach, 43-year-old Graham James. While Feld did say he regretted what had occurred, he criticized Kennedy for not "being a man" about the situation and dealing properly with this "fag behaviour": "I'll say it, if someone had come up to me when I was fifteen years old, sixteen years old, I'm big enough to fucking do something about it. Do something, even if – you know, you go up to the guy – you've got to do something about it: this guy's a fucking fag!" (Feld 1997). It is clear that terms such as "fag," or any other homosexual epithet, associate homosexuality with deviancy and informally dismiss it as a viable way of life within the group. In addition, when the players choose to derogate via antigay terminology, they are aligning themselves with a greater homophobic tradition. What violence these acts potentially impose upon the players is overshadowed because of what they contribute to a larger history of violence: the repeated denial of, and attack on, gay rights. Not only do these utterances legitimize and perpetuate the collective homophobia of the hockey community, they also contribute to an ongoing homophobic discourse; their utterances carry with them an illocutionary force that marginalizes and violates homosexual experiences.

These violent and derogatory speech acts, as seen here, are littered throughout hockey; they are heard from players, training staff, and coaches. The fact that what is uttered is often not perceived as injurious speech, or not understood as injurious in a larger historical context, does not diminish the effects and affects of language. These words and phrases are not accidentally maintained within the hockey tradition; the tradition is intrinsically homophobic and misogynistic and the "word" is instrumental in perpetuating perceptions and beliefs. The word becomes a subordinating act that has been normalized through time and consistent usage. But it also serves as a linguistic code of behaviour that contributes to the aforementioned conceptualization of masculinity. Clearly, these illocutionary utterances are not only violent acts toward that which is perceived as "other"; they also naturalize the hockey identity. The power of the word, then, can be understood as furthering the homogenization process and the reduction of human experience.

PLAYING AT BEING MASCULINE

The violence of speech within the Reds' community is a vivid articulation of an overbearing masculinity often referred to as hypermasculinity. This hypermasculine model becomes intriguing, however, when we consider that much of the players' behaviour does not fit within this superior, macho male image that is so often verbally expressed. Rarely do the players assume behaviours that validate this masculine image; in fact, their behaviour often appears to run counter to the male posturing typical of many male working-class cultures. In contrast to behaviour that is excessively macho or self-aggrandizing, the players express themselves, both privately and publicly, in a manner that appears to subvert the dominant male image. To explain, it would be useful to consider the experience of Tim Chip, an acquaintance of mine who for over five years has played professional hockey in both the NHL and AHL.

At one point in his career Chip was considered to be not only one of the toughest men in the NHL, but also one of the scariest. As an "enforcer" in professional hockey, he faced the predicament that losing a fight meant potentially losing his value as an intimidating force on the ice. Every night his hypermasculine role was put to the test, just as his occupation was similarly put on the line. This predicament was later commented upon by emerging enforcer Ted Simms, a Troy Reds forward, who listed what what he had to do and be to achieve success in the league: "be a physical presence; have the ability to fight; have the gift of being able to win [fights] on a consecutive basis; hit; and be able to put fear in an opponent's eyes" (Simms 1997). But as Marc D. Weinstein et al. point out, this role is precarious because while "demonstrating control over an opponent is a method of earning respect from adversaries, backing down is a way of losing it. A player is expected to fight in order to earn respect" (1995, 837). During his interview, well aware that I knew the lore surrounding him as a professional hockey player, Chip did not feel he had to establish any more of a masculine identity than he already had through his on-ice performances. Instead, like the other men interviewed, he downplayed the tough, macho exterior he displays on the ice. At one point he stated: "Well, yeah, people who first meet me, who don't know me, just think I'm the same person on the ice, but I'm not. So, I guess they expect me to be loud, and aggressive and stuff. But I'm not" (Chip 1996). Interestingly, this failure to perpetuate such an image off the ice (I have known him for about seven years) is consistent with the behaviour of other players.

Chip and the other players I interviewed display an artificial process of emasculation. I use the term "artificial" here because this emasculating process is essentially a paradox: it is a means of maintaining a definitive masculine identity within the group. I asked Chip if he was accorded special status being a hockey player, and he responded, "Yeah a little bit, but nah – I don't know – if you're a star, yeah, but if you're a slug, no" (Chip 1996). Because this individual throughout his career has played a defensive style of game – one that is highly valued on the team, but often overlooked by the public – he comfortably acknowledges his "lunch bucket" status. Incidentally, the metaphor "slug" connotes both mindlessness and insignificance, yet simultaneously signifies perseverance and durability. What is taking place here is similar to what Dunk observes in his study of male working-class culture in Thunder Bay, Ontario. During an annual lob-ball tournament (a modified softball game), Dunk recognizes that the men express their masculinity in paradoxical fashion: "In the context of the lob-ball game, professional baseball players serve as a model; perhaps more than other professional athletes, they exude a casual air which is echoed in the Boys' [the men from Thunder Bay] style of movement. A great deal of effort is put into appearing casual. One does not want to give the impression of being too eager or of trying too hard" (1991, 75). Like Chip's manner, this artificial complacency expressed by the "Boys" actually resonates with subtle expressions of esoteric masculine validation. As Dunk later explains: "Popularity is partly based on being good at a wide range of practical skills and physical activities without *seeming* to work at them" (1991, 75; emphasis added). It seems that these men successfully confirm their identities through artificial self-deprecation.

Chip, in the same interview, explains that professional hockey has stunted his development as an adult. He told me: "You're [hockey players] playing a game for a living: you're never serious and you're with a bunch of guys who think exactly the same as you do. You never really have to grow up. So I think it makes you regress instead of progress" (Chip 1996). It is interesting, however, that personal regression does not appear to be of great concern to him, since when I asked what he disliked most about hockey, he was unable to come up with an answer: "What do I dislike the most? Uhm [pauses and then laughs]. That's a tough one. Actually, I like everything about it" (Chip 1996). This particular individual was able to assert a level of self-confidence and security by openly directing me to weaknesses that are in fact deemed positive qualities (at least by hockey players). This is a paradoxical pattern that also unfolds through more physical actions.

For example, former professional hockey player John Doe began describing the various forms of physical interaction that players engage in, quite deliberately, in the public eye. The following exchange of dialogue began when I asked if and how the players behaved differently outside their occupational environment:

DOE: Let's see, how would I put this? This is kind of weird. You kind of think that you're gay sometimes.
ROBIDOUX: [I laugh and try to put him at ease] Don't worry about that.

DOE: You kind of grab the guy's ass or something like that in public –
you don't really care. But we don't really care what people think of us
anyway. So I don't really think it's changed too much, no.
ROBIDOUX: Actually that would be something that I didn't touch on.
When you grab a guy's ass or whatever –
DOE: Or grab a guy's nuts or something like that. You always have fun
doing shit like that.
ROBIDOUX: And why could behaviour like that happen? I mean, why
could you do that?
DOE: Because you know the guy so well. Like, [pause] I don't think I ever
– you talked about this before – but I don't think I have any school-boy
friends that I could do that with. I have a couple of very close friends that
I never went to school with, like my brothers or cousins or whatever, that
we used to fool around like that with, but the only other guys I could
ever do that with would be guys on the hockey team that you know so
well, and intimately, and – intimately, like I don't mean –
ROBIDOUX: Yeah, yeah. No that's okay.
DOE: You know, inside-and-out kind of thing. (Doe 1996)

All of the players either alluded to, or discussed outright, the
intimacy present in their inner group relationships. Doe relates the
high level of intimacy to the players' ability to open up to one
another: "But, I think the main thing is just, is just opening up.
You know – just speaking about stuff you wouldn't normally speak
about to anyone. And as soon as you open yourself up by saying
that, you automatically become closer to that person" (Doe 1996).
And while this explains how grabbing another man's testicles is
allowed, it does not necessarily explain *why* grabbing another
individual's genitalia is an accepted form of expression. All the
players indicated that they could say and do anything around the
"boys," and that that is what has made their relationships as tight
as they are. Why, then, is this specific outlet of expressing intimacy
employed as consistently as it is?

It must be stated here that grabbing another male's genitals is a
multivalent gesture, capable of withstanding a multiplicity of interpretations. As in all cultural texts, we are forced to interpret
meaning through our own perceptions, which act as filters, modi-
fying the world around us to suit our intellectual capabilities (Fish
1981, 10). The mock sexual interaction evidenced here has been
commonly interpreted as an expression of latent homosexuality
and/or homophobia.[3] While I agree that the professional hockey

environment is homophobic, I feel it is important to resist reading this behaviour as an expression of sexual desire. Although the behaviour lends itself well to such an interpretation, such a reading, while likely true in individual cases, refuses to acknowledge the voices of the actual individuals involved. If we believe that the majority of these players, who claim to be heterosexual, are in fact heterosexual, the behaviour being expressed may be – and I would argue is – signifying something other than sexual attraction.

Aside from intimacy, I feel the players are simply expressing their desire to fulfill the macho image expected of them as hockey players. By employing this tactic, however, the players are once again performing in a manner that undermines the strictly hetero-sexual notion of masculinity, while keeping their masculinity up front. In order for a player to grab another male's genitalia, a trust must have already been established regarding not only his status within the group but also that of his so-called victim. The fact that players "grab a guy's ass" in public establishes further this idyllic level of security in themselves as men; that is, they fall into the paradox of maintaining masculinity by superficially assuming a role that subverts the tough, macho exterior that is, in reality, being expressed. As opposed to stereotypical macho behaviour evidenced in many male working-class cultures, professional hockey players are able to maintain a masculine image through the very nature of their occupation. The need, then, to maintain a hypermasculine exterior does not appear to be critical to them as men, although the desire to express the various ways in which they are different from, or similar to, women and other men is still very real. The pattern therefore consists of the players *artificially* removing their masculine exteriors to downplay their need to validate their status as men. What is evident is that through these expressive behaviours – whether verbal or kinesic – the players collectively articulate what it means to be male, which in turn serves to perpetuate a pre-existing masculine identity. How, then, does this limited construc-tion affect both individual and group development?

CHALLENGING THE BORDERS OF MASCULINITY

Arguments have been made by certain individuals, such as B. Mark Schoenberg, that it is necessary to reassert a *definitive* masculine identity in order to correct what, he believes, is responsible for much turmoil and uncertainty in contemporary societies. Schoenberg writes that traditional "concepts of maleness and masculinity provided men with a set of behavioural guidelines as well as an explicit code of ethics that formed a foundation for personal construct development" (1993, 5). Without these "traditional concepts of maleness," he claims, boys have few opportunities to identify with males from their family or their community and, therefore, lack the ability to take on different roles (1993, 7). He stresses that, in order to remove these *perceived* dangers of blurring gender division, societies need to return to a more codified experience of gender, where definitive boundaries are maintained to guarantee the roles and behaviour of the sexes. Through the establishment of these unique boundaries, society will, he says, be freed from any uncertainty and/or psychological turmoil.

To establish these divisions, Ray Raphael has suggested that North Americans need to reincorporate the formal rituals that tribal peoples used to signify the transition from boyhood to manhood, to reestablish two distinct gender orders.[4] According to Raphael, the absence of these formal "rites of passage"[5] in contemporary societies has profound negative effects upon the male population. He points out that even "if traditional initiations no longer appear to be objectively necessary, the psychological function they once served is still very real. The psychic needs of contemporary males have not always been able to keep pace with sex-role liberation and a computerized economy and nuclear warfare, all of which contribute to the obsolescence of traditional initiations" (1988, xii). If contemporary societies did incorporate these formal rituals as signifiers of the transition from childhood to manhood, what would be the end product? In other words, what qualities would this "man" have to have to be properly called a man?

In effect, Raphael, and in turn Schoenberg, are calling for males to reassume the highly competitive qualities that define their gender, and that have been traditionally introduced to young men through rituals. The sporting arena, which provides men with a forum to symbolically display their ability to conquer and lead, fulfills the qualities Marc Feigen Fasteau assigns to the ideal male: "The male machine is a special kind of being, different from women, children, and men who don't measure up ... He has armour plating which is virtually impregnable. His circuits are never scrambled or overrun by irrelevant personal signals. He dominates and outperforms his fellows" (1974, 2). Fasteau argues that there should be no confusion when it comes to the sexes, and that men should reassert themselves in their *proper* patriarchal position. In case people need to be reminded of exactly what this position entails, Tony Simpson points out that it "is not normal for a male to be in submission to a female and like it ... These so-called males are in submission to the warped standards of females who like to set the dress and grooming standards for their mousy husbands, their pantywaist boyfriends or their feminine sons" (1992, 262). The complete absurdity of these positions is noteworthy because of their unfortunate appeal to many North American men; more importantly, here they are symbolically played out within the "male-preserve" of hockey, where specific male qualities are celebrated, and others demeaned. The "male-preserve" of hockey therefore needs to be fully explored, if we are to examine how male exclusionary practices validate one male experience and debase others.

To begin, let us turn briefly to David Whitson's essay "Sport in the Social Construction of Masculinity," where he proposes two basic concepts. First, those in sport who establish themselves in "forceful and space-occupying ways" learn "to associate such behaviour with being a man." Second, "sport as a 'male preserve' has served as an important site in the construction of male solidarity," one that encourages "men to identify with other men and provides for the regular rehearsal of such identifications" (1990, 21). What quickly became evident from my study of the Reds was that the construction of male solidarity is an act of power that attempts to reduce the status of all other experience, while strengthening this one limited model of masculinity. The extent to which the "male preserve" attempts to remain intact, and how it occupies all facets of the players' lives, needs emphasizing. For example, the fact that players are expected to spend the majority of their time together as a team as opposed to with their families clearly illustrates the imposition of team unity. Even married team members are required by coaches to spend long periods of time with the team, as former professional hockey player Doe indicates in the following discussion:

ROBIDOUX: Okay, would even the married guys, though, spend most of their time with the guys, do you think? Or would it be more with their family do you think?
DOE: I think [pause] –

ROBIDOUX: Like throughout a twenty-four hour time span?
DOE: Probably more with the guys on the team. I bet eighty percent of
the time would be spent with the guys on the team. (Doe 1996)

In effect, the family at home is replaced by the family provided by
the hockey organization. As Reds goaltender Jack Hammer states:
"You know the guys in the dressing room are your family almost.
It's kind of overused, but it is. It's who you're with all the time,
and you go through ups and downs with them" (Hammer 1996).
Hammer, who is currently contemplating retirement after fifteen
years in the NHL, later said to me, "I have two daughters that live
in Atlantis all the time. And you know, last season I didn't see
them for eight straight months." He was still having difficulty,
however, deciding who he was going to place first in his life, his
family or his team: "And you know, it comes to a point, do I still
want to [pause] put [pause] do I still want to put hockey before
my family, or do I want to put my family before my hockey
career?" (Hammer 1996). The commitment these players are
required to make to their teams is profound. Instead of resisting
these demands, however, the players generally appear to revel in
the "homosocial" environment.

LOOKING CRITICALLY
AT THE HOMOSOCIAL ENVIRONMENT

The concept of homosociality is especially useful when examining
the male preserve of professional hockey. Although the term signifies same-sex interaction, it does not connote homosexual relations.
As Eve Kosofsky Sedgwick asserts, "'Homosocial' is a word occasionally used in history and the social sciences, where it describes
social bonds between persons of the same sex; it is a neologism,
obviously formed by analogy with 'homosexual,' and just as obviously meant to be distinguished from 'homosexual'" (1985, 1). The
distinction between "homosocial" and "homosexual" is an important one that directs us to the notion of the separative experience
of homosociality. The shared male experience of professional
hockey not only promotes segregation between men and women,
it also segregates and devalues other men that do not fit within this
hegemonic structure (Bird 1996, 121). But the male power symbolically played out in the professional hockey arena is ultimately

illusory. This power remains intact *only* within the framework of the team: when players venture outside of the male preserve, much of the power associated with physical supremacy erodes. Put simply, physical dominance has limited currency in contemporary society; thus, this somewhat archaic model of masculinity is generally ineffective. It is not surprising that players willingly chose to spend eighty percent of their time within the enclosure of the team, denying themselves not only of family but of other life experiences as well. What, then, are the ramifications of living within this limiting environment?

If we listen to the players describe life within their exclusively male domain, we see remarkable male bonds that, according to the players, would likely not develop in any other context. Sean Pack, a former Junior and Varsity hockey player, explained to me: "Oh yeah! I was by far the closest to John Doe when I played for the [Junior team], simply because I also lived with the guy. He was almost two years older, and I know I am sort of straying off your questioning here Mike, but he was almost a brotherly figure, so to speak. So it almost transcended the fact that we played hockey together. He was almost, you know, a brother" (Pack 1996). In an interview I conducted with NHL veteran Don Maxwell, he informed me that there is certainly a special bond between players:

You know I've played with guys in the past, who for two or three years I might be lucky to see for two or three days a year on a good year. But for that one or two years, they were someone that you just hang out with constantly. That you could speak [to] about anything, and freely. And not worry about it going any farther than that. And it was just like a place where you could release. And vice versa. You know, it seems like every player – or pretty well every player – has someone on a team that they're a little bit tighter to than the other guys. You know, maybe there's two or three guys, but there's always a little bit tighter of a group that would do anything, whether it was on the ice or off the ice. (Maxwell 1996)

All the players clearly indicated that through hockey they experienced personal relationships that exceeded mere friendship, that were more of a brotherly kind of bond. Nevertheless, while these relationships on the surface appear to be both genuine and appealing, an underlying problem exists that can potentially pose a serious danger to a player's personal development.

To begin, the intimacy found within this community is somewhat dubious, inasmuch as the players are coerced into these special relationships. Clearly, success in hockey is highly dependent on the players coming together and working/playing as one; measures – such as rituals – are used to ensure this unified dynamic. But the competitive nature of professional hockey means that players are constantly competing against one another. This competition could simply entail working oneself up onto the top line; it could mean becoming the starting goaltender. (In the case of the Reds, the players compete to work themselves up into the NHL.) If players do not maintain this competitive edge within what is clearly a precarious environment, others will take their job, or even steal their opportunity for advancement. Listening to the players talk about this "dog-eat-dog" world only underlines the real superficiality of the so-called special bonds between players. For example, Darren Feld, who has been with the Reds longer than any other current Reds player and is regularly overlooked by the parent club for younger and more skilled players, has a pragmatic outlook about his relationship with the rest of the team:

When you play hockey for a living, you get very competitive, and you see it in everything that you do. You go out to shoot pool; there is always a little bet on the go. Like chess, there's a little bet on the go. You want to win – very proud. Guys play cribbage, they lose, they get pissed off. I think you have to have that to be a professional athlete. If you don't want to take buddy's job beside you, you're the one that is in trouble. And if you're waiting to let the guy take your job, you're out. So you can't have it both ways. Even if it's a team sport, I want buddy's job right beside me. You know what I mean. (Feld 1997)

Feld's comments call into question how real these inscrutable bonds in professional hockey are; in fact, his comments suggest that one's fellow players are seen as obstacles to success as opposed to a source of intimate relations.

The struggle for success in hockey appears to overwhelm any notion of fraternity, making the profession much more individualistic than the usual portrayal. Jack Hammer articulates further the need for players to put themselves first: "I mean because that's what it all depends on. You have to be better than the other goalie, you have to be better than the shooter in all the games. That's how I grew up; that's why I've made it to where I am today. Because I have just striven for that all the time. But at some point in your life, you have to put that aside; you can't live everyday like that you know" (Hammer 1996). Instead of describing a harmonious atmosphere using familial metaphors, some players speak of behaviour that is more typical of vultures. Just as a wounded animal becomes a victim of prey, so too does the hockey player: "You know when I was first breaking into the NHL, there would be games where my hand was so sore from fighting I couldn't even close or open it, but I'd still play. I wasn't going to say I couldn't play because sometimes, you know, you sit out one game, and somebody steps in and does your job: and then you're out of a job!" (Falk 1997).

The basis of relations in hockey is competitiveness; that exemplifies the capitalist framework in which it is housed. Performance and production are actually alienating processes that pit one person against another in the struggle to succeed. Early in his career the hockey player learns that his profession is built on self-interest, and that every man sees "in other men not the *realization*, but rather the *limitation* of his own liberty" (Marx 1963b, 25). Because the foundation of this system of relations promotes individualism, the possibility for intimate relations is seriously reduced. What is deemed most positive about the homosocial environment, then, is largely superficial. If we compound this with the limited viability of a man whose power is based entirely on his ability to be physically dominant, the failings of this homogeneous, homosocial existence become that much more profound.

CHALLENGING ETHNIC DISTINCTION

The well-defined structure that the professional hockey community provides needs to be recognized as the discriminatory[6] environment that it is. We have already determined how it discriminates in terms of gender. But its limitations encroach on all aspects of life. More specifically, the hockey identity does not draw only on a "definitively male model," it is also definitively North American, Caucasian, and, as Marc Lavoie convincingly argues in *Désavantage Numérique*, prejudicially English-speaking.[7] However, these discriminatory measures are very subtle, for they are deeply ingrained in the development of hockey players. In fact, when players were asked how they respond to teammates of different ethnicity, they said ethnicity really makes no difference. Indeed, the players seem to be truly accepting of both African-Canadian and African-American players, as well as of the increasing number of European players arriving in North America to play professionally. But on closer inspection, the players' responses indicate that their acceptance is conditional. In one interview I asked Tim Chip how he felt about playing with European-born players, and he replied:

CHIP: Good. Good, I lived with one this year: a Russian.
ROBIDOUX: Oh really eh?
CHIP: Yeah, they're good guys. Guys are guys, no matter where they are. (Chip 1996)

I do not question Chip's sincerity here. Nor do I doubt that he had an enjoyable experience with the Russian player. But what is problematic is the length to which the Russian player had to extend himself to become a "regular guy," just like everyone else.

What I am arguing here is that ethnicity – and as already discussed, masculinity – is accepted if it is expressed within the pre-existing homogeneous framework. A Russian is a "good guy" if he abandons cultural traits that make him distinct from the group and conforms to the model of behaviour with which he has become acquainted through such things as rituals and language. Czech Republic–born player Mikel Zakov, when asked about his experience of coming to Canada to play hockey, indicated, as expected, that the transition had been tremendously difficult. He explained that in the "first year, I was unhappy and I didn't want to be here. I just wanted to go home all the time because I couldn't speak English; I was going to school with little kids to learn" (Zakov 1997). He said that he disliked the pressures placed on him to become more like a North American player, when, ironically, it was his distinctly European style that made him a valuable asset to teams in North America. "They're telling us that we're not tough enough, or we're not hitting enough, but that's not really what I came to do here. You know, they have thousands of people who can hit and who can fight and who can do all those things, but they have only a few people who score and who can make good passes so you can win the game" (Zakov 1997). And these demands to be more like North American players do not stop on the ice. Zakov continues to struggle to reconcile the pressures of assimilation with the desire to remain true to himself and his ethnicity: "Like with [pause] my closer friends I'm really just myself – really European style and whatever. But, but between people who I don't really know as well, I just try – not pretend – but try to be more like Canadians. And I don't know why I'm doing it. Because I don't even like that, but I'm doing it. You know, I just – probably to be a bit closer. I don't know, I don't really know why I'm doing it" (Zakov 1997). As he explained this to me he became visibly upset, and, understandably, his command of the English language quickly began to deteriorate. Taken aback by this sudden outburst, I simply sat as Zakov continued, painfully, to describe the results of homogenization in hockey. As he spoke, I became increasingly incensed at the thought that his resistance to assimilation would only jeopardize his career as a hockey player in North America.

At one point in the interview, Zakov actually discussed the futility of trying to counter the forces that reduced his, and other European players', identity. He was referring specifically to Don Cherry's weekly attacks on European players on *Hockey Night in Canada* and to Cherry's call for fellow Canadians to keep the game Canadian. Zakov admitted: "It hurts when you see him [Cherry] on TV. But you can't really make a big deal of it because if you say something against him, there's ten million people behind him, saying, 'Well you're not right, he's right.' Because I know how Canadians just love him" (Zakov 1997). The result is that instead of resisting this North American model, European players seek acceptance and praise for abandoning their so-called weaker style of play and appropriating a tougher, more violent brand of hockey. In a recent article in the *Troy Examiner* profiling the Russian rookie, Reds defenceman Nicolas Yeltsin, both the author and players interviewed legitimize Yeltsin's worth because of his ability to conform to a North American style of play. In the article, Jim Falk states: "A lot of European defencemen like to play a controlled game, let the puck do the work," but "Nicky is a throwback to the old defencemen. He does anything to win. He'll block a shot, take a hit, give a hit … anything" (1997a). The article begins with the author setting the tone with a vignette intended to capture the hearts of North American readers: "Nicolas Yeltsin extends his right hand, fingers curling to form a fist. He shows off a battle scar, a half-inch wound on the large knuckle. He smiles as I inquire about the condition of the person on the receiving end of the blow.

The Troy Reds' rookie rearguard didn't mash his hand swatting hockey helmets. Instead, an unsuspecting Moscow car thief learned the hard way Yeltsin is one hombre you don't mess with" (1997a). Clearly, the framework has been laid out for "Nicky," and his ability to succeed therein has quickly made him one of the franchise's top prospects.[8] It is evident, too, that the pressures to conform are enormous: not only must players contend with becoming "one of the guys" off the ice, but they must also become a *true player* on the ice. Otherwise, they suffer the consequences of social and professional ostracism.

What must be understood, however, is that the barriers faced by would-be professional hockey players are not limited to the fact that they belong to an ethnic minority, or that they are women or homosexuals. Rather, it is that any experience that does not fit within the specific hegemonic paradigm is discriminated against. In fact, discrimination in the hockey community exceeds ethnicity, gender, or class. Examine coach of the AHL Springfield *Spartans* and former hockey star Bob Carlyle's explanation of the basic principles of hockey: "It's like black and white players: we have Bruce Coles, a black player on our hockey team who I admire, who I think is a good hockey player. He works very very hard. And it's a very simple philosophy, you know if you look at it. If the players work hard – if we had a woman who could get the job done, and she earned it, she would play" (Carlyle 1997). In other words, if someone can simply *just be a guy* he (or she) will have no problem adjusting to life as a hockey player and will be well received within the community. What has historically not been understood, however, is that while some players may take pleasure in fulfilling these traditional expectations, others simply do not fit this mould. As Zakov attests, they suffer terribly, either forcing themselves to assume this normalized behaviour or, having rejected it, facing the scrutiny of an intolerant group. Jackson Katz explains: "There is evidence that many men are uncomfortable with other men's bragging about sexual exploits, dislike men's preoccupation with commenting on women's bodies, and misperceive the extent of other men's sexual activity. These men may belong to a 'silent majority' who keep their discomfort to themselves rather than express disagreement or intervene in an environment which they perceive as unsympathetic" (1995, 166). Players outside this framework are therefore forced to suffer silently, while those within it exist in a constructed universe removed from larger society.

Throughout this chapter, I have explored the manner in which gender identities are constructed in the homosocial realm of professional hockey. Unlike those who look to a single, absolute image of masculinity to alleviate many of the difficulties today's men go through as gender perceptions become increasingly ambiguous, I contend that *absolute* constructions of identity limit human interaction and subsequent experience. The security a particular group receives from perceiving itself as homogeneous makes involvement outside the group not only unnecessary, but potentially threatening. Therefore, when Chip, a professional hockey player and personal acquaintance of mine, claims that "guys are guys, no matter where they are," and, "I find it's always easier to deal with guys than with women [accompanied by a quiet chuckle]" (Chip 1996), he evokes the comfort some players find when dwelling within these rigid boundaries. These statements – however misleading – illustrate the severe limitations faced by players immersed in their own closed environment.

Moreover, these statements are, in fact, erroneous. The environment is not as "intact" as it initially appears; in reality, the competitive nature of the occupation pits players against one another. In order to survive within the league, players must be opportunists; they must place their own welfare above others or another player will soon replace them. The players are constantly reminded of this threat, as when coach Murphy verbally accosts the players for their "gutless" performances the night previous: "Lots of guys want your fucking jobs, so just think of that next time you step onto the ice!" (Field Notes 1996). Any comfort the players are able to draw from this brutally competitive environment is therefore cherished; paradoxically, it serves as the only real sense of stability in the players' lives. More specifically, the ability to perform within a team dynamic is crucial to individual success; if team success is dependent upon team unity, forming special bonds within the group (superficial though they may be) serves as a means to an end for player empowerment. As a result, the group, as the primary source of power, dictates the manner in which the players respond within it and how they articulate its significance. The homogenized male, then, must be understood as a product of the process of player empowerment, as players attach themselves to this predefined team/ group identity. But the question then becomes, is power truly achievable within this closed and discriminatory environment? In the next chapter we shall explore how expressions of power are manifested through group solidarity, while simultaneously contributing to group and individual powerlessness.

CHAPTER EIGHT

Power, Play, and Powerlessness

The celebrated status of professional hockey players in Canada is a phenomenon experienced by the players in virtually all aspects of their lives. In addition to the adoration of fans during the games – their cheering and holding up of signs showing their admiration for the players – the players also receive privileged treatment away from the arena. In *The Game*, Ken Dryden discusses this preferential handling of hockey players, saying "this kind of special treatment we have grown accustomed to, and enjoy. We have been *special* for most of our lives. It began with hockey, with names and faces in local papers as teenagers, with hockey jackets that only the best players on the best teams wore, with parents who competed not so quietly on the side ... On the street, in restaurants and theatres, you are pointed out, pointed at, talked about like the weather" (1983, 158). The players are international celebrities and are treated as such by the public. Reds athletic therapist Jones, in an interview, explained to me that the players are "professional athletes, and everyone wants to be associated with a professional athlete. So you make friends pretty quickly. And the guys, they get a lot of stuff, and they want to give you stuff. Because they want to be with you. You know, free meal, fifty-percent discount on clothing; they want to give you this, that, and the other thing. And the guys eat it up" (Jones 1996). The public's privileging of professional hockey players naturally means the players live with a sense of importance and a sense of power. They see themselves as highly fortunate. Reds forward Jerry Wall one day asked me rhetorically: "What would you rather be doing on a Tuesday night than playing a hockey game in front of thousands of people?" (Wall 1996b). Yet this privileged position does not guarantee power. In fact, the celebrated status of professional hockey players ironically contributes to their vulnerability in the labour process.

The game of professional hockey is riddled with paradox. Fundamentally, it is the product of big business. Yet the business aspect of the game is perceived by the media, the public, and many players and coaches as the bane of hockey's existence. The players are praised for playing for "the love of the game" and scorned and considered selfish if money takes precedence in their career decisions. As a result, players have generally avoided the business aspect of the game, focusing instead on the game itself and leaving themselves ignorant of league and franchise operations. The fortune associated with being a professional hockey player and the special status that accompanies it have seriously prevented the players from scrutinizing their role within the labour process. When I asked veteran Reds goaltender Paul Proux if he resented any of the demands placed upon him by this franchise, such as curfews or the general monopolization of his time, he responded indignantly: "You're paid – you're expected to do that job and it's a great job. And you realize that a lot of other people are trying to get your job. So, no, I think that somebody who would not respect that would be a fool, because it's such a great job" (Proux 1996). Unfavourable labour circumstances are rationalized by the players and interpreted merely as occupational hazards to be quickly dismissed. Within this chapter we shall consider professional hockey as the disadvantaged process it is, as opposed to the occupation of power that it is perceived to be. Moreover, the players' responses to the demands of labour will be explored, in the hope of elucidating what can be best understood as a disadvantaged negotiation of power.

FROM CHILDHOOD DREAM TO LABOUR

The National Hockey League Players' Association (NHLPA) and the Professional Hockey Players' Association (PHPA)[1] have made great strides in informing the players and the public of the injustices done to professional hockey players over the years by both the leagues and the team owners. The two associations have also been instrumental in raising minimum league salaries and providing suitable benefits; that is, health plans and pensions.[2] Yet that said, from my discussions with the Reds and other players around the league, it seems that the majority are barely cognizant of their rights as pro-

fessional hockey players. As Bob Tucker, a player represent[a]
for one of the visiting AHL teams during the Reds season, expl[a]
to me, "It's a really funny situation, because I don't think players
really realize their rights until something negative happens to them"
(Tucker 1996). Furthermore, it appears that the players have no
real interest in learning about their rights. When I asked the Reds
player representative, Jerry Wall, if the players were concerned
about what their union offered them in terms of protection or bargaining power, he responded: "No, well I mean it's not something
that we worry about. I mean we're here to play hockey. I think it's
nice to have that [the player's association], but as far as concern, I
mean, we know it's there, so it's just a comfort I guess" (Wall
1996b). Because the opportunity to play professional hockey is, for
most players, the fulfilment of a childhood dream, few scrutinize
their job and/or working environment. Because they perceive themselves to be fortunate, they do not look critically at their role within
the labour process. Thus, they are left highly vulnerable in an
already disadvantaged employer-employee relationship.

Despite the players' apparent complacency, however, they are
quick to point out that what they do is in fact labour intensive,
and that their experiences playing hockey are quite different from
their expectations on first entering the league. A former hockey
acquaintance of mine, currently playing in the NHL, when asked a
year prior to my ethnography of the Reds about his experiences
playing pro hockey, responded that while those "outside" hockey
may perceive it as a game that grown men are paid to play, it is
seen quite differently from the "inside":

You know, it's been something when you're a kid you always watch – you
never think it can happen – [that] there's a chance. And when you do get
a chance, you just want to play that one game, just to say that you did
it. And then once you do it, then you just want to – okay, I want to play
a year. And then it just snowballs and snowballs. And you know what it
is, it's an accomplishment, and it's a job, and it's a living. And what I
found out after, after the novelty of making the NHL wore off: you know,
you can look at it and, being on the inside, it's not a game like what people
see from the outside, it's a job. There's good days, there's bad days. There's
days you just don't want to go. And then there's days where you couldn't
have imagined doing anything else. But people look at it, and you know,
you can talk to anyone, I'm sure, and they would say, "but you're in the

NHL; I would do anything to play in the NHL." And it's easy for them to say that. And it's also easy for me to say that it's not all that it's cracked up to be. Because it is great. You know, it's premier, but it's a hard go. You got to take the good with the bad. (Maxwell 1996)

The public perceptions of professional sport are generally based on the glimpses provided by the media via either live game telecasts or interviews conducted before, during, and/or after the actual games played. These brief and often skewed images of professional sport, along with the seemingly recreational language used to discuss the experience – such as "games," and "played" – inadequately represent life as a professional hockey player. In fact, Reds goaltender Proux responded angrily to my comments in an interview about the potential fun a hockey player experiences while living on the road:[4]

ROBIDOUX: I noticed just now in the practice that this was probably one of the most playful practices you guys have had in awhile. And I'm wondering if it's because you guys are going together as a team on this road trip. Do you guys generally have fun taking these road trips?
PROUX: Fun! You know, they're not always fun. You know they're hard – a lot of times they're hard. Today we are starting in Troy and tomorrow night we travel for five or six hours on the bus. The next morning we get up and then we play that night. I don't know how you would call [laughing] that fun! It's hard; it's not easy when you finish a game and you are just drenched, and you are tired and stuff, and you have to go sit on the bus two-by-two, in a bus for six hours. I'm not too sure guys would[n't] rather be at home and just go back to their place. So, no, I don't think so. (Proux 1996)

Despite the players' claims that playing hockey is a propitious situation, it was evident early on that they were consistently expressing sentiments that actually undermined this apparent contentment. While the players all spoke highly of their trade, they seemed to struggle, consciously and unconsciously, with their predicament.

While examples of these conflicting messages are numerous, I will focus on two that are especially revealing. The first centres on one individual, Jack Hammer, who was sent down from the Reds' parent club in November – meaning he was demoted – after playing in the NHL for over fifteen years. As an older player in the league (thirty-eight years of age), his skills were not as sharp as they once were and his services had become redundant. In order to demote Hammer, the parent organization was required to place him on waivers, meaning that any other team was free to pick up his contract. However, Hammer had signed a large contract three years earlier, which prevented teams from selecting him. In other words, Hammer was now a financial burden who easily cleared waivers, thus forcing the demotion. He thus had two options: to continue to play for the Troy Reds and hope to be traded by the Reds' parent club; or to retire. I truly felt sorry for Hammer; I had watched and admired him throughout his career and was curious to find out what his intentions were.

We met for an interview after a mid-week practice; Hammer brought me into the dressing room after the other players had departed. Because he had just finished undergoing therapy for a shoulder injury, he was wired to a device during the interview which, he said, sent electric pulses through his shoulder in hopes of healing damaged muscle tissue. So as not to waste time, I began asking him about his response to the demotion. Did he, for example, have any ill feelings towards management. "Well," he replied, "I can't complain about the way they treated me and my family. And I think they do respect the fact that I put in a lot of time. But, you know it's results, and if there are no results they have to make a change. And you know I respect that, just like the fact that if I'm playing well I want to play more often. So you know, I can't complain about the organization at all. I mean they're first class ... it all depends on your, you know, results and I wasn't getting results when I played so they had to do something" (Hammer 1996). As the interview progressed, however, Hammer's positive articulations of his experience in professional hockey were slowly overshadowed by brief and somewhat awkward expressions of bitterness:

Well, you know, to be quite frank, it [hockey] probably cost me one marriage. I mean I'm remarried again. And you know I'm willing to accept that my first wife couldn't handle what hockey brought. Because once I got traded, from Atlantis, where I was living, things seemed to fall apart. So you know, it probably cost me that. So you know – yes, there is no doubt that it puts a lot of strain on being away all the time, and on your kids. I mean I have two daughters that live in Atlantis all the time. And you know, last season I didn't see them for eight straight months. You know, from the start of the season I went to training camp until the season was over; I went back there in the summer. And when I talk to them it's not the same. You know when they're young like that, it does put a strain on your family. (Hammer 1996)

Later, Hammer began talking about the inevitable end of his career, which furthered this critical introspection:

If you're good at one thing, then that's pretty good ... but once hockey's put aside – when I don't have hockey I don't have anything else really. But once hockey's put aside and I'm done playing, is there something else that will give me that same gratification? I think that's where a lot of guys have trouble when they've done their pro-careers; [it] is making that adjustment to something else, to get that satisfaction from everyday like you do in hockey. There may not be anything, and there hasn't been anything for a lot of guys ... it's like I have to find something else that I'm good at, and well, this is all I know. (Hammer 1996)

Despite Hammer's self-acknowledged troublesome situation (and he is better off, both financially and in terms of career longevity, than the majority of players who have played professional hockey), he has not abandoned his positive stance towards the league and the way he was treated. It is this desire to remain part of the game that keeps Hammer in Troy, working furiously in the hope of becoming, once again, desirable to an NHL franchise; it is his desire that makes him that much more vulnerable to exploitation, and thus, virtually powerless.[5]

Hammer's commentary is especially illuminating if we consider remarks such as, "I can't complain" (which he says twice in the opening passage) and "you know, I respect that" (Hammer 1996). Even after a broken marriage, alienation from his children, and virtually no practical life skills to help him make the transition out of hockey, he publicly supports the league and its ideology. But Hammer's puzzling stance is less troubling when we hear his team-mate Peter Copper naturalize the exploitative situation of professional hockey. My discussion with Copper began when I asked him to explain the "waiver" rule in pro-hockey. He responded:

Guys that have played over three years are eligible to be picked up by other teams before being sent right down to the minors – the minor league system. But nowadays, not many players are really touched. It's very rare that a guy gets picked up. Except for the waiver draft, and that's a different example, where guys do get picked up because it is an official day. In other words, I think that the GMs [general managers] just say, "don't touch my guy and we won't touch yours." And leave it at that. So that's basically how the waivers go. And there's two weeks conditioning too, where guys get sent down just for two weeks, but they don't have to clear waivers. (Copper 1996)

When I sought clarification, asking Copper if "the waiver system [is] supposed to free up players," he answered: "It's supposed to be good for the player, but it hasn't really worked out to the benefit of us. It pretty much came in about two years ago when they [NHLPA] signed the new agreement with the NHL owners. Unfortunately, we figured as players it would work a little better where guys would get picked up – go on other teams and get opportunities elsewhere. Or maybe another team needed a player; the type of player that's being sent down by another club." Again I asked, "So it seems like management and ownership seem to be able to keep their stranglehold on where players are playing?" He responded, "Yeah, kind of, kind of. Yeah. I mean, we as players have a little more leeway than we used to. Before they pretty well controlled everything, but we got a little bit more out of our last agreement that could benefit us as players." The fact that Copper was clearly aware of what was happening to him, yet resisted being critical of his situation, fascinated me.

I pursued the matter further, asking Copper how he felt about being sent down to the minors[6] after spending so much time playing in the NHL. His response is noteworthy. Not only did he accept his situation, he actually commended the team for treating him in that way: "Well, it's part of the business of hockey. Right now for me, I'm injured and I haven't played in a month. So, as a matter of getting healthy, I'm coming to play some games. And you know if I was running a team, that's what I would do with the players too. Cause it's the business side. You don't want your people sitting around when they could be getting better, or [be] improving their skills by playing elsewhere. And that's pretty much how the teams deal with them nowadays. And as players, it's our job to accept that and work our way back to where we want to be" (Copper 1996). What Copper does not reveal here, however, is that "getting better" or "improving their skills" comes at an enormous price for the players because the vast majority have signed "two-way" contracts. What this means is that players will receive a certain sum of money playing in one league and another sum if they are demoted to a lesser league. In the AHL/PHPA bargaining agreement, a two-way contract is described as follows: "A Player on an AHL contract which contains specific provision for assignment to lesser leagues shall receive only those benefits which are provided to players in such a league, during period of assignment" (16). The NHL contracts are fashioned around the two-way clause as well; thus, players, although they may sign an enormous contract to play in the NHL, must actually play in the NHL to receive the money for which they initially signed. Moreover, the discrepancy between the two salaries is considerable, meaning substantial financial losses for time not spent in the NHL.

A concrete example of the two-way payment system can be seen in the case of the Reds goaltender Paul Proux. An article in the *Troy Examiner*[7] says that "Proux will earn $400,000 Cdn if he remains in the NHL, and only $55,000 if he's relegated to the minors" (1997b). Therefore, for the time Proux spends playing with the Troy Reds as opposed to the parent organization, he will be losing approximately eighty-six percent of his salary. Some players have managed to sign one-way contracts, but those players with the bargaining power to make such a deal – the exceptionally skilled players – will likely not be demoted; thus, the one-way contract is of little or no consequence to management or to these few fortunate individuals. Hence, the significance of Copper's rationalization of his predicament becomes that much more difficult to comprehend if we consider the huge financial consequences of his perceived opportunity to work his "way back to where he wants to be." To make matters worse, aside from a few brief stints with the parent organization, Copper remained in Troy to finish up the season; thus, he never did move back to where he wanted to be. But instead of expressing any resentment, he accepts his situation as "part of the game," saying "that's just the way it works" (Copper 1996).

The players' description of their situation within professional sport is often paradoxical, their love of and pride in their work countering the expressions of maltreatment. Both Hammer and Copper are cognizant of their precarious position within the labour process, yet both refrain from directly criticizing the league or speaking out against the way it has treated them. Instead, the difficulties encountered are rationalized as being "part of the job" and most often articulated as a positive experience:

You knew which way the game was going when Wayne Gretzky got traded. I mean there's the greatest hockey player ever, and a guy can look at him and say – still with great years left in him – we're going to trade him, because for some reason it's going to be better for the team. So if he can get traded, anybody in the league can get traded. And that's what happens you know, they look at you as a commodity or as a piece of meat, and they say we got to move you on because we want this guy here. You know, it happens a lot. It's a lot harder for people with families and kids who are in school; they have to move them out. So I guess in that way I'm a little lucky and have no one travelling. You know in my younger years I didn't mind it. It was a lot of fun, single guy, travelling all over North America. (Falk 1997)

Despite the fact that Falk is describing professional hockey as a corporate structure that treats players as chattels to secure franchise prosperity, he accepts it as part of the trade; he turns it into an opportunity to see parts of the world he would not have seen otherwise. Falk and I then discussed the various injuries he had incurred over the years playing in over sixteen cities. Again, the same thinking process is disturbingly evident:

FALK: There's always the minor injuries that keep you out for a couple of games here and there. But they add up over the years.
ROBIDOUX: What kind of injuries would they be?
FALK: Broken knuckles, broken fingers [pause], pulled muscles [pause], minor separated shoulder; all kinds of stuff like that.
ROBIDOUX: Cuts and stuff like that?
FALK: Yeah, cuts. I had one of my testicles split in half in Junior with a slapshot [we burst out laughing]. So I was out for a couple of games.
ROBIDOUX: So these injuries are quite common for hockey players?
FALK: Yeah, I think, depending on what you do, injuries are going to be there. I guess they say now it's people who sit in front of a computer all day [who] are coming up with these problems, these health problems and stuff. So, my point of view is that, you know hockey's a rough fast game and there's going to be a greater chance of more serious injuries, but you

also have a chance to get injured just walking down the street and so on. So, that's about it.

ROBIDOUX: Do you feel any chronic pain at all?

FALK: I feel a little, mostly [in] my hands; I guess it would be a little arthritis. Each morning I get up and I can hardly tighten up my skates. But then again, that's – everyone gets arthritis don't they? I mean I'm turning thirty-one next week, next month, so I'm getting up there in age. It feels like some mornings I wake up and my whole body is sore: muscles and everything, shoulders and that. You know its probably got something to do with my age and playing the game. (Falk 1997)

Falk equates "split testicles," the "inability to tie his skates" and chronic muscle and joint pain to natural aging processes and the potential danger of "walking down the street." His response is typical, inasmuch as few players challenge their predicament within the labour process. This makes Ken Dryden's response to his situation especially significant: "It has never seemed right to me that someone should have that power over me, or over anyone … I simply find it demeaning. And whenever I've lingered with the thought long enough to confront myself, I've always come to the same conclusion – that if I were ever traded, no matter where, I couldn't accept the helpless, shabby sense of manipulation I would feel and [I would] retire" (1983, 147).

Dryden's comments now seem ironic, given his 1997 hiring by the NHL Toronto Maple Leafs as team president and general manager. In this new position – which involves, among other things, making player trades to improve the team – Dryden has been criticized for unsound human resource management, most notably the poor treatment of goaltender Felix Potvin. After the acquisition of superstar goaltender Curtis Joseph in a free-agent signing in the 1998 off-season, Potvin's services were no longer needed; his contract was a financial burden for the organization. Although the Leafs made efforts to trade Potvin, they were unable to make a trade they believed to be satisfactory for the *team*. Showing total disregard for Potvin's personal predicament, the Leafs traded him two-thirds of the way into the season. Potvin, who had sat out for almost the entire season, was negatively affected by this work stoppage and had tremendous difficulty performing for his new club, the New York Islanders. After a disappointing year with the Islanders, Potvin was again traded, this time to the Vancouver

Canucks. There he did show signs of regaining his confidence, and his play improved significantly.

In his book *The Game*, Dryden discusses his powerless position as a player within the Montreal Canadians' organization; he sees retirement as the only escape from being traded. Without education or any real formal training in something other than hockey, however, retirement for most players is not a real option. Reds athletic therapist Jones once told me in an interview that the majority of the team's players "don't even know how to go to a bank and open up an account. They've never done this before because their Mommies or their hockey teams have done it for them. They haven't been exposed to those things that people have to do, like renting homes, buying food, and getting car insurance. All those things: getting a telephone installed; getting cable installed" (Jones 1997). Do players, then, articulate a response to their subordinate role in the labour process? Or do they passively accept the "business" of hockey and try their best to function within the system in place?

It is crucial to note here that, despite their apparent passivity the players *are* aware of the conflicting relationship at the core of the labour process – the relationship whereby the demands of one group involve the exploitation of another. And it is through this fundamental acknowledgement that the conflict arises. Although the players are rarely seen challenging the existing hegemony, they resist the demands of labour both consciously and unconsciously to create their own relevant work world. What perhaps is most difficult to understand is behaviour that is oppositional, yet not intellectually motivated or perhaps even understood by the individuals involved. In other words, if the players are not fully cognizant of their own role within this power/manipulation dynamic, how real can this antagonistic relationship be?

But resistance in fact does exist as players enter into a relationship with a dominant managerial corporate culture, where labour is typically exploited for the financial success of ownership. The players' resistance is most often simply achieved without the means or desire to rationalize their experience within the labour process; often, moreover, its form is not easily identifiable. For Reds players, it was manifested through play. Briefly, the greatest difficulty that players face while playing professional hockey is the pressure placed on them to perform flawlessly on every occasion. This emphasis on success and winning only undermines the nature of sport, since losing is experienced far more often than winning.[8] Hence the "winning is everything" sensibility of professional hockey is quite illogical. By refusing to acknowledge the value of losing, ownership has altered the dynamic of the performance: "play" is no longer possible. No longer engaged in play, the players now work at producing "victories." Without winning, the game is lost in both senses of the word: the "losers," who have failed to produce, lose whatever points would have been available to them through victory; moreover, what was presented as a game is also lost, as the process of playing is inconsequential if victory is not achieved.

The players struggle, then, to regain control of the labour process by turning back into play what management has turned into work. While the business of hockey has been, and continues to be, seen as outside the players' control, the game itself becomes contested by the players. Peter Jackson explains:

During the games you basically can control what happens out there, because you're out there playing. It's not the management, it's not the coach or anything. And you know, you can control what's happening during the game. But it's the things that happen after the game, or outside the game, or [the] different moves the organization makes that you can't control ... things like that. But during the game, as long as you're playing – as long as you're on the ice – you have control over what happens ... so basically when you're on the ice, you pretty much control your own destiny. I mean there's five guys out there, but, your job – everyone else has a job with a role – and you can pretty much control it. (Jackson 1997)

Thus, the players discuss hockey as a dichotomous experience where there are "two things: one is the business part of it; and two, is the love of the game. And you always have to keep that love of the game there. If you take it too far, where I mean the game is coming into a lot of money and you don't have that love of the game, you're not going to succeed. And you just have to make sure you keep the game fun, and just keep going out there and working hard every day" (Toll 1996). The occupation of professional hockey player can be seen, then, in terms of any capitalist labour institution. Just as the labourer in any other work culture attempts to "gain informal control of the workplace," the hockey player "transforms work into a game" – one in which there is informal resistance to "the intensity of exploitation in the labour process" (Dunk 1991, 7). As a result, *play* within the workplace can be a cultural signifier that communicates individual and group empowerment.

PLAYING FOR POWER

It was at the conclusion of every practice, when the Reds "played" at hockey as opposed to working at the game, that I appreciated the importance of their play. In chapter four, where I alluded to aspects of the games the players played and the enthusiasm with which they played, I made the comparison to children at play. During an especially playful time, I wrote in my field notes, "These guys are also 'pros' at play." My comment was made because the players' behaviour did not seem to simply consist of random moments of horseplay, but rather of a variety of games with a definite structure and purpose. Two primary games made up the players' repertoire of play; both were orally constructed and reconstructed over the season. As I watched the players make rules and instruct and reprimand those who either did not know the rules or intentionally tried to break them, it was evident that the game-making process was just as important as the play itself. The players were relatively loyal to the game frameworks they designed, which suggested that the games were important and meaningful to them as a group. The first game was called "Juice-Boy"; the second was known as the "Rebound Game."

The first game – Juice-Boy, better known as "Showdown" – is one of the first forms of hockey players learn when they come to the sport. Although they play the game during informal practice times, it has traditionally been played as a form of road hockey. Quite simply, the game involves one player approaching the net in an attempt to score a goal, while another player stands in net trying to prevent the goal from occurring. The game, although it can be played with a minimum of two players, has no maximum number of players. The point of the game is to score; if someone fails to score he is out, and the last remaining player to score wins the game. If there is only one shooter, the point of the game is to score more goals than the goaltender can stop; the goaltender, on the other hand, must stop more goals than the shooter scores. The game's appeal is threefold: first, it is simple; second, its structure allows for as many players as there are people available to play; and third, the game captures the most exciting moment of hockey:

the breakaway. It is a time, too, where players can put their skills on display, unfettered by the constant checking that would occur in an actual game. Similarly, it affords goaltenders the opportunity to make spectacular saves without worrying about the repercussions of letting in a goal. As a result, the game is filled with flair and excitement, exciting for those participating and those awaiting their turn.

The game Show-down was renamed Juice-Boy during the Reds' practices. It was also slightly modified. Although the game still maintains the principle of moving in one-on-one with the goaltender and attempting to score, additional stipulations have been added to make the game more interesting. First, as opposed to one shot, the shooter now has two opportunities to score. If he does not score, he is placed in the non-scoring group; if he is the only one in the non-scoring group he automatically loses. Second, the players are now required to start approximately ten feet from the goal, and they have the option of shooting from a standstill or moving in on the goalie in a breakaway fashion. Third, after the first attempt, the player must come to a complete stop at the place of origin before taking his second shot. If the player scores on his attempt but did not come to a complete stop, his goal is disqualified and he ends up losing a turn. Finally, those players who score on either their first or second attempt are removed from the competition and are safe from becoming "losers"; this is where the game distinguishes itself from the typical showdown format. Instead of there being one winner in Juice-Boy, the game is designed so there is only one loser, who assumes the title "Juice-Boy." The remaining players are winners.

As I watched the players engage enthusiastically in their game, those players who had already scored could be seen teasing those who had been unable to score and were now shooting to avoid losing and becoming "Juice-Boy." The players who did not score on their first attempt would play off against one another until only one person was left "goal-less." For example, if only two players remained and the first person scored on his first attempt, the next player would have two shots to try and get a goal, the objective being to "stay alive." If he was successful, the process would be repeated again and again, until only one scoreless player remained. I did not know the significance of the term "Juice-Boy" until I spoke with Reds forward Peter Jackson, who explained: "That's where everybody gets two shots at about the hash-mark. And you can deek or shoot. And whoever doesn't score just keeps playing. And whoever doesn't score goes again until there is one guy left, and he's 'Juice-Boy.' And he gets the Gatorade for all the guys who played the game after in the dressing-room. He kind of serves them like a waiter, so we call him 'Juice-Boy'" (Jackson 1997). The game, then, can be seen as a highly playful contest with players humiliating and admiring one another along the way. The players playfully mock those who fail, and at times those who succeed, but always remain faithful to the game itself. When veteran and infamous tough-guy Jim Falk failed to score during one particular practice and was tauntingly acclaimed "Juice-Boy," Falk cursed and scowled at his hecklers; he nevertheless fulfilled his duties and served drinks to the younger and weaker players after practice. By abiding by the tenets of play, this seemingly insignificant frivolity becomes a highly valued time during which players construct their own system of meaning, and set their own standards of excellence and/or failure. In this case, players have constructed a game that enables all players, except one, to be winners. This runs counter to the professional hockey premise which is, ultimately, an annual search for *one* champion and a host of losers. Players here successfully establish an alternative discourse by reinventing the "winning is everything" ideology imposed upon them from above. Moreover, the ideological value of the play helps us to understand the enthusiasm with which players engage in these, at times outrageous, playful episodes.

The other diversion in which the Reds' players eagerly participated throughout the season was the Rebound Game. In this game, the players work together as a team, as opposed to the individual challenges of Juice-Boy. The only team member who provides opposition in this game is the goaltender, who tries to prevent the players from scoring. In this respect, the goaltender's position is unidimensional, in that stopping pucks becomes his only task. The goaltender's unique position places him at odds with the remainder of the team during games and scrimmages; thus, the goaltender is primarily the adversary in the players' constructed framework of play. In this particular game, the goaltender is pitted against at least five forwards who, together, try to score within the game's boundaries.

The game itself is quite simple. One forward who stands approximately fifteen feet away from the goal is the initial shooter. His

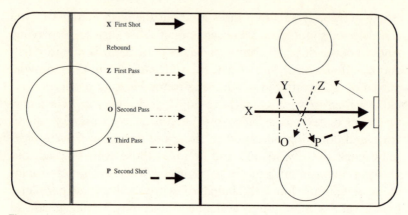

Figure 2
The Rebound Game.

role is to shoot the puck at the net in the hope of either scoring or generating a rebound (off the goaltender) so as to allow the remaining players to enter into the game. The remaining players – generally four – stand in pairs on either side of the goaltender, forming a horseshoe shape with the initial shooter (see Figure 2). After the initial shot is taken, a rebound usually occurs, and the players who are alongside the goaltender gather up the puck and attempt to score before the puck comes to a standstill. The players have several options: they can either pass the puck to one of the three other players, shoot the puck themselves, or fake the pass and shoot.

If the players cannot gather the puck before it stops, the puck is termed "dead" and a point goes to the goaltender. If the goaltender is able to corral the puck and smother it, not giving up a rebound, he is also awarded a point. The players thus have to be somewhat selective in their shooting, so as to prevent the goaltender from stopping and covering the puck.

The Rebound Game afforded the players much amusement and horseplay. Indeed, I often found myself laughing at their antics. On one particular day my field notes included the following observations: "Much laughter and joking is going on here. It is funny watching the guys make the rules to suit their needs. The guys keep score and after each play, Czech Republic–born Mikel Zakov calls out the score. When the puck nearly dies [puck comes to a standstill] the initial shooter yells 'Go Stevenson!! He got it!! He got it!! No, it's not 'out'!!!'" That an "alive" puck – one not "out" –

allows the play to continue to develop indicates that the players willingly let the rules of play govern their actions. By making this allowance, the players were able to operate within the play framework and, thus, draw pleasure from these puerile behaviours. One player's plea that the puck be kept "alive" was not made in jest, but rather with every intention of allowing his team another chance to score. Day in and day out the players could be found engaging in these playful scenarios – some more intense than others. It was apparent that the concept of play was highly valued: the games themselves were the articulation of this ideal. Thirty-one-year-old Reds defenceman Jim Falk stated: "I think there's always going to be the "game" in it: the fun. You know, we're just a bunch of kids. A lot of these guys are still twenty-one, twenty-two, twenty-three-years old. And we're, like you said, playing a game. And, it's fun to me. If I was a plumber on the other hand, if it weren't fun for me, I wouldn't be doing it. You know, I definitely wouldn't do anything that I'm not having fun at. And anybody out there not having fun at what they're doing, they should move on, because life is too short to be worrying, in misery over a job" (Falk 1997). Thus, play is ultimately seen by the players as a direct means of achieving ownership of their trade; conversely, once play and fun is lost, so too is their occupation: "Well, it [play] is important I think. You have to have fun to do real well, and you know I have to admit, of late, it hasn't been a lot of fun. And I don't think I've played as well as I can play" (Hammer 1996). By establishing play as a vital component of the labour process – through games such as Juice-Boy and the Rebound Game – players reorder their work world. And in turn, they subvert the "work-behaviour" dynamic imposed upon them by management.

CREATIVELY RESISTING SYSTEMIZATION

In addition to recognizing play as a valuable means of resisting the business of hockey, players understand it as a means of returning to the essence of the sport: to the game itself. As I stressed earlier in chapter four, professional hockey has become systematized to the extent that the so-called game aspect has been arguably removed from the sport. Journalists and fans often lament the apparent loss of the Canadian game of hockey, an outgrowth of "long northern winters uncluttered by things to do" (Dryden 1983,

134). A game "once played on rivers and ponds, later on streets and driveways and in backyards" is now played in "arenas, in full team uniform, with coaches and referees, or to an ever-increasing extent we don't play at all" (Dryden 1983, 134). The romantic sentiments expressed here are instrumental to establishing and perpetuating the mythological dimensions of hockey in Canada. Typical here is the concern that what has made hockey – and in mythological terms, what has played a part in the making of a nation – has been put in jeopardy by technology and corporate greed. The lament is that hockey has been removed from the ponds and the streets to become a booming corporate enterprise that is destroying the heart and soul of the game and, ultimately, the heart and soul of the players.

The truth is that the game of hockey has *not* been removed from frozen ponds and backyards; people of all ages across Canada are still seen playing "pond hockey" and "road hockey." More importantly here, however, is that hockey was never a game exclusively played in these more informal settings; nor, for that matter, was it ever solely the property of "the folk." In fact, the earliest forms of hockey in its vernacular sense were played by "upward striving businessmen and professionals committed to the values of individual achievement through commerce and public service" (Gruneau and Whitson 1993, 41), as opposed to the masses that romanticists would have us believe. The irony is that it was through the professionalization of hockey that underprivileged classes (whether economically or ethnically defined) were allowed access into the game; it was the professionalization of hockey that played a significant role in its popularization and its ultimate status as Canada's national pastime. What must be stressed is that by opening up the sport to those outside the dominant culture, the game itself was transformed from an amateur/bourgeois pastime to a game that reflected the commercial interests of the working-class culture that consumed it. Richard Gruneau informs us that hockey's "popularization and incorporation into a commodity form for mass consumption occurred when the game was taken over by industrial entrepreneurs, was stripped of its amateur trappings, and was reconstituted as a violent spectator sport in the mining towns of Cobalt; Haileybury; Timmins; Sault Ste. Marie; and Houghton, Michigan" (Gruneau 1983, 120). Gradually, as the game moved from the petit bourgeoisie to larger corporate enterprises, athletes from working-class backgrounds became mercenaries bound to the corporate framework that employed them.

It is not surprising, then, that in the contemporary hockey era, the division between players and owners/management continues to exist. The game continues to function as a highly successful capitalist institution, and continues to be played by contracted athletes who live largely outside the business of sport. The players openly admit to remaining outside the business decisions and finances that surround the game: "I don't like to get involved in that [finances]. I like to have someone deal with that so I can just deal with my hockey" (Jackson 1997). However, the game itself provides players with a means of asserting themselves as owners because "once everyone puts their skates on and helmet on, they go out there. We play the game you know. And it doesn't matter how much money you make, everybody wants to play hard. And everybody is proud" (Feld 1997). It is on the ice that performance is achieved and, for "most players, performances of physical excellence are an expression of self, a side of themselves they miss when they leave the game" (Gruneau and Whitson 1993, 114). The players' comments about success on the ice demonstrate that for performance to be fully realized, play/fun is essential. Incorporating and maintaining elements of play in the labour process (both formally and informally) are therefore critical steps for individual and group success; they inject creativity into the potentially oppressive systems of play that critics of the game believe lie at the root of hockey's demise.

As systems in hockey have become increasingly scientific and mechanized in their design and execution, the players, in order to produce within these systems, must find ways of circumventing them. It is nonsensical to say that "games are not won on good plays, but by others' mistakes, where the safe and sure survive, and the creative and not-so-sure may not" (Dryden 1983, 132). In order to capitalize on one's mistakes a player must do something creative with the puck – not only to create a scoring opportunity, but to actually score. Dryden's statement assumes that once a mistake is committed, a goal is an inevitable outcome. This is simply not the case. On the ice, players are constantly forced to imagine, to be creative, albeit within the systems in place; they must either compensate for human error (or the intangible misfortunes that occur throughout the game), or overcome the systems of defence that, in theory, are infallible.[9] More important, the players themselves discuss creativity and heightened behaviour on ice as something beyond what is taught or learned and, in some cases, beyond articulation.

One particular Reds player, Jason Dodd, astounded me throughout the year – in practices and in games – with the magic he performed on the ice. I use the term "magic" here deliberately, to suggest behaviour that defies natural law and human limitations. During one particular practice, Dodd performed a series of moves to go around a defender that left the other player standing still in utter disbelief, his mouth open. I wrote in my field book: "The pure talent of Jason Dodd is amazing to watch. He turns the mechanical into an art form" (Field Notes 1997). Three days later, when I asked Dodd to talk about this elevated form of performance, he said:

I think it's something tough to teach – creativity on the ice, anticipation on the ice. I think I just have a knack for anticipating where my players are: maybe where the puck's going to go ahead of other guys ... and I think that's probably why I've had some success. How to explain it, it's [pause] – like I said before, I don't really think you can teach things like that. It's just something probably that I developed over the years, playing with other creative guys. I've watched Wayne Gretzky growing up: I think he plays a lot like that. Or Stevie Yzerman, guys like that. They've just got that instinct ... I think probably a high percentage of it is just instinct. Just for example, if I'm not on my game, if I'm really not concentrating, I have a bad game. Or I don't do as well, because I'm not focused on what I have to do. And I think it's more instinctual than probably anything else. (Dodd 1997)

Dodd accredits his success to this instinctual level of play that simply defies explication. It is common for players to discuss this level of play with clichés and exoteric language, for the simple reason that it is performed outside of everyday experience. "When I'm having a good game, like a really good game – one of my better games – guys call it that in you're 'in the zone,' or whatever, I guess. I don't know if it's that, but I feel that I can go out there and do things, and I know that I'm not going to mess up. I'm going to do the right play all the time. Or, you know, ninety-eight percent of the times. You're still going to have mistakes, but I'm going to make the right play, the right decision when my total mind set is focused, and I'm totally prepared for that shift or that game" (Dodd 1997). Similar sentiments were expressed by goaltender Jack Hammer in our conversation earlier in the season:

ROBIDOUX: I'm wondering about those times during a game when you make a really great save or something, or you really feel yourself in sync with the game. Can you reflect on those moments? Or is the play so intense you can't really think about it?

HAMMER: No. I mean it's real, you're conscious of that, and you kind of play in sub – you know, unconscious – but you're really conscious of it when you feel great. And I think over time when you learn about yourself, you know when you're heading into – I guess the "zone" it's called – and you realize that you're in the middle of it. But you get to know how to get there. And when you're approaching it. And it's a great feeling to know that. And so when you're not in that zone, you know you're working to get that. It's frustrating sometimes when you can't get there. Sometimes you just can't get there for whatever reason, and you – but you're always striving to get there.

ROBIDOUX: You can feel yourself in it though?

HAMMER: Yeah! Oh yeah, you know! I mean you know when you're not going to get scored on. You know you're right on top of things, yeah! I mean for me anyway, it's real conscious.

ROBIDOUX: Is it totally mental or is it physical as well?

HAMMER: Oh it's physical! Because all of a sudden you're just so energized! And you know, you just [pause] the game's easier, but you don't realize that you're working that hard. It's just your energy level gets up so high, and you put everything else aside. You just play the game, and you just seem to make all the right moves. I mean it's a great feeling; you just feel you can't do anything wrong. (Hammer 1996)

Within this state – the zone – the players are performing at a level that is beyond comprehension, and thus beyond what is taught and learned. While systems and scientific approaches to the game tend to overintellectualize hockey and challenge players' creativity and individuality, they simultaneously force players to respond with higher levels of artistic performance, ultimately perpetuating player ownership and the intellectual/moral superiority of their trade.

Furthermore, players are conscious of the fact that in order to enter the zone they must resist all that surrounds the game and simply "play." The appeal of play becomes even more significant if, in doing so, these elite athletes achieve what Mihaly Csikszent-mihalyi describes as a "flow state" where "action follows upon action according to an internal logic that seems to need no conscious intervention by the actor. He experiences it as a unified flowing from one moment to the next, in which he is in control of his actions, and in which there is little distinction between self and environment, between stimulus and response, or between past, present, and future" (1977, 36). The level of control professional hockey players derive from this state turns it into a fundamental means of resistance. Thus, it is only while "playing" that players escape, at least temporarily, the oppressive forces that dictate virtually every other aspect of their lives. As Chip puts it: "Everything is – you're told when to get up, when to go to bed. Your travel plans are made for you. You never have to make any decisions. So [laughing], you come out of hockey without having ever made a decision in your life" (1996).

It is not surprising, then, that play manifests itself not only on the ice, but also during the informal times when the players are together. The intense schedules and long hours that players are required to spend in some team-related capacity (whether it be collectively on buses, or time spent in off-ice training) often makes hockey a gruelling and unenviable occupation. Players have told me that it is "hard to get going every night. Sometimes you don't feel like doing it. But even if you don't care about the fans and everything, you've got to do it because someone is chasing your job" (Feld 1997). Others have stated that it is "a big sacrifice to play professional hockey. There are no givens; it's not an easy profession" (Carlyle 1997). In fact, in an interview I conducted with a former professional hockey player before my research with the Reds, the individual not only described certain difficulties he had faced as a player, but also expressed strong resentment towards the way he was treated by those who ran the organization. As he put it: "If you didn't perform they'd ship you right out to somewhere else. So you kind of get treated like a piece of meat. If you did well you stayed; if you didn't, you're playing somewhere else" (Doe 1996). Clearly, the daily difficulties of playing professional hockey seriously challenge what players love about the game and force them to reinsert their own meaning back into the profession.

"ACTING STUPID TOGETHER"

Play becomes a response to the players' predicament in the labour process as well. Just as the seemingly frivolous acts of play on the ice can be read as acts of empowerment, play in more informal periods is also imbued with meaning. The pranking and verbal jabbing that take place behind closed doors are typical of these behaviours. Jim Falk explains that "the guys go around and play little pranks and fill shoes up with shaving cream, and skates and everything – and Vaseline in the gloves. And when Wally [referring to teammate Jerry Wall] says something stupid we got to [we both laugh] we got to jump on it. [He laughs harder] It's all in good humour and everyone gets a good laugh out of it" (Falk 1997). Athletic therapist Jones, who oversees and overhears much of the players' "doings" during these informal periods, states that the players spend much of their time playing, telling stories, and entertaining via other forms of oral humour. He explains: "Guys like to tell stories. Guys like to have other guys listen to their stories. You get a lot of that. You know 'last night I did this, this and this'; 'I was with this person,' whether it was male or female or whatever. And there's a little bit of – you know the guys want to shock the other guy. They want to be king for a minute or something. They want to have a good story because they have all heard great stories, and they want to be the one telling great stories. So you do get a lot of socializing before practice. And I think it's good: it lightens things up" (Jones 1996). It is important to note the immediate recognition in both Jones's and Falk's accounts of the benefits of this behaviour: it raises the players' spirits and relaxes them. Yet the significance of these moments of jocularity and playfulness remains unarticulated. Attempts by players to articulate these informal experiences have tended to trivialize the behaviour, rather than illuminate what many players contend are the most cherished aspects of their occupation. The exception is Dryden's account, which reads: "With no appointments to keep, no agents, no lawyers or accountants to interrupt us, it is our chance to rediscover the team. It happens over a meal, at a table of empty beer bottles, on planes or buses, in card games or golf games, wearing clothes that seem right, but laughingly are not, in the awful outrageous stories we tell that we've told too often before; it is our time, as Pete

Mahovolich once put it, to 'act stupid together'" (1983, 92). It seems that even if the performance of these expressive acts appears highly trivial and often absurd, it is precisely the silliness of the acts that imbues them with value and meaning.

In one of the few works that seriously approaches the presence of "humour" in professional hockey – Richard Gruneau and David Whitson's *Hockey Night in Canada: Sport, Identities, and Cultural Politics* (1993) – the authors discuss these informal periods of play as an integral aspect of the professional hockey experience. Their conclusions, however, do not move beyond recognizing the entertaining, socially interactive qualities of expressive behaviour. While they are certainly correct in saying that these humorous episodes within the dressing rooms are part "of what is remembered most warmly" by players reflecting on their past hockey experiences (1993, 120), an adequate analytical discussion of the behaviour itself is missing. To appreciate fully the value of humour within this occupational context, a broader understanding of the dynamics of working-class culture is needed. This "jock humour" is not unique to sport; it serves a vital function in most male occupational groups.

Looking at parallel behaviours within male culture in southeastern Spain, we are informed by Stanley Brandes that "jokes and joking are so important, in fact, that they can be said to provide the main fabric by which men are bound to each other on a daily basis" (1980, 97–8). Brandes explains that humour is one of the more profound expressive outlets for a group whose members are generally unwilling to express themselves to one another. He adds that the men of this particular region, through jokes, are able to "reveal and share their most deeply buried anxieties with one another"; the jokes, he says, are "a safe, jocular release" (1980, 98). Without any great risk of being taken seriously, men in Spain – like men in a North American culture – are able to open themselves up to one another in a non-threatening fashion. The cathartic value humour provides would understandably make it a favourite, and cherished, form of expression. A.E. Green affirms this position by discussing the value of humour in a coal-mining context. For a miner, "money and beer can be repaid, the saving of a life probably cannot; therefore, in a community which sets great store by reciprocity and co-operation yet mistrusts ceremonious behaviour, formal release from the debt through the informal mechanism of kidding is the logical answer" (1981, 58). As an outlet, it allows individuals to express those concerns that would otherwise be left unsaid because of the uncertainty or sensitive nature surrounding the information. According to Brandes, the humour generated in this particular group is a product of sexual anxiety. To a certain extent, this may be true of the male working-class culture in North America. However, as Green rightfully indicates, other anxieties and other manifestations of humour, such as those in direct response to the individual's position within the labour process, need exploring as well.

To begin, we must acknowledge that hockey players, as with any other working-class group, enter the workforce with a general understanding that their "social and cultural needs ... are generally seen as antithetical to the efficient execution of the labour process" (Dunk 1991, 65). As a result there is a certain level of antagonism among the workers, who express their discontent in ways that run counter to the models of efficiency provided by management and ownership. It has been pointed out that athletes entering the professional ranks, disillusioned with what the owners have done to their game, respond with their own counterproductive leisurely pursuits. Not surprisingly, then, there are similarities between the mill workers' responses in Thunder Bay (Ontario) and those of professional hockey players. Dunk explains that the "Boys [the mill workers] have a variety of leisure pursuits. In terms of the number of hours spent on a given activity, watching television may be the most important. As in many modern homes, the Boys' living-rooms are arranged around the television, symbolizing its importance in the household" (Dunk 1991, 67). The high value placed on the daily watching of television by this particular work group reminds me of the professional hockey player's explanation that watching the television program *Cheers* was cherished in his work environment. In addition to watching TV, however, Reds players revel in a series of other mundane activities, of equal significance to the group. For example, when asked what they do with their time away from the formal demands of the job, players typically respond, "We try to hang out as much as we can, outside of practice and stuff like that. You know, we don't know a lot of people from the town. So guys like me, we do hang out quite a bit. The same guys get together after practice, go out for dinner, and stuff like that. On the road, we get to hang out more as a team. We do a lot of things: we go out for dinner and when we get a chance after the game, we go out together as a group" (Jackson 1997). Similarly, Steve Toll states: "You know you're always together; you're always doing something. So, there's not too many times when you're lonely ... right now it's a lot of fun. Guys go out, and we do what we want" (Toll 1996). What is common to all of these leisure activities is that they are politically and symbolically charged. Hence, these mundane acts need to be interpreted as occasions rich with meaning – more than simply the product of men playing a game for a living.

Through this time of "just hanging out," the players are able not only to reinsert play back into their occupation, but also to liberate themselves further by openly defying the seriousness and efficiency of professionalization. The demands of labour are subverted by engaging in activities that signify something other than productivity or toil, thus allowing labourers to temporarily feel in control of the labour process. In this way, players/workers are able to resist the existing hegemony and to express themselves within their own meaningful occupational reality. As a result, these informal periods are invaluable to the players, despite the seemingly commonplace nature of the activities. But certain questions remain: how real is this resistance? and are the players truly empowered in the labour process?

ILLUSION OF POWER

Unfortunately, the so-called power that workers (players) experience is often illusory. Hegemony consists of a give-and-take relationship between the dominant and dominated classes; thus, it is inevitable that those in power will occasionally concede minimal victories in order to secure their own dominant position. In the case of professional sport, the athletes' resistance to a subordinate role has actually contributed to their own subordination. The decision to contest the "game" as the site of worker control has meant that players commit themselves totally to the team and to the overall concept of teamwork. Mastering their trade has meant dedicating themselves – during the season, as well as the off-season (their so-called holidays) – to arduous training routines that help in the strengthening, conditioning, and developing of specific skills. As Peter Jackson explained, "It [hockey] consumes all my time and all my energies. And that's all I think about. Even in the summer I work on off-ice training, working out and weightlifting to try and build up my strength for the upcoming year. It's basically a year-round

job for me, and that's all that's on my mind ... for me, it's a hundred
percent hockey – I live hockey basically. That's my life" (Jackson
1997). In Jackson's situation with the Reds, his admirable dedication was highly beneficial: his status changed from that of a marginal player to that of a top offensive forward. And his achievement
was felt by both the team and the franchise, since a franchise is
dependent on team success. Generating surplus capital in professional sport is achieved by producing a winning product. Certainly,
Jackson's devotion to the game helped ensure corporate revenue.

Turning the game that has been systematized by game strategists
back into play *is* a resistive act by the players. But their resistance
simultaneously complies with the mandate that owners and game
strategists initially set out to fulfill in the first place; that is, to put
together a quality product and to win. In effect, while this relationship first appears to be complementary – in that success is achieved
by both players and owners – it is highly exploitative. Dedication
to a team sport requires that players dedicate themselves to a team
philosophy, which, in its most basic sense, places the team first and
the individual second. Through this same philosophy, the players
who are seen taking refuge in the comfort of the team dynamic,
and who use team dynamism as a response to the oppressive forces
that surround the game, end up celebrating their subordinate positions. To be a team player requires not only a selfless approach to
the game, but also a subservience to the structures in place. In fact,
subservience is celebrated by the players: it becomes a marker for
individual commitment and dedication to the game.

"Celebrated subservience" can be illustrated through various situations in which the players willingly subject themselves to positions of subservience in highly expressive manners. For example,
during practice, when a coach blows his whistle, players must immediately stop what they are doing and turn their attention to the
coach(es). If the coach wants his players to gather around him for
more detailed instructions, there will be a second command – either
vocal or kinesic – that draws the players towards him. It was stated
earlier that formal practice time is used efficiently, that players are
constantly moving through their drills or assembling for the next
one. Therefore, when the coach signals to the players to gather
round, he does not want them to casually convene; rather, they must
rush over and stand or kneel in front of him, waiting for the next
bit of instruction. Although the expectation is already perpetuating

subordinate behaviour, the manner in which the Troy Reds carry out the behaviour actually celebrates the premise by turning it into a race. Instead of players simply complying with the command and gathering around the coach, the Reds players race one another to the coach and the last person to arrive must sprint one lap of the ice. Interestingly, this game's structure resembles that of Juice-Boy, where there is only one loser and the rest are winners.

Once again, the race needs to be recognized as the multivalent act that it is. In effect, the players have turned their subordinate roles into a game, and the act now serves as a means of subversion. However, the act simultaneously expresses the utmost compliance, and the player who complies least – finishes last – must suffer the consequence of conditioning himself further by skating the extra lap. In reality, this only contributes further to the player's subservience to the demands of labour. By racing towards Murphy, the players are articulating the fundamental goal of management, which is to attain maximum control over activities while achieving a measure of voluntary compliance. In other words, the players are racing towards their own subordination through their efforts to reinsert some level of control into the labour process. The paradoxical reality is typical of any hegemonic relationship. As Dunk states, "Given the tools the working class have to work with, their response sometimes is ineffectual and generates further complications" (1991, 153). Although hockey players, and the working class generally, may "resist it and react against it," they "are trapped in a veritable hall of mirrors. The commoditization of all aspects of life gives rise to appearances which mask or distort reality. In their attempt to escape this hall of mirrors and find a world where things are what they seem, they must use the images reflected in the mirrors ... The sole reward for their effort is, often, to become further embedded in the world they were trying to escape" (Dunk 1991, 160).

In fact, much of the resistive behaviour that transpires both formally and informally within professional hockey reduces the player's status even further, in an already disadvantaged relationship. I found one particular episode during a Reds practice to be especially revealing. The situation involved veteran NHL goaltender Jack Hammer – after being demoted to the Reds – attempting to express himself as an equally subordinate member of the Reds team. Hammer is one of the few players signed to a one-way NHL contract who is playing in the AHL because of certain circumstances (elucidated earlier in this chapter). This particular season he had one more year in his contract, which was paying him $962,500 (US) – $907,500 more than the average salary of an American Hockey League player, and thus, of his Reds teammates (NHLPA Compensation). During one of the competitions described above, in which the players race to the coach after he calls them, Hammer finished last. Because goaltenders have the disadvantage of wearing heavier and bulkier equipment than their teammates, they are exempt from the contest. Despite this, and his status as a star player within the franchise, Hammer willingly accepted the loser's fate. In my field notes I wrote: "Hammer, a recognized star, finishes last and skates the symbolic lap around the ice. This says much, as Hammer equalizes himself among players by willingly accepting the punishment. He is a star but wants to illustrate he is no better than anyone, which really endears him to the rest of the team" (Field Notes, 5 March 1997). The qualities of selflessness expressed by Hammer are noble, and as such (and for many other "sacrifices" throughout the season) Hammer is a favourite among the players and team personnel. At one point, I overheard the team and media relations co-ordinator say about Hammer's demotion, "He's really got a good attitude about it."

A plethora of scenarios illustrate still further these imposed acts of subordination. Examples include Ted Simms taking on more work by skating exceptionally hard and long so that another player would not lose his turn in a drill; or players going on the ice early or staying late for extra practice. The greater the act of subservience, the greater the dedication and commitment to becoming "a player" and, without hyperbole, becoming a Canadian hero. Thus, the illusion of power is twofold. On the one hand, players appear to maintain control over their workspace and are celebrated by a nation for their dedication. On the other, their acts are actually empowering those they are attempting to resist, which magnifies the futility of their actions. Bruce Kidd captures poetically the irony of the labourer in professional hockey, "Hockey players became Canadian Prometheuses, imprisoned by the gods of capital and guarded by vultures for the temerity of exciting our national ambition and pride" (1996, 228). The heroic status of the players contributes to the illusion of power. And as long as they continue to be masters of their trade, they will receive the acclaim that perpetuates the illusion.

Consequently, players often express themselves as powerful and secure individuals and are often perceived as such by an adoring public. Veteran defenceman Jim Falk told me that in response to their privileged status "players are a little egotistical" (Falk 1997). He explained further: "When I played in the NHL and just watching some of the guys and, you know maybe even myself, when we're a group going out to dinner or something, we kind of take on the big-shot role. I think that's just the way hockey is. It's just the way any sport would be. They put you on a different level and then take your privacy away when it's your time-off. So sometimes guys get a little, they think they're big shots" (Falk 1997). The success the players achieve on the ice extends into their daily lives; players *are* "put on a different level." But as success on the ice is fleeting, so too is their public appeal. The power is short-lived as well. And the players seem to feel cheated by this. As Feld puts it: "I think people forget about you pretty quick, you know. I think people forget about you big time" (1997). It is not surprising, then, that the players' attachment to hockey is profound, for it serves as a life-support system. Moreover, time away from hockey or from the group reduces any feelings of power or security. As Falk states, players "find their way back into it [hockey] somehow, either as a scout, because they just want to be around the guys they play with; or [so] they can walk into the dressing-room and say 'Hey guys how ya doing,' and stuff like that. I mean a lot of people, maybe hockey players are insecure too. They like the group – they feel the 'big shot' when they're in the group, but when they're by themselves it's a whole different story. I definitely think that's the situation" (1997). The players quickly become dependent on hockey; this in turn makes them highly vulnerable to the exploitative forces of labour and, ultimately, turns them into individuals with little power. As the significance of the group and the time spent within the group becomes that much more apparent, it also paradoxically increases player vulnerability.

The players consistently resort to a group mentality which is not only tolerated by management but also, somewhat cynically, encouraged. It is not accidental that dressing rooms throughout the professional leagues are now furnished with a number of luxuries: game rooms, whirlpools, televisions, and sophisticated sound systems. Players find it "very easy to spend half a day there. And that's done most times now. You know, just hanging around, and talking, and what not" (Maxwell 1996). The meaningful reality constructed by players in response to their occupational demands is actually furnished by the owners, which then circumvents the intended process of deliberate subversion. In effect, the power that the players believe exists when they create their own meaningful work world has resulted in a closed social group, where outside influence is generally unwelcome. Because any bridges formed with those outside the group potentially threaten group cohesion and unity, contact is minimal. As a result, while the team dynamic found within professional sport culture is obviously of great value to the players, for managers and owners it is even more beneficial, for the simple reason that a team's success directly corresponds to its ability to function as a whole: the closer the team dynamic, the better the team.

More specifically, the closed social environment of professional hockey retards the players' ability to grow in almost every respect – except as hockey players. As already mentioned, the players refer to themselves as "boys" and as people "who do not want to grow up"; once again, this increases their dependency on the team (Toll 1996). In response, team officials treat the players as children both on and off the ice. It starts from the moment the players enter the dressing room, where their lives are not only ordered by their physical surroundings – from labeled seating to the two sticks of gum placed on their seats before and after games/practices – and continues through the rules and procedures the players must follow, or suffer monetary fines. Athletic therapist Jones explains the Reds' fine system:

Actually it works on three or four different levels. The players issue their own fines to themselves for certain infractions. There are certain infractions that are issued by the coach in terms of on-ice violations – if you take this type of a penalty, it's this kind of money. If it causes a goal, it's even more. Things like that. There are also fines for penalties, like a stick violation: if you get caught with an illegal stick, that's so much money. If they score on it, it's so much more. And Joe Sell [equipment manager] will have certain fines. These are more common sense things to remind them [the players] to keep the place clean; to respect the place that you work in because, if you respect it, it will respect you back ... that type of thing. And the people who work for you, like myself, Jonesy and Selly, then we'll have respect in return. And things like throwing your jersey on the floor: that's a fine. I mean that's disrespectful to your jersey. You put the jersey on, you wear it proudly. If you take it off and throw it on the floor, what does that mean? It's not a lot of respect for the team you play for, and so on. There's a place that Joe wants them put, and if you don't put them there, that's a fine. Intentionally breaking a stick in practice – slamming it against the glass because you are mad for some reason, well that's a fine. And that's issued by Joe. I have one or two fines: if you miss any kind of a doctor's appointment that was made by me, it's a twenty-five-dollar fine. You do it again, it's a fifty-dollar fine. I take the time to make these, and the doctors take the time to see you; you should have enough respect to go and meet those commitments. And I have other little ones, too, which are not as strict as those things. If you miss treatment, that is considered missing an appointment. If I told you to be here at 8:30 and you miss it completely and without a good reason, it's twenty-five dollars. You come late, and expect me to treat you right now, you go to the end of the line. I take care of the next person. That's the way I have usually done it, and that's the way it's worked. (Jones 1996)

It is evident from this fine system that management treats the players as if they were incapable of making any responsible decisions. At the same time, the fine system contributes to the players' inability to take control of the decision-making process and to assume proper control of their lives, thus perpetuating player dependency. Furthermore, it is difficult to move beyond this dependency when the players see themselves as "kids," requiring special attention. One player informed me that "we're away from home, and we're – a lot of us are young kids. And you know, we stick together" (Toll 1996). The players have little opportunity to mature within the profession and often leave hockey with the same social skills they possessed on entering the game.

Some players do recognize the limitations of this closed environment and attempt to connect themselves to life outside of hockey. However, these efforts are often unproductive because of occupational demands. For example, Lester Dell explained to me that he found the endless hours of hanging out with the team tedious and often found himself without anything to do. Yet his new team informed him that continuing his post-secondary education throughout the season would be too difficult. As Dell put it: "I went to school last year. I went to college and I did sign up for university here, but our scheduling – I wasn't able to fit it in, because I'd be there for a class, I'd miss two. I'd be there for two – there's so much travelling. So I was kind of disappointed about that. There's a lot of free time here. I found it the biggest thing; there's so much free time on your hands after practice" (1997b). For whatever reason, catching up on missed classes was not an option for his "free time" and, as a result, Dell was denied not only academic development, but access to a social network outside hockey. During the year prior to coming to the Reds, Dell had been "living with billets and going to school" and "found it easier to meet people"; yet as a professional, he didn't really have "the opportunity to meet too many people ... besides the guys on the team here" (1997b). Dell's situation is, unfortunately, far from unique. As Reds Al Jones informed me, a player's inability to develop himself socially and intellectually is a fate common to most players:

The guys that come to us straight out of Junior for the most part are already professional hockey players. You've played junior and you understand that they're practising and playing almost every day. And its hard for them to do school at the same time – some do but some don't. And basically all they've done then is finish high school, maybe; some guys haven't even finished high school. They're concentrating on their hockey as it's going to be their livelihood ... but they're very limited in their knowledge of all these day-to-day things that have to be done. So I find that the guys from junior have problems.

Then you have guys that are coming from American colleges and these guys are older. These guys may have gone one, two, three, [or] four years and may have even finished college. And they're coming here, and they've done a lot of stuff for themselves. But at the same time, these American college kids are treated like gold. Like they don't have to do anything, buy anything; they get everything. Especially from the big schools like Michigan ... they come from these universities, and they didn't have to do a thing. They get housing, they get food, they get vehicles – they get all this shit. They get it all free as an incentive to play there. So again, they don't have to do a lot of things for themselves. But they have a better idea of what they have to do in terms of outside stuff.

When the Europeans come over, they're just lost. I mean, we have to lead them by the hand, and it can be difficult. But for the most part, they're just good kids and they just want to play hockey, and they get a lot of help from the front office. (Jones 1997)

With limited life skills and education, players seldom seek contact with those outside their occupational community; indeed, on the limited occasions where contact is necessary, it is done with a certain degree of trepidation. Accordingly, the constructed universe of the game has actually consumed the players, to the extent that leaving the game is not only undesired but feared. The world of hockey consists basically of "a game day or an off-day. I mean it all revolves around the game itself: what time the game is, and then preparing for the game right from the start of the season right to the end. That's the way it is, and I really find that only after a few months – by the end of the summer – I'm just starting to get comfortable in everyday life: like away from hockey and dealing with that kind of stuff. So I mean the dressing room is where your whole life is focused for eight or nine months of the year. And that's a little space – I mean you don't get out" (Hammer 1996). Because the players are truly in a precarious situation within the labour process, acquiring control of the workplace may appear to be an act of empowerment; actually, though, it contributes to the players' vulnerability and subsequent exploitation.

The hockey players' status within the labour process has not been presented positively in this chapter: players are seen to be virtually powerless. The illusion of power, however, is actually increasing for both the players and we, the general public. For one thing, there is an enormous increase in the players' salaries and prestige. As well, players are developing an increased awareness of their worth within the billion-dollar industry that is professional hockey. Up until recently, hockey superstar Eric Lindros successfully resisted NHL hegemony by refusing to play with the organization to which he was drafted; eventually, he signed with a team in a more lucrative American market. His decision was made possible because "Eric Lindros is one of the few hockey players ever to understand that when the NHL does something for *the good of the game* it really means for the *good of the owners*. And he's determined to turn that understanding to his advantage" (Cruise and Griffiths 1991, 356). Lindros has remained steadfast in his decision to ensure his own financial well-being; to the chagrin of the league, owners, and many fans, *he*[10] has dictated his own future within the league. Yet this stance has recently been jeopardized as Lindros's injuries have multiplied, the most recent setback being a series of career-threatening concussions. These injuries have seriously reduced

Lindros's bargaining ability, and, at twenty-seven, he is unable to demand the same attention he once did. In fact, one NHL official referred to him as "damaged goods" (Panaccio 2000, E1). And an unnamed player agent is quoted in the *Philadelphia Enquirer* as saying that when "he [Lindros] came into the league, he was bigger than the game, but now the game is bigger than him ... GM's won't allow themselves to cave this time ... He's not bigger than the sport" (Panaccio 2000, E5).

Significant shortcomings, then, can be seen in the players' struggle for power within the labour process. First, and perhaps most important, the players see compensatory measures almost exclusively in terms of dollars. Victory is being equated with financial success. And with the players' sky-rocketing salaries, tremendous gains have been achieved. Yet against those few players who have access to enormous salaries must be balanced those players who remain intellectually and socially challenged, although now with more wealth. The players choose, usually still voluntarily, to place themselves outside their own financial and business affairs, rendering them largely oblivious to the decisions made around them. Even players who make relatively little, compared to potential earnings, hand over their financial concerns to experts: "I have an agent and I have to give him a percentage.[11] Whatever I make, I give him a percentage. And then I've invested a little bit; my agent introduced me to someone who works in the bank or whatever. So I save my money because I have to think about a future and [all] that" (Dell 1997b). According to another player, "Everyone's got an agent; I do myself. And they pretty much take care of all of that so you don't have to worry about it as much as you might think. I know a lot of guys – some guys don't like their agent – are having problems with them. But I haven't had any problems with mine yet. And they do take care of all of that kind of stuff. I just like to have someone deal with it so I can deal with my hockey" (Jackson 1997). Moreover, the players continue to receive little to no education; as Jack Hammer states, the players end up being "behind a few years compared to the guys coming out of college; you probably don't have a college education – a lot of guys don't" (Hammer 1996). Thus the players remain disadvantaged in every aspect of their lives except in terms of capital.

The flaws of capitalist-motivated bargaining strategies become particularly evident as the players, gradually forced out of the game

early in their lives, are left to consider life outside hockey. Despite
their financial earnings, the players often know nothing other than
the game; indeed, they have invested everything in an occupation
that quickly finds their services obsolete. Moreover, their sense of
worth and self-esteem is directly related to their identity as a hockey
play. As such, players are seen clinging to a career that inevitably
discards them for younger and more desirable prospects. In *Life
After Hockey*, Michael Smith presents the results of twenty-two
interviews he conducted with various professional hockey players
about their careers and the transition periods they encountered as
they left the game. While certain players were able to make a
smooth transition from the game, the more typical responses
echoed the statements of Tom Williams: "I think that maybe my
last year in Washington I had a feeling … I probably wasn't going
to sign another contract. I was just kind of like a big wave rolling
along having a great time and enjoying it and not really thinking
about paying attention to what's going on around me" (Smith
1987, 47–8). Ron Ellis's remarks are also typical: "It has been
difficult. Not financially, nothing like that. Just trying to find a part
of me that enjoys doing something other than playing hockey. I
need to find that same thing that's going to give me that same
amount of satisfaction, the same drive and willingness to get up
each morning and work at it" (Smith 1987, 274). It is often years
before players are able to disassociate themselves from the game,
and, as already noted, many simply return in some other capacity:
as a scout, coach, sport broadcaster, or team executive.

For the majority of players, their situations are even worse because
they will not have the opportunity to acquire the financial security
made possible by playing multiple years in the NHL, signed to a lucrative contract. Statistics show that in the late 1980s, the "average age
of players in the NHL is twenty-five and careers there last an average
of five years" (Staudohar 1989, 148). Players who play the average
number of years in the NHL receive an average salary of approximately $500,000 a season. That is a rough figure calculated from the
salaries – provided by the National Hockey Players' Association – of
the 900 players who played in the 1999–2000 NHL hockey season
(*NHLPA.COM* 2000). Although the listed figures provided by the
NHLPA (see Appendix B for listed salaries and calculations) actually
show the average salary to be approximately $1,136,375 per season,
this figure is distorted because the top five players were making

upwards of $10 million a year.[12] Salary parity increases dramatically as we move down the list of players. For example, the twentieth highest-paid player made about $5 million less than the top-paid player, while the four hundred and fifty-sixth player on the list made only $200,000 more than the seven hundred and ninety-seventh player, a difference of only $340,000 over a span of 341 players. The salary median – approximately $700,000 – is clearly a more accurate representation of the average players' salary.

The figure of $700,000, however, also needs qualifying since many of the players on this list, such as previously mentioned Reds goaltender Paul Proux, are on two-way contracts. For the 1999–2000 season, Proux is listed as making $450,000 a year; however, because he spent only a short time playing with the parent organization, his yearly salary was $135,000, as opposed to the listed $450,000.[13] We can conclude, then, that average and marginal players are making substantially less than the $700,000 median, further reducing this figure to approximately $500,000 a year. Thus, a high percentage of NHL players are, for perhaps five years, making substantially less than the $1,136,375 average and are also being forced out of the game before the age of thirty. Moreover, these are NHL players, which, alas, the majority of AHL players never even become. Therefore, most of the players in this study will never have access to the larger NHL monetary packages; with careers limited primarily to the minor leagues, they will make on average $55,000 per year for approximately the same five-year period. The reality, then, is that unless players are investing their money scrupulously and/or living below their means, they not only retire from the game socially and educationally delayed, but without the capital gains that initially appeared to be the only real compensation. The limited power achieved through monetary gain is therefore often non-existent – a further illustration that professional hockey players are generally disadvantaged individuals. The illusion of power made possible through large salaries, group cohesion, group self-sufficiency, and the celebrity status of the players ironically contributes to their powerlessness, inasmuch as players subsequently choose not to venture outside of this dynamic. Moreover, their inevitable exit from the group – too often before they are prepared to do so – forces them to cope with life in the real world with little or no formal education, few job prospects, and inadequate life skills.

Conclusion

Throughout this discussion of a professional hockey community, I have attempted to provide the reader with a series of narratives that illustrate the exclusive nature of this occupational group. Clearly, the vast amounts of time players spend working, playing, and living within this closed environment ultimately affect their personal and professional development. Yet the question remains, what is the product of this personal/professional development? Or, more bluntly, what is the ultimate product of the trade? We have seen that as players enter the life of hockey they undergo a rite of passage, emerging as something other than what they were on entering. What, then, are the effects of being "gelled into one" for the sake of group unity and overall team success?

To begin, the players are forced to contend with the homogenizing forces that shape them as hockey players, and as men. The physically dominant male construct is articulated repeatedly through occupational demands and the informal behaviours of the workplace. The limited perception of what it means to be male denies the multiplicity of masculine roles and achieves what Sharon Bird characterizes as the perpetuation of *a* legitimized masculine identity. As she puts it: "The presumption that hegemonic masculinity meanings are the only mutually accepted and legitimate masculinity meanings helps to reify hegemonic norms while suppressing meanings that might otherwise create a foundation for the subversion of the existing hegemony. This presumption is especially prevalent in male homosocial interactions, which are critical to both the conceptualization of masculinity identity and the maintenance of gender norms" (Bird 1996, 122). In order to be male within this context, the players are forced to throw out that which does not fit this limited model and, ultimately, to deny all other experience.

To ensure that this masculine identity remains intact and that the representation of hockey player/hockey man is perpetuated, initiation rituals have been established to celebrate, collectively, a young player's change of status. The initiation rituals are not only symbolic representations of the player's transformation on entering professional hockey, they are also a means of divesting the young player of undesirable (that is, unmanly) qualities so as to ensure his new status within the group. The rituals expose the rookie to behaviours suitable to him as a hockey player, while at the same time exploiting and mocking inferior qualities – vulnerability and individualism – as counterproductive to him as a player, and to the team as a whole. The value of the rituals is underlined by the fact that they are performed indirectly under the supervision of team officials appreciative of their unifying potential. The more willing the younger player is to accept the traditional behaviours expressed in these cultural performances, the more likely the group is to achieve the cohesive structure necessary for success. The pressures a player faces in conforming to these entrenched attitudes and beliefs are enormous: not only does his own personal professional status depend upon his assimilating into the group, but that assimilation contributes, once again, to the construction of a hockey identity. As a result, what it means to be a hockey player is generally indistinguishable from being a man. The result is debilitating: not only are players denied their own personal development but, through expressive behaviours, they contribute to the reductive forces inherent in a univalent masculine identity.

This reduction of experience is significant for yet another reason. In addition to their portrayal in terms of this homogenized male construct, hockey players have become something else: a product of the trade, *a commodity*. As commodities, they are employed to create new values, such that their "purchaser can then realise the value thus created in the form of profit. That commodity is labour-power, or the capacity of an individual to work for an agreed period of time and in return for the receipt of a money payment" (McAll 1990, 13). The players dedicate themselves entirely to achieving success in the workplace. The more able they are to achieve this goal, the more they satisfy the essence of capitalist production. But the power and privilege professional hockey players receive from achieving excellence in their sport only increases their commodity status further, generating greater revenues and profits for those exploiting labour power for capital gain. Despite the lucrative monetary rewards high-profile players finally do receive for their services, their high-profile status contributes to the economic growth of the industry; in other words, their work is, in part, a means of acquiring their own subsistence, but also a means of producing "surplus value for the capitalist. Their working day is made up of ... necessary labour on the one hand and surplus labour on the other" (McAll 1990, 14).

The players' commodity status within the workplace is under-lined throughout the daily operations of the sport. Just like any other commodity in the market place, they are *purchased, sold, drafted* and *traded*. Indeed, the distinction the AHL holds as a "farm system"[1] for the NHL could not be a more profound illustration of the capitalist mode of production. The players are literally culti-vated "on the farm"[2]; only those with suitable qualities are "picked" to be used in the NHL market. The cultivation period, moreover, is limited, and those who do not develop sufficiently are eventually replaced with new "stock." Reds captain Darren Feld explained that his time to make it into the NHL was running out: "I'd like to go the next level [the NHL], but I'm twenty-five years old, and it's getting a little hard. But I still want to play until they take the skates away from me" (1997). "Until they take the skates away" has also been phrased more crudely as "being left to rot on the farm."[3] The agricultural metaphor encapsulates wonderfully the manner in which players are developed within the hockey system; it also captures the temporary nature of the commodity being produced. The player's body, like a fine-tuned engine, is driven to exhaustion; once the body expires the player becomes superfluous. For example, after playing more than fifteen years as an exceptional goaltender in the NHL, Jack Hammer was suddenly forced to consider the possibility that his time in the NHL was finished:

The only thing that bothers me about the whole thing [about being sent down to the Reds] is that it's because I didn't play, which is the biggest reason why I'm here. I mean I sat a whole month – over a month – without starting a game. And you know my track record: I've never played well under those circumstances. And I never played my best when I did get in there. And you know what followed [he is referring to being sent down]. I was trying to stay positive and was thinking, "oh, I can handle this, I can play well." But it didn't happen ... I mean I tried it and it didn't work, and because of that I'm in the minors because I didn't get any starts. And that's probably the only thing I resent about it. (Hammer 1996)

Hammer's career, however, was longer than most; players generally learn of their "expiration date" earlier in their careers, that is, if they even get the chance to play NHL hockey.[4]

The situation is even more disheartening when one considers actual transition rates. Since my research began with the Reds almost three years ago, I have seen only three Reds players successfully make the transition from the AHL to the NHL. Initially, it looked as though four players would have permanent jobs with the parent organization, but because of a trade made by the NHL team during the off-season, one player's position became redundant and he was returned to the Reds. The absence of job mobility cannot be attributed to a dearth of positions available to upcoming Reds players; in fact, the parent club's 1997–98 roster had five rookie positions, only one of which was occupied by a former Reds player. In recent years, NHL franchises have increasingly selected hockey players from abroad, partly because the players from Eastern bloc countries, denied access to the league before the collapse of communism, are now available. The American presence in the game has also developed considerably, as hockey's popularity in the United States has grown. As a result, more leagues – both professional and amateur – are producing highly skilled players and, thus, increasing job competition.[5] It should therefore come as no surprise that only twenty percent of the vacancies on the Reds' parent club were filled by Reds players, the other eighty percent being players from American Colleges (40%), Canadian Junior leagues (20%), and the European Hockey League (20%) (*Slam Hockey* 1998).

Tenure for players playing in the AHL is generally precarious, given the enormous odds against their ever acquiring a permanent position in a NHL lineup. But their situation becomes even more volatile now that a new crop of players is drafted every year; not only do these players have the potential to steal a spot on the NHL club rosters, but the new players – those no longer eligible to play Junior hockey and who have not made the NHL team – must fight for a position on the farm (whether the farm system is located in the AHL, IHL, or wherever). For example, the Reds' 1997–98 season season lineup had eleven new players on its twenty-one man roster, and, at the time, only one of the players no longer in the lineup was playing in the NHL. This does not mean that the other ten absentees were demoted, for certain players such as former team captain Darren Feld and the Reds' leading scorer, Jason Dodd, had opted to pursue an alternate route to the NHL by signing contracts with

IHL teams.[6] What this does suggest, however, is that stability in the AHL is virtually non-existent and labour turnover is enormous. Clearly, then, player vulnerability is excessive in this volatile industry. The surplus labour pool guarantees worker productivity, which, in turn, means that players are forced to produce or be replaced by any one of ten other men willing to do the job (Falk 1997).

The realization that professional hockey thrives on a capitalist system of production should hardly be surprising, given the capitalist framework on which the industry is based. What is somewhat difficult to accept is the players' lack of effective resistance within this exploitative system of production. As already noted, all hegemonic relationships retain a definite struggle between resistive and controlling agents; power is never static. However, the struggle in professional hockey is unfortunately subdued, as resistive acts inevitably secure owner/league hegemony. In few other occupations – given the players' total commitment to achieving their goal of playing professional hockey – is worker dedication more apparent. This does not necessarily mean that hockey players feel a sense of loyalty to individual franchises or even to the league; nevertheless, their loyalty to themselves, to achieve personal professional success, requires their subservience to the dynamics of professionalism. In return, by demanding total commitment from their players, these organizations gain complete autonomy over almost all aspects of the players' lives.

By and large, the limited signs of players' resistance manifest themselves in some form of avoidance, the players removing themselves as far as possible from the business of hockey. By remaining outside the business operations of hockey, the players see themselves as being true to themselves and to the game. Indeed, this attitude tends to be seen as the recipe for achieving success in the sport. But this form of resistance comes at a price: the denial by the players of other forms of experience as they dedicate themselves to the game. Reds forward Peter Jackson explained that he shuts out life's concerns in order to focus entirely on hockey. His comments are even more troublesome when we realize that he believes the other components of life – such as a future outside of hockey – will be easily dealt with once success in hockey is realized:

If I start worrying about that now [life outside of hockey] it's going to take away from my game and my focus. And I think, for me, if I can work maybe the next day on how I can improve myself and how I can get better and how I can just play as hard as I can, I think that later on in life, that [other life] will just take care of itself. If I can extend my career and play hockey at the highest level I can, and for as long as I can, well then I think that, maybe, I can last ten years in this game and make a living at it. And then once I'm done, you know, I think you make certain connections along the way. Or have an idea, or in the back of your mind [be] thinking what you might want to do. But for me, if I can prolong this career as long as I can, well that will take care of itself, and then I can worry about life after hockey when I come to it. (Jackson 1997)

Considering that Peter Jackson was only twenty-three years old at the time of this interview, his career will terminate at age thirty-three if he meets his ten-year objective. Keeping in mind the average NHL career of only five years, and his, at best, mediocre status as a professional AHL hockey player, the chances of an extended career are minimal. However, even if he did beat the odds and achieve his desired level of success, he would still leave the game a young man, without a post-secondary education, without any real life skills, and with only an "idea in the back of his mind" as to what he might want to do.

The reality of the situation is that professional hockey hegemony in Canada is overwhelming and, to date, has had no real significant challenge to its authority. The players' only gains have been monetary, although, in certain cases, these have been substantial. Moreover, players have had to pay an enormous price to achieve such lucrative financial compensation. Witness how they deprive themselves of experience outside their occupational domain in order to focus on hockey. For instance, players often refer to their families as "forsaken"; they regularly endure chronic ailments; they generally lack a formal education; they lack confidence in performing basic life skills; and they are often unable to pursue meaningful relationships outside of hockey. Furthermore, once players face the inevitable end to their careers, they are usually left struggling with questions about life outside the game. Listen, once again, to the Reds' goaltender, Jack Hammer: "Well, is this what I'm going to do? And is this what I'm going to be good at, because I don't know if that's what I'm going to think when I'm out there? What's going to be important?" (Hammer 1996). Of even greater concern is that the majority of players, who will never achieve the success that warrants a huge salary, are thus left potentially lacking all these qualities and without the financial means to struggle through the transition they will ultimately be forced to make. Finally, by seeking empowerment through the resistive measures described above, players further compromise their positions within the labour force and, as a byproduct, secure the hegemony of the professional hockey industry.

From this discussion of a professional hockey community, based as it is on my own experiences studying a professional team for an entire season, one clearly sees that my assessment of the players' situations, and of the industry itself, is unfavourable. Perhaps even more disheartening is that as the industry continues to grow, so too will the precariousness of the players' positions. Moreover, as the game tends to become more corporate in its business operations, the players will continue to misunderstand the extent to which their profession – and, ultimately, their lives – is dictated. It is for this reason that I believe professional hockey must be reintroduced to the players (and to the millions of people who celebrate them) for what it is – an occupation. In doing so, the players will have a better opportunity to contribute to, or challenge, the industry that now has virtually unlimited control over their lives. Until then, the players will continue to exist within hockey's self-centredness, ignoring the outside world as having little consequence or relevance and, thereby, further diminishing themselves as workers and as men.

Profiles

TROY REDS PLAYERS

Defence: Best, Colin
Born: Ontario, Canada, 1973
Previous Amateur Association
   (PAA): Ontario Hockey League
Previous Professional Experience
   (PPE): 2 years

Right Wing: Coles, Chris
Born: Manitoba, Canada, 1971
PAA: Western Hockey League
PPE: 2 years

Left Wing: Copper, Peter
Born: Ontario, Canada, 1969
PAA: Ontario Hockey League
PPE: 11 years

Left Wing: Dell, Lester
Born: Ontario, Canada, 1975
PAA: Ontario Hockey League
PPE: 0

Goaltender: Dent, John
Born: Washington, USA, 1976
PAA: Western Hockey League
PPE: 0

Centre: Dodd, Jason
Born: Ontario, Canada, 1971
PAA: American College
PPE: 4 years

Defence: Falk, Jim
Born: Ontario, Canada, 1966
PAA: Ontario Hockey League
PPE: 10 years

Defence: Feld, Darren
Born: Quebec, Canada, 1971
PAA: Quebec Major Junior
   Hockey League
PPE: 5 years

Goaltender: Hammer, Jack
Born: Ontario, Canada, 1961
PPA: Ontario Hockey League
PPE: 17 years

Centre: Jackson, Peter
Born: Ontario, Canada, 1973
PPA: American College
PPE: 2 years

Left Wing: Jones, Todd
Born: Ontario, Canada, 1974
PPA: Ontario Hockey League
PPE: 2 years

Goaltender: Proux, Paul
Born: Quebec, Canada, 1973
PPA: Quebec Major Junior
   Hockey League
PPE: 3 years

Left Wing: Simms, Ted
Born: British Columbia, Canada,
   1971
PPA: unknown
PPE: 1 year

Defence: Smith, Bill
Born: Saskatchewan, Canada, 1971
PPA: Western Hockey League
PPE: 5 years

Centre: Smith, Pat
Born: Saskatchewan, Canada, 1976
PPA: Western Hockey League
PPE: 0

Centre: Stevenson, Woody
Born: Minnesota, USA, 1973
PPA: American College
PPE: 4 years

Defence: Toll, Steve
Born: Ontario, Canada, 1973
PPA: Western Hockey League
PPE: 2 years

Left Wing: Vest, Frank
Born: Saskatchewan, Canada, 1975
PPA: Western Hockey League
PPE: 1 year

Right Wing: Wall, Jerry
Born: Saskatchewan, Canada, 1975
PPA: Western Hockey League
PPE: 1 year

Right Wing: Zakov, Mikel
Born: Czech Republic, 1975
PPA: Ontario Hockey League
PPE: 1 year

Defence: Zeal, Sid
Born: Alberta, Canada, 1975
PPA: Western Hockey League
PPE: 1 year

AHL PLAYERS FROM TEAMS
OTHER THAN THE TROY REDS

Defence: Bélanger, Marc
Born: Quebec, Canada, 1971
PPA: Quebec Major Junior
   Hockey League
PPE: 6 years

Goaltender: Boland, Sam
Born: Quebec, Canada, 1976
PPA: Quebec Major Junior
   Hockey League
PPE: 1 year

Defence: Tucker, Bob
Born: Manitoba, Canada, 1965
PPA: American College
PPE: 12 years

PLAYERS MENTIONED FROM OUTSIDE
THE IMMEDIATE ETHNOGRAPHIC FRAMEWORK –
OCTOBER 1996–APRIL 1997

Defence: Chip, Tim
Born: Ontario, Canada, 1968
PPA: Ontario Hockey League
PPE: 6 years
Current hockey status:
   professional hockey player

Centre: Maxwell, Don
Born: Ontario, Canada, 1970
PPA: Ontario Hockey League
PPE: 5 years
Current hockey status:
   professional hockey player

Defence: Doe, John
Born: Ontario, Canada, 1968
PPA: Ontario Hockey League
PPE: 1 year
Current hockey status: retired

Defence: Pack, Sean
Born: Ontario, Canada, 1970
PPA: Ontario Hockey League
PPE: 0
Current hockey status: retired

NON-PLAYERS MENTIONED

Head Coach, Springfield Spartans:
   Carlyle, Bob
Born: Canada
Professional coaching experience:
   1 year
Prior professional playing
   experience: 11 years

Head Coach, Troy Reds:
   Murphy, Hal
Born: Ontario, Canada
Professional coaching experience: 0

Assistant Coach, Troy Reds:
   Dig, Sam
Born: Ontario, Canada
Professional coaching experience: 0

Assistant Trainer, Troy Reds:
   Penn, Lou
Born: Newfoundland, Canada
Professional experience: 5 years

Equipment Manager, Troy Reds:
   Sell, Joe
Born: Ontario, Canada
Professional experience: 5 years

Athletic Therapist, Troy Reds:
   Jones, Al
Born: United Kingdom
Professional experience: 3 years

Players' Salaries: Calculations for the 1999–2000 NHL Hockey Season

SALARY BRACKET	NO. OF PLAYERS IN SALARY BRACKET	% PLAYERS IN SALARY BRACKET
$10.3 – 5.4 million	20	2%
$5.4 – 1.5 million	160	18%
$1.5 – 600,000	329	37%
$600,000 – 150,000	391	43%

TOTALS:

Salary sum = $1,022,737,810
Salary average = $1,136,375
Salary median = $700,000

Notes

INTRODUCTION

1 I use the term "vernacular" here to signify play as it is experienced "by the people," in contrast to organized play that is unattainable for reasons of class, gender, and/or skill (Rapoport 1969, 3).

2 See Appendix A for a list of players and profiles.

3 I had only stopped playing competitive hockey seven years prior to conducting this research (1989). Most recently I had played in the Ontario University Athletic Association (OUAA). Before the OUAA, I played in a variety of Junior leagues but was initially drafted by a franchise in the Ontario Hockey League (OHL) in 1986. For those unfamiliar with hockey, Junior hockey in Canada is the primary location from which NHL organizations draft or select their players. Appendix A lists the teams for which the players in this study played prior to professional hockey – eighty-three percent of the people interviewed for this project played Junior hockey prior to playing professional. The various leagues, both Junior and professional, will be discussed in detail in the chapters to follow.

4 The use of the term "fictional" here does not imply "falsehood" or "something merely opposed to the truth," but rather "the partiality of cultural and historical truths, the ways they are systematic and exclusive" (Clifford 1986, 6).

5 A mere sampling of this literature would include works by R.A. Berger (1993), G.A. Fine (1993), and R. Cintron (1993).

6 In *Triste Tropiques*, Lévi-Strauss writes: "Intentionally or unintentionally, these modern seasonings are falsified. Not of course, because they are of a purely psychological nature, but because, however honest the narrator may be, he cannot – since this is no longer

possible – supply them in a genuine form. For us to be willing to accept them, memories have to be sorted and sifted; through a degree of manipulation which, in the most sincere writers, takes place below the level of consciousness, actual experience is replaced by stereotypes" (1955, 39).

CHAPTER ONE

1 These acts have also been referred to as acts of sabotage by Martin Sprouse in *Sabotage in the American Workplace*. He defines sabotage within the workplace as "anything that you do at work that you're not supposed to do" (1992, 3).

2 Donald A. Messerschmidt's collection of essays, *Anthropologists at Home in North America: Methods and Issues in the Study of One's Own Society* (1981), considers the possibilities of doing anthropology at home, in one's own society, in order to study the familiar and the ordinary instead of the exotic and the unfamiliar.

3 Marshall McLuhan's critical analysis of popular and vernacular culture in *The Mechanical Bride* (1951) predates Barthes's analysis by six years.

4 See such works as Lois Bryson's "Sport and the Maintenance of Masculine Hegemony" (1987) and Michael Messner's "Boyhood, Organized Sports, and the Construction of Masculinities" (1990).

CHAPTER TWO

1 French Imperialism also played a role in Canada's development. But as Richard Gruneau indicates in *Class, Sports and Social Development*, Britain's ultimate domination of Canada meant a more apparent British influence (1983, 94).

2 Richard Holt in *Sport and the British* provides an example of one of these loosely organized events called "purring," which was a "ferocious shin-kicking contest fought between pairs of men in heavy clogs" (1989, 60).

3 Eileen Yeo writes of the struggle to "suppress or regulate cultural forms through state authorization" and working-class resistance to these measures in her essay "Phases in the History of Popular Culture and Power Relations in Britain, 1789 to the Present" (1988, 138).

4 Unless otherwise stated, the author has done the translations.

5 The Caughnawaga Indians and the Montreal Shamrocks are examples of First Nations and working-class teams that were dominant in the early stages of the modern development of lacrosse (1860–85). In *Canada Learns to Play*, Alan Metcalfe states: "The Shamrocks were ... the most successful team prior to 1885." He continues, "They were out of place both socially and athletically. Social misfits on the middle-class playing fields, the Shamrocks were Irish, Roman Catholic, and working class" (1987, 196).

6 This system also discriminated against race for when the National Lacrosse Association (NLA) "incorporated the word amateur in the title of the organization" it excluded First Nations peoples "who were legally prohibited from participation in amateur sport" (Metcalfe 1988, 46).

7 I have used the term "ice hockey" here to make the distinction between ice hockey and field hockey. In the remainder of the book, I avoid using the prefix "ice," allowing the term "hockey" to signify "ice hockey."

8 Selected works that offer theories on the origin of hockey include Don Morrow and Mary Keyes' *A Concise History of Sport in Canada* (1989); Donald Guay's "Les Origines Du Hockey" (1989); Neil D. Isaacs's *Checking Back: A History of the National Hockey League* (1977); Alan Metcalfe's "The Growth of Organized Sport and Development of Amateurism in Canada, 1807–1914" (1988); and Garth Vaughn's *The Puck Starts Here* (1996).

9 David Cruise and Alison Griffiths explain that there "was competition from two other leagues – the Pacific Coast Hockey League and the Western Canadian Hockey League ... By 1926, however, only the NHL, headquartered in Montreal, was left" (1991, 31).

10 Eric Lindros's "selfish" stance has returned to haunt him. A series of injuries has kept Lindros out of the Philadelphia Flyers' line-up over much of his career, and the Flyers' management have called into question Lindros's commitment to the game and to his team. *Philadelphia Enquirer* reporter Bill Lyon writes: "Lindros has been convinced for quite a while now that there are those within the Flyers organization who say he lacks the old-time, fang-toothed, if-they cut-off-both-my-legs-then-I'll-crawl-out-for-my-next-shift mindset" (2000, A8). And because of this Lindros has felt pressure to prove his loyalty to the team, to the game, and to the fans, unwisely playing three games "despite having the classic symptoms of yet another concussion. His memory began to fog over. He began to sleep to the

point of narcolepsy. He threw up between periods. He was wracked by raging headaches" (Lyon 2000, A1, A8). There is a disturbing irony here as Eric's younger brother Brett was forced to retire early from professional hockey because of concussion-related injuries.

CHAPTER THREE

1 In "Fifty of Years of the American Hockey League," by Larry Halloran, Al Arbour is quoted as saying that "You could have taken some of the [AHL] teams and put them right into [NHL] expansion" (1986, 23).

2 Note that in my calculation of salary averages I have not included players on one-way NHL contracts. This is because only eighteen of the 430 AHL players were on one-way NHL contracts, and the average salary for these eighteen players is approximately $260,000 (US). By including these figures, I would therefore be grossly inflating the AHL average salary. More will be said about "one-way" and "two-way" contracts in chapter seven.

3 Since conducting this study of the Troy Reds, only three of the twenty-one players have been able to play in the National Hockey League for an extended period of time. In other words, eighty-six percent of the players never moved beyond the AHL.

4 See the appended table of National Hockey League Salaries.

5 I soon learned that this particular individual – Ted Right – was a dedicated Reds follower who, in addition to being a loyal fan, had helped provide certain players with temporary lodgings in the city and, occasionally, had provided rides for the players if no other rides were available. His presence will be discussed further in the sections to follow.

6 See Rory Turner's and Phillip H. McArthur's article "Cultural Performances: Public Display Events and Festival," which reads: "We know when we have entered into one of these *times out of time* ... when "we are seeing or participating in something a little different than normal life" (1990, 82).

7 CCM and Bauer are two of the major sporting goods manufacturers in North America. Since this study was completed, Bauer/Canstar was purchased by Nike Inc. for 395 million dollars.

8 At least this was the case on that particular day and most days in general. Some days, however, the players did not get the drills right, and the subsequent chaos often incited anger in both the coaches and the players.

9 "On the fly" simply means while in motion.

10 Two players of African descent were on the Reds team; Ted Simms, from Canada; and back-up goaltender, John Dent, an American. John Dent was demoted from the team at Christmas, leaving only one African-Canadian player on the team.

CHAPTER FOUR

1 A new stadium has not yet been built, and the Reds remain in the city of Troy. The debate concerning a new stadium has not yet been resolved.

2 A complete reference is withheld for the sake of anonymity.

3 Again, a formal reference is withheld for the sake of anonymity.

4 On the night previous, the two teams met and the Mustang player mentioned here struck Jerry Wall over the hand with his stick. He struck Wall with no time remaining in the game, which meant that the Reds could not retaliate for this "cheap shot." They had to wait for the following night to seek revenge.

5 Asking someone "to go" means asking someone to fight.

6 Roger Caillois echoes Huizinga in his book *Man, Play and Games* when he writes: "As for the professionals ... who must think in terms of prize, salary or title," when "they play, it is at some other game" (1961, 6).

7 The Reds faced this losing scenario later in the season.

CHAPTER FIVE

1 The practice to which I am referring occurred two days after the Reds' win against the Mustangs. I have chosen this second day's practice because the first day's practice was optional. I note this not only to be faithful to the chronology of events, but to show the basic reward system that is in place. Reds player Steve Toll explains: "You know, we're at home here and we're winning a few games in a row. And we had six games in eight days, so a lot of those days you try to get your rest, and get back just to keep your intensity level up so you can get back at it the next day. So, you know, you might have a day off here, and if you're losing it might be a little different" (Toll 1996).

2 Out of nine attempts to take the puck down to the other end and score, only two successful attempts were made. That is a success rate of only twenty-two percent.

3 Formal reference is withheld for the sake of anonymity.

4 I am referring to the majority of the players in the lineup, as opposed to those players wearing the gray jerseys, who would be required to do extra conditioning drills at the end of practice.

5 Even when players stop to sign autographs or address fans personally, the sheer numbers of fans seeking a response makes it impossible for players to address more than a minute percentage of their admirers.

CHAPTER SIX

1 I am employing the strategy used by Clifford Geertz in "Deep Play," which is that rituals are texts to be interpreted and decoded (1973, 414). I am using this approach with caution, however, as Geertz himself warns that approaching rituals as texts is "a thoroughgoing conceptual wrench" (1983, 30).

2 For example, Steve Toll who played for the Rochester Americans the year before signing with the Reds, was not initiated, because he was not a league rookie.

3 It is worth repeating that Junior Hockey in Canada – the Canadian Hockey League (CHL), which is comprised of the Quebec Major Junior Hockey League (QMJHL), the Ontario Hockey League (OHL), and the Western Hockey League (WHL) – is the principal source of NHL draftees. It is here that males between the ages of sixteen to twenty are trained to be professional hockey players.

4 This particular person has been called Sean Pack throughout the book. He said that he wished to remain anonymous because of some of the personal information he provided throughout the interview.

5 A squat rack is a piece of exercise equipment used to support large amounts of weight. It consists of a metal frame that stands approximately nine feet in the air.

6 The player who received individual treatment resisted the shared rites imposed upon him by the veterans, and thus suffered alone. This singular treatment will be considered in a section to follow.

7 The rituals also serve to exclude certain players from the group, which will become evident when we consider the effects of ritual behaviour in hockey.

8 The Peterborough Petes is a Junior team in the Ontario Hockey League (OHL).

9 The two-way contract is discussed in detail in chapter seven.

CHAPTER SEVEN

1 When I asked Darren Feld if the dressing-room banter often consisted of narratives that reiterated the players' sexual exploits, he responded, "No, you know, I think it's a personal thing. Like, if the guy wants to say it, he'll say it and we'll laugh at the story, but, most of the times, guys keep it to themselves. And you know, we don't want to hear about it" (Feld 1997).

2 The periodic banning of *The Adventures of Huckleberry Finn* from certain schools would indicate that innocuous intentions do not necessarily remove the injury of speech. In 1996, an attempt, detailed below, was made to remove this novel, along with William Faulkner's short story "A Rose for Emily," because of racist overtones.

> In Tempe, objections [surfaced] to the short story "A Rose for Emily" by William Faulkner in an anthology, and *The Adventures of Huckleberry Finn* by Mark Twain, both in use in the honors freshman English class, for containing racial slurs. "Why should African American students' and other minority students' right to a fair and equal education always be destroyed for another race of people's educational benefit?" the objector asked. Removal from the required reading list and placement on the optional reading list [was] requested.
>
> OBJECTOR: Parent.
>
> RESOLUTION: On appeal, the school board upheld the recommendation of a review committee to retain the books on the required reading list. "Rather than ignoring words that are offensive and hoping that the words and the evil thoughts behind them will go away, our high school students would be better served by being allowed to explore the historical development of such bigotry and to uncover the ignorance behind it," the principal said. In fact, the objector's child was given the option of choosing an alternate assignment, which she opted to do, and was allowed to pursue independent study in the library during class discussion of Huckleberry Finn.
>
> In addition, the school and the school board decided to form a committee to ensure that materials are taught with cultural sensitivity. Teachers and administrators are also getting a general training to ensure that cultural sensitivity exists all over the school. "As far as the specific complaints, the issue is dead. However, the issue is not dead as a whole. It got people to see that there is

always more than meets the eye. In this case we saw that [the school] needed to take a look at its literary choices and we are doing just that," the principal said. For her part, the objector decided to join the curriculum committee, and "be part of the solution," one teacher said.

That notwithstanding, the objector has decided to sue the school in court to get the books removed from the required reading list. Said one supporter of the objector, "We're going to make you pay." (*People for the American Way* 1996)

3 See such works as Alan Dundes's "Into the Endzone" (1978) and Peggy Reeves Sanday's *Fraternity Gang Rape* (1990).

4 There is room for only two possible gender orders in this model: Raphael does not recognize anyone other than male/female heterosexuals.

5 Raphael speaks of the absence of rites of passage in larger North American society, but he recognizes their presence in various subcultures such as the realm of sport (Raphael 1988, 110).

6 Although I use the term "discriminatory" here, it has taken on a much greater significance ever since I read Pauline Greenhill's book *Ethnicity in the Mainstream: Three Studies of English Canadian Culture in Ontario* (1994).

7 Marc Lavoie examines at great length why there is a shortage of French-Canadian players in the NHL, despite statistical analysis that indicates that French-Canadian players, on average, outperform their English-Canadian counterparts. His research exposes the levels of discrimination French hockey players must endure trying to make it into the NHL, successfully illustrating that "les Canadiens anglais – les dépisteurs, les directeurs généraux, les entraîneurs – préféreront recommander ou engager des joueurs anglophones plutôt que des joueurs francophones de talent égal" [English Canadians – scouts, general managers, coaches – prefer to recommend or hire English players rather than French players of equal talent] (1998, 81).

8 Nicolas is one of the three players successfully promoted to the parent organization.

CHAPTER EIGHT

1 The NHLPA (1957) and the PHPA (1967) are the two players' associations organized to address the working needs of professional hockey players and to collectively represent the players in their dealings with management and their respective professional leagues.

2 Within the past five years of the NHL two strikes have occurred, the only strikes in the league's history. The strikes are indicative of two phenomena: the players' increased involvement in hockey as a business, and the growing power of the NHLPA.

3 Each professional hockey team elects a player representative (player rep) who represents the players in the event of individual or collective grievances during the season.

4 I made this assessment because of numerous players' comments that described hockey road trips as pleasurable, male-bonding experiences. Mustangs' goaltender Sam Boland stated "It's [life on the road] fun, because we're always with the players, hanging around ... and, it's just fun being around with the boys. And it's a great part of hockey I think" (Boland 1996).

5 Jack Hammer played brilliantly for the Reds throughout the season. But he was not picked up by an NHL club and was eventually shipped to an independent (without NHL affiliation) International Hockey League (IHL) franchise in the southern United States. This move to the IHL reduced Hammer's chances of returning to the NHL even further.

6 Peter, like Jack Hammer, has previously been with the Reds' parent club, but had recently been demoted and was currently playing with the Reds.

7 For the sake of anonymity, a fictitious title has been substituted for the real name of the paper.

8 A professional hockey league season is in essence a series of competitions where *one* team becomes champion through a process of defeats. Teams play off against one another until only one team remains.

9 A zero-zero outcome is virtually non-existent in professional hockey, thus thwarting any notion of perfectly executed hockey games. Moreover, fans would not pay to see games that lacked drama. The unpredictability of North American sport is its appeal; literally anything can happen on any given night.

10 Or at least his agent (formerly Rick Curran; now Eric Lindros's father, Carl Lindros) directs career decision making.

11 Lester Dell made $45,000 in 1999–2000.

12 The players and their salaries are as follows: Jaromir Jagr $10,359,852; Paul Kariya $10,000,000; Peter Forsberg $9,000,000; Theoren Fleury $8,500,000; Eric Lindros $8,500,000.

13 The figures for Proux's annual earnings were provided by the Professional Hockey Players' Association (PHPA) – along with all the other minor league salaries for the 1999–2000 season.

CONCLUSION

1 "Farm teams" are not exclusive to professional hockey. The word "farm" is a generic term used in the sport industry to describe developmental leagues or teams – whether they revolve around baseball, hockey, rugby, or whatever.

2 "He's been sent to the farm" is an expression commonly used to indicate that a player has been sent down to the AHL.

3 Approximately half way through the season, a player who had been repeatedly called up to the Reds' parent organization and repeatedly sent down was returned to the Reds for what looked like the last time in his career. Long-time Reds supporter and fan Ted Right looked at me when this particular player skated onto the ice for practice and said: "That's it for him; he's here to rot for good."

4 I am basing this on Paul D. Staudohar's somewhat generous estimate of five years as an average NHL career (1989, 148).

5 In addition to the already existing areas for hockey development in North America, such as the Canadian Junior League (CHL), the International Hockey League (IHL) and the American College hockey system, there are Elite Leagues throughout Europe, such as the European Hockey League, that provide players from Europe with the necessary exposure to gain entrance into the NHL. The European Hockey League is made up of teams from Finland, Germany, Sweden, Slovakia, Austria, Norway, Switzerland, Russia, France, Italy, and Great Britain (*European Hockey League*).

6 Both players' contracts terminated with the Reds at the conclusion of the 1996–97 season; they were then "free" to sign with any team that appealed to them.

Bibliography

AHL/PHPA *Collective Bargaining Agreement: September 1, 1994–August 31, 1998.* N.d. N.p.: Professional Hockey Players' Association.

Arendt, Hannah. 1958. *The Human Condition.* Chicago: The University of Chicago Press.

The Articulate. 1996. 2 October.

Austin, J.L. 1962. *How to Do Things With Words.* Cambridge: Harvard University Press.

Back, Les. 1993. Gendered Participation: Masculinity and Fieldwork in a South London Adolescent Community. In *Gendered Fields: Women, Men and Ethnography.* Eds. Diane Bell *et al.* New York: Routledge. 215–33.

Baker, William J. 1979. The Making of a Working-Class Football Culture in Victorian England. *Journal of Social History* 13(2): 241–51.

Bakhtin, Mikhail. 1968. *Rabelais and His World.* Trans. Hélène Iswolsky. Cambridge: MIT Press.

Bale, John. 1994. *Landscapes of Modern Sport.* Leicester: Leicester University Press.

Barnes, John. 1988. *Sports and the Law in Canada.* 2d ed. Toronto: Butterworths.

Barthes, Roland. 1957. *Mythologies.* Trans. Annette Lavers. New York: Hill and Wang.

Beamish, Rob. 1988. The Political Economy of Professional Sport. In *Not Just a Game: Essays in Canadian Sport Sociology.* Eds. Jean Harvey and Hart Cantelon. Ottawa: University of Ottawa Press, 141–58.

Beers, W. G. 1867. National Game. *Montreal Gazette,* 8 August.

Belanger, Marc. 1996. Interview by the author. Tape recording, 23 October.

Bell, Catherine. 1992. *Ritual Theory, Ritual Practice.* Oxford: Oxford University Press.

Bell, Diane. 1993. Introduction 1: The Context. In *Gendered Fields: Women, Men and Ethnography*. Eds. Diane Bell *et al.* London: Routledge, 1–19.

Bell, Michael J. 1984. Making Art Work. *Western Folklore* 43(3): 211–21.

Berger, Roger A. 1993. From Text to (Field)Work and Back Again: Theorizing a Post(modern)-Ethnography. *Anthropological Quarterly* 66(4): 174–86.

Bird, Sharon R. 1996. Welcome to the Men's Club: Homosociality and the Maintenance of Hegemonic Masculinity. *Gender and Society* 10(2): 120–32.

Boland, Sam. 1996. Interview by the author. Tape recording, 23 October.

Bourdieu, Pierre. 1993. How Can One be a Sports Fan? In *The Cultural Studies Reader*. Ed. Simon During. London: Routledge, 339–58.

Boyd, Todd. 1997. Preface. *Out of Bounds: Sports, Media and the Politics of Identity*. Eds. Aaron Baker and Todd Boyd. Bloomington: Indiana Press, vii–ix.

Brandes, Stanley. 1980. *Metaphors of Masculinity: Sex and Status in Andalusian Folklore*. Philadelphia: University of Pennsylvania Press.

Braverman, Harry. 1974. *Labor and Monopoly Capital: The Degradation of Work in the Twentieth Century*. New York: Monthly Review Press.

Bryson, Lois. 1983. Sport and the Oppression of Women. *Australian and New Zealand Journal of Sociology* 19(3): 413–26.

– 1987. Sport and the Maintenance of Masculine Hegemony. *Women's Studies International Forum* 10(4): 349–60.

Burawoy, Michael. 1979. *Manufacturing Consent: Changes in the Labor Process Under Monopoly Capitalism*. Chicago: The University of Chicago Press.

Burstyn, Varda. 1999. *The Rites of Men: Manhood, Politics, and the Culture of Sport*. Toronto: U of T Press.

Butler, Judith. 1995. Burning Acts – Injurious Speech. In *Performativity and Performance*. Eds. Andrew Parker and Eve Kosofsky Sedgwick. New York: Routledge. 197–227.

Caillois, Roger. 1961. *Man, Play, and Games*. Trans. Meyer Barash. New York: Free Press, Macmillan Publishing.

Canoe Limited Partnership. 2000. "AHL, NHL Announce Marketing Alliance: Agreement to Allow Leagues to Jointly Promote Game." 1998. Online. Available HTTP: <www.canoe.com/AHLNews/nov16_market.html>.

Carlyle, Bob. 1997. Interview by the author. Tape recording, 8 January.

Chip, Tim. 1996. Interview by the author. Tape recording, 28 April.

Cintron, Ralph. 1993. Wearing a Pith Helmet at a Sly Angle: Or, Can Writing Researchers Do Ethnography in a Postmodern Era? *Written Communication* 10(3): 371–412.

Clifford, James. 1986. Introduction: Partial Truths. In *Writing Culture: The Poetics and Politics of Ethnography*. Eds. James Clifford and George E. Marcus. Berkeley: University of California Press, 1–26.

Cohen, Sheila. 1987. A Labour Process to Nowhere? *New Left Review* 165: 34–50.

Copper, Peter. 1996. Interview by the author. Tape recording, 14 November.

Cruise, David and Alison Griffiths. 1991. *Net Worth: Exploding the Myths of Pro Hockey*. Toronto: Viking.

Csikszentmihalyi, Mihaly. 1977. *Beyond Boredom and Anxiety*. San Francisco: Jossey-Bass Publishers.

Culler, Jonathan. 1989. Convention and Meaning: Derrida and Austin. In *Contemporary Literary Criticism: Literary and Cultural Studies*. 2d ed. Eds. Robert Con Davis and Ronald Schleifer. New York: Longman, 215–28.

Dell, Lester. 1997a. Interview by the author. Tape recording. 10 February.

– 1997b. Interview by the author. Tape recording. 10 October.

Derrida, Jacques. 1977. Signature, Event, Context. In *Limited Inc., abc …* Baltimore: Johns Hopkins University Press, 1–23.

– 1989. Structure, Sign, and Play in the Discourse of the Human Sciences. In *Contemporary Literary Criticism: Literary and Cultural Studies*. Second Edition. Eds. Robert Con Davis and Ronald Schleifer. New York: Longman, 230–48.

Dodd, Jason. 1997. Interview by the author. Tape recording. 12 February.

Doe, John. 1996. Interview by author. Tape recording, 30 April.

Dryden, Ken. 1983. *The Game: A Thoughtful and Provocative Look at a Life in Hockey*. Toronto: Totem Books.

Dundes, Alan. 1978. Into the Endzone for a Touchdown: A Psychoanalytic Consideration of American Football. *Western Folklore* 37: 75–88.

Dunk, Thomas. 1991. *It's a Working Man's Town: Male Working-Class Culture in Northwestern Ontario*. Montreal: McGill-Queen's University Press.

European Hockey League. N.d. Online. Available HTTP: <www.penza.sura.com.ru/~dizelist/eng/eurolea1.htm>.

Falk, Jim. 1997. Interview by the author. Tape recording, 21 March.

Fasteau, Marc Feigen. 1974. *The Male Machine*. New York: McGraw-Hill.

Feld, Darren. 1997. Interview by the author. Tape recording, 5 March.

The Fifth Estate. Thin ice. Narrated by Linden MacIntyre. Produced/ Directed by Leslie Fruman. Associate producer Sheila Pin. CBC, 29 October 1996.

Fine, G.A. 1993. Ten Lies of Ethnography: Moral Dilemmas of Field-Research. *Journal of Contemporary Ethnography* 22(1): 267–94.

Fish, Stanley. 1981. Why No One's Afraid of Wolfgang Iser. *Diacritics* 11: 2–13.

Foucault, Michel. 1977. *Discipline and Punish: The Birth of the Prison.* Trans. Alan Sheridan. New York: Pantheon Books.

– 1983. The Subject and Power. In *Michel Foucault: Beyond Structuralism and Hermeneutics.* 2d ed. Eds. Hubert L. Dreyfus and Paul Rainbow. Chicago: University of Chicago Press, 208–26.

Freud, Sigmund. 1961. *Civilization and Its Discontents.* Trans. James Strachey. New York: Norton.

Geertz, Clifford. 1973. Deep Play: Notes on the Balinese Cockfight. In *The Interpretation of Cultures.* New York: Basic Books, 412–53.

– 1983. *Local Knowledge: Further Essays in Interpretative Anthropology.* New York: Basic Books.

Green, A.E. 1981. Only Kidding: Joking Among Coal-Miners. In *Language, Culture and Tradition: Papers on Language and Folklore Presented at the Annual Conference of the British Sociological Association, April 1978.* Eds. A.E. Green and J.D.A. Widdowson. Sheffield: University of Sheffield Printing Unit, 47–76.

Greenhill, Pauline. 1994. *Ethnicity in the Mainstream: Three Studies of English Canadian Culture in Ontario.* Montreal: McGill-Queen's University Press.

Gruneau, Richard. 1983. *Class, Sports and Social Development.* Amherst: University of Massachusetts Press.

– 1988. Modernization or Hegemony: Two Views on Sport and Social Development. In *Not Just a Game: Essays in Canadian Sport Sociology.* Eds. Jean Harvey and Hart Cantelon. Ottawa: University of Ottawa Press, 9–32.

Gruneau Richard and David Whitson. 1993. *Hockey Night in Canada: Sport, Identities and Cultural Politics.* Culture and Communication Series. Toronto: Garamond Press.

Guay, Donald. 1989. Les Origines Du Hockey. *Canadian Journal of History of Sport* 20(1): 32–46.

Hall, Stuart. 1993. Encoding, Decoding. In *The Cultural Studies Reader.* Ed. Simon During. London: Routledge, 90–103.

Halloran, Larry. 1986. Fifty Years of the American Hockey League. *Goal* 13: 23–6.

Hammer, Jack. 1996. Interview by the author. Tape recording. 13 December.

Hargreaves, John. 1986. *Sport, Power and Culture: A Social and Historical Analysis of Popular Sports in Britain.* New York: St. Martin's Press.

Hawkins, Joyce. 1988. *The Oxford Paperback Dictionary.* 3d ed. Oxford: Oxford University Press.

Holt, Richard. 1989. *Sport and the British: A Modern History.* Oxford: Clarendon Press.

Howell, Maxwell L. and Reet A. Howell, eds. 1981. *History of Sport in Canada.* Champaign, Ill.: Stipes Publishing.

Huizinga, John. 1950. *Homo Ludens.* New York: Roy Publishers.

Issacs, Neil D. 1977. *Checking Back: A History of the National Hockey League.* New York: Norton.

Jackson, Peter. 1997. Interview by the author. Tape recording, 20 January.

Jameson, Fredric. 1975–6. The Ideology of the Text. *Salmagundi* 31(2): 204–46.

Janson, Gilles. 1995. *Emparons-Nous du Sport: Les Canadiens Français et le Sport au XIXe siècle.* Montréal: Guérin.

Jarvie, Grant, and Joseph Maguire. 1994. *Sport and Leisure in Social Thought.* London: Routledge.

Jet Ice. N.d. Online. Available HTTP: <www.jetice.com/paints.html>.

Jones, Al. 1996. Interview by the author. Tape recording, 9 November.

– 1997. Interview by the author. Tape recording, 11 July.

Katz, Jackson. 1995. Reconstructing Masculinity in the Locker Room: The Mentors in Violence Prevention Project. *Harvard Education Review* 65(2): 163–74.

Kidd, Bruce. 1996. *The Struggle for Canadian Sport.* Toronto: University of Toronto Press.

Klein, Alan M. 1993. *Little Big Men: Bodybuilding Subculture and Gender Construction.* Albany: State University of New York Press.

Laba, Martin. 1992. Myths and Markets: Hockey as Popular Culture in Canada. In *Seeing Ourselves: Media Power and Policy in Canada.* Eds. Helen Holmes and David Taras. Toronto: Harcourt Brace Jovanovich Canada, 333–44.

Langness, L. L. 1974. Ritual, Power, and Male Dominance. *Ethos* 2(3): 189–212.

Lavoie, Marc. 1998. *Désavantage Numérique: Les Francophones dans la LNH.* Hull: Vents d'Ouest.

Lévi-Strauss, Claude. [1955] 1974. *Tristes Tropiques*. Trans. John and Doreen Weightman. New York: Atheneum.

Lyon, Bill. 2000. A Player Desperate to Prove Himself. *The Philadelphia Enquirer* 16 (March): A1, A8.

MacAloon, John J. 1984. Olympic Games and the Theory of Spectacle in Modern Societies. In *Rite, Drama, Festival, Spectacle: Rehearsals Toward a Theory of Cultural Performance*. Ed. John J. MacAloon. Philadelphia: Institute for the Study of Human Issues, 241–80.

Marx, Karl. 1963a. Economic and Philosophical Manuscripts. In *Karl Marx: Early Writings*. Trans. T.B. Bottomore. New York: McGraw-Hill.

– 1963b. On the Jewish Question. In *Karl Marx: Early Writings*. Trans. T.B. Bottomore. New York: McGraw-Hill.

Marx, Karl and Frederick Engels. [1888]. 1967. *The Communist Manifesto*. Trans. Samuel Moore. New York: Penguin Books.

– 1972. "Feuerbach: Opposition of the Materialistic and Idealistic Outlook." In *On Historical Materialism: A Collection*. Moscow: Progress Publishers.

Maxwell, Don. 1996. Interview by the author. Tape recording, 4 May.

McAll, Christopher. 1990. *Class, Ethnicity, and Social Inequality*. Montreal: McGill-Queen's University Press.

McCarl, Robert S. 1974. The Production Welder: Product, Process and the Industrial Craftsman. *New Folklore Quarterly* 30: 243–54.

McLuhan, Marshall. 1951. *The Mechanical Bride: Folklore of Industrial Man*. New York: Vanguard Press.

Messerschmidt, Donald A., ed. 1981. *Anthropologists at Home in North America: Methods and Issues in the Study of One's Own Society*. Cambridge: Cambridge University Press.

Messner, Michael A. 1990. Boyhood, Organized Sports, and the Construction of Masculinities. *Journal of Contemporary Ethnography* 18(4): 416–44.

– 1992. *Power at Play: Sports and the Problem of Masculinity*. Boston: Beacon Press.

Metcalfe, Alan. 1987. *Canada Learns to Play: The Emergence of Organized Sport, 1807–1914*. Toronto: McClelland and Stewart.

– 1988. The Growth of Organized Sport and the Development of Amateurism in Canada, 1807–1914. In *Not Just a Game: Essays in Canadian Sport Sociology*. Eds. Jean Harvey and Hart Cantelon. Ottawa: University of Ottawa Press, 33–50.

Morinis, Alan. 1985. The Ritual Experience: Pain and the Transformation of Consciousness in Ordeals of Initiation. *Ethos* 13(2): 150–74.

Morrow, Don. 1989. Lacrosse as the National Game. In *A Concise History of Sport in Canada*. Eds. Don Morrow, Mary Keyes, Wayne Simpson, Franck Cosentino, and Ron Lappage. Toronto: Oxford University Press, 45–68.

Murphy, Dennis. 1996. Interview by the author. Tape recording, 12 December.

NHLPA Compensation. N.d. NHLPA Compensation in Descending Order – All Players. Online. Available HTTP:<www.nhlpa.com/nhlpa/comp/compall.html>.

NHLPA.COM. 2000. The Official Site of the National Hockey League Players' Association. Online. Available HTTP: <www.nhlpa.com/>.

Nietzsche, Friedrich. 1967. *The Birth of Tragedy and the Case of Wagner*. Trans. Walter Kaufmann. New York: Vintage.

Pack, Sean. 1996. Interview by the author. Tape recording, 28 April.

Panaccio, Tim. 2000. Consensus: Lindros is Finished in Philly. *The Philadelphia Enquirer*, 25 March 2000. E1, E5.

People for the American Way. 1996. Attacks on the Freedom to Learn '96. Online. Available HTTP: <www.pfaw.org/attacks/Afl96002.htm>.

Proux, Paul. 1996. Interview by the author. Tape recording, 28 October.

Radner, Joan Newlon. 1993. Preface. *Feminist Messages: Coding in Women's Folk Culture*. Ed. Joan Newlon Radner. Urbana: University of Illinois Press, vii–xiii.

Raphael, Ray. 1988. *The Men from the Boys: Rites of Passage in Male America*. Lincoln: University of Nebraska Press.

Rapoport, Amos. 1969. *House Form and Culture*. Englewood Cliffs: Prentice-Hall.

Reds' Magazine. 1996–97a. 6(1): 7.

Reds' Magazine. 1996–97b. 6(2): 29.

Robinson, Laura. 1998. *Crossing the Line: Violence and Sexual Assault in Canada's National Sport*. Toronto: McClelland and Stewart.

Rojek, Chris. 1985. *Capitalism and Leisure Theory*. London: Tavistock Publications.

Rutherford, Jonathan. [1988] 1996. Who's that Man? In *Male Order: Unwrapping Masculinity*. Eds. Rowena Chapman and Jonathan Rutherford. London: Lawrence and Wishart, 21–67.

Sanday, Peggy Reeves. 1990. *Fraternity Gang Rape: Sex, Brotherhood, and Privilege on Campus*. New York: New York University Press.

Schoenberg, B. Mark. 1993. *Growing Up Male: The Psychology of Masculinity*. Westport: Bergin and Garvey.

Sedgwick, Eve Kosofsky. 1985. *Between Men: English Literature and Male Homosocial Desire*. New York: Columbia University Press.

September 1972. 1997. Narrated by August Schellenberg. Written by Ian Davey. Produced by Ian Davey and Robert MacAskill. Directed by Robert MacAskill. CTV.

Shogan, Debra. 1999. *The Making of High-Performance Athletes: Discipline, Diversity, and Ethics.* Toronto: U of T Press.

Simms, Ted. 1997. Interview by the author. Tape recording, 12 February.

Simpson, Tony. 1992. Real Men, Short Hair. In *Sport and Religion.* Ed. Shirl J. Hoffman. Champaign: Human Kinetics Books, 261–4.

Simpson, Wayne. 1989. Hockey. In *A Concise History of Sport in Canada.* Eds. Don Morrow, Mary Keyes, Wayne Simpson, Frank Cosentino, and Ron Lappage. Toronto: Oxford University Press, 169–229.

Slam Hockey. 1998. *1997–98 Parent Club* ROSTER. Online. Available HTTP: <www.canoe.ca/StatSHKN/BC-HKN-LGNS-TORROS-R.html>.

Smith, Michael A. 1987. *Life After Hockey: When the Lights are Dimmed.* St. Paul: Codner Books.

Sohn-Rethel, Alfred. 1978. *Intellectual and Manual Labour: A Critique of Epistemology.* London: Macmillan Press.

Spivak, Gayatri Chakravorty. 1989. Imperialism and Sexual Difference. In *Contemporary Literary Criticism: Literary and Cultural Studies.* 2d ed. Eds. Robert Con Davis and Ronald Schleifer. New York: Longman, 517–29.

Sprouse, Martin, ed. 1992. *Sabotage in the American Workplace: Anecdotes of Dissatisfaction, Mischief and Revenge.* San Francisco: Pressure Drop Press.

Stallybrass, Peter, and Allon White. 1986. *The Politics and Poetics of Transgression.* London: Methuen.

Staudohar, Paul D. 1989. *The Sports Industry and Collective Bargaining.* 2d ed. New York: Industrial and Labor Relations, Cornell University Press.

Toll, Steve. 1996. Interview by the author. Tape fecording, 11 November.

Troy Examiner. 1997a. From Russia with heart. 1 November.

Troy Examiner. 1997b. Proux caught between the rock and a hard place. 18 September.

Tucker, Bob. 1996. Interview by the author. Tape recording. 13 November.

Turner, Bryan S. 1991. Recent Developments in the Theory of the Body. In *The Body: Social Press and Cultural Theory.* Eds. Mike Featherstone, Mike Hepworth and Bryan S. Turner. London: Sage Publications, 1–35.

Turner, Rory and Philip H. McArthur. 1990. Cultural Performances: Public Display Events and Festival. In *The Emergence of Folklore in Everyday Life: A Fieldguide and Sourcebook.* Ed. George H. Schoemaker. Bloomington: Trickster Press, 83–94.

Turner, Victor. 1969. *The Ritual Process: Structure and Anti-Structure.* Ithaca: Cornell University Press.

van Gennep, Arnold. 1960. *The Rites of Passage.* Trans. Monika B. Vizedom and Gabrielle L. Caffee. Chicago: University of Chicago Press.

Vaughan, Garth. 1996. *The Puck Starts Here: The Origin of Canada's Great Winter Game: Ice Hockey.* Fredericton: Goose Lane Editions and Four East Publications.

Veblen, Thorstein. [1899] 1994. *The Theory of the Leisure Class.* New York: Penguin Books.

Vigil, James Diego. 1996. Street Baptism: Chicano Gang Initiation. *Human Organization* 55(2): 149–53.

Visweswaran, Kamala. 1994. *Fictions of Feminist Ethnography.* Minneapolis: University of Minnesota Press.

Wagner, P. 1981. Sport: Culture and Geography. In *Space, Time and Geography.* Ed. A. Pred. Lund: Gleerup, 85–108.

Wall, Jerry. 1996a. Interview by the author. Tape recording, 24 October.

– 1996b. Interview by the author. Tape recording, 11 November.

Weinstein, Marc D., Michael D. Smith, and David Wisenthal. 1995. Masculinity and Hockey Violence. *Sex Roles* 33(11): 831–47.

Wheeler, Robert F. 1978. Organized Sport and Organized Labour: The Workers' Sports Movement. *Journal of Contemporary History* 13: 191–210.

Whitson, David. 1990. Sport in the Social Construction of Masculinity. In *Sport, Men, and The Gender Order: Critical Feminist Perspectives.* Eds. Michael A. Messner and Donald F. Sabo. Champaign, Ill.: Human Kinetics Books, 19–30.

Williams, Raymond. 1977. *Marxism and Literature.* Oxford: Oxford University Press.

Wolcott, Harry F. 1990. Making a Study "More Ethnographic." *Journal of Contemporary Ethnography* 19(1): 44–72.

Yeo, Eileen. 1988. Phases in the History of Popular Culture and Power Relations in Britain, 1789 to the Present. In *Working Class and Popular Culture.* Amsterdam: Stichting Beheer IISG. 135–46.

Zakov, Mikel. 1997. Interview by the author. Tape recording, 17 April.

Index

Amateurism: defined, 42; as discrimination, 42; in terms of lacrosse 42–3, 201

American Hockey League (AHL), 6, 51–4; as farm system, 52, 190, 202; initiation ritual, 101–4, 122–4; salaries, 53–4, 186–7, 202

Apollo and Dionysus, 119–25

arena: corporate imagery, 55–6; prior to game, 66–8; as unnatural landscape, 56–7, 98–9

Arendt, Hannah, 17–18

Austin, J.L., 130–1

Back, Les, 13

Baker, William J., 36

Bakhtin, Mikhail, 72–3

Bale, John, 98

Barnes, John, 105

Barthes, Roland, 23–5, 200

Beamish, Rob, 46–7, 89

Beers, George, 39

Bell, Catherine, 100, 103

Bell, Diane, 13

Bell, Michael J., 20

Berger, R.A., 199

Bird, Sharon R., 142, 188

body: as docile, 27–30; dualism, 29–30; gender, 29–30; in hockey,

26; in production, 25–30, 27–8, 30

Bourdieu, Pierre, 34, 36

Boyd, Todd, 28

Brandes, Stanley, 174–5

Braverman, Harry, 18, 29

Bryson, Lois, 128, 200

Burawoy, Michael, 21

Burstyn, Varda, 28

Butler, Judith, 130–3

Caillois, Roger, 16, 79, 203

Canada: historical development of sport, 37–43; lacrosse, 39–43; nationalism, 3, 32, 179

capitalism: in terms of the body, 28–30; in hockey, 45–7, 144–5, 162, 168–9, 177, 185; in labour, 20–3

carnivalesque, 72–3

Central Hockey League (CHL), 53

Cherry, Don, 147

Cintron, Ralph, 9, 199

class: in labour, 20–1; control, 33–37, 175–6, 192; as disadvantaged, 28–30; working-class, 136–7, 168–9

Clifford, James, 9, 199

Cohen, Sheila, 20, 21, 22

Cruise, David and Alison Griffiths, 47, 48, 105, 184, 201

Csikszentmihalyi, Mihaly, 172

Culler, Jonathan, 131

Derrida, Jacques, 112, 131–2

dressing room, 95–8

drills: as conditioning, 62–3; as flow, 58–60, 87–8; as illusion, 60; pre-game drills, 68–9

Dryden, Ken, 29, 63, 151; on humour in hockey, 114–15, 173–4; on worker control in hockey, 160–1, 167–9

Dundes, Alan, 206

Dunk, Thomas, 18, 21, 22; on worker resistance, 30–1, 49, 162, 175, 178; on working-class men, 136–7

East Coast Hockey League (ECHL), 53; salaries, 53–4

emasculation, 136–9

enforcer, 136

Engels, Friedrich, 17, 18

England: class division, 33–7; football 35–6; in terms of sport development, 32–7

Esposito, Phil, 3

ethnicity, 145–50

ethnography, 9–13; definition 10–11;

ethnographic responsibility, 11–13; as fiction 9–10; as influenced by feminism, 13; reflexivity, 12–13
exploitation, 20–1

fans: as participants, 79–83; prior to game, 66–8; and protocol, 69; as removed from hockey, 70–1; and spectacle, 70–6; as voyeurs, 124–5
farm system, 8, 190, 208
Fasteau, Marc Feigen, 140–1
Fine, G.A., 199
First Nations peoples, 39–43, 201
Fish, Stanley, 138
flow state, 172
football, 35–6
Foucault, Michel, 27, 29, 119
French Canadian, 145, 206
Freud, Sigmund, 119–25

Geertz, Clifford, 204
gender: as competitive, 144–5; in ethnography, 13; as homosocial, 142–5; in terms of masculinity, 127–50, 136–7, 140–1, 188–9, 141
Green, A.E., 118, 174
Greenhill, Pauline, 206
Gruneau, Richard, 3, 200; on Canadian sport development, 38, 39, 45, 168; on humour in hockey, 169, 174
Guay, Donald, 43, 201

Hall, Stuart, 103
Halloran, Larry, 52, 202
Hargreaves, John, 34, 35
Hawkins, Joyce, 133

hegemony, 4, 30, 176; definition, 21
Henderson, Paul, 3
hockey: as bricolage, 44; in Canadian nationalism, 32; discrimination against European players, 146–50; discrimination against French Canadian players, 145, 206; dressing room, 95–8; ethnically divisive, 145–50; as exclusive, 94–5, 99, 141–2, 180–4; as homoerotic, 138–9; as homosocial, 142–5; as influenced by capitalism, 45–7, 144–5, 162, 168–9, 177, 185; as myth, 47, 167–8, 179, 189–94; as occupation, 4–5, 73–9, 152–87; origins, 43–5, 48–9; as play, 78–6, 162–76, 178; as privileged, 151–2; retirement, 186, 190–1; as spectacle, 72–6; as subordinating, 177–85, 189–94; as systemized, 88–9, 167–70; as working-class, 136–7
Holt, Richard, 200
homoeroticism, 138–9
homosocial, 142–5
Howell, Reet and Maxwell Howell, 37–8, 42
Huizinga, John, 78–9, 203
humour, 91–3, 115–16, 163–7, 173–6

initiation. See ritual.
International Hockey League (IHL), 53; in terms of salaries, 53–4
Isaacs, Neil D., 44, 201

James, Graham, 134
Jameson, Fredric, 101

Janson, Gilles, 37
Jarvie, Grant and Joseph Maguire, 33, 34
Jocularity, 91–3, 115–16, 163–7, 173–6
Junior hockey, 204; initiations within, 104–23; as professional, 105

Katz, Jackson, 148
Kennedy, Sheldon, 134
Keyes, Mary, 201
Kidd, Bruce, 179
Klein, Alan, 12

Laba, Martin, 47
labour: in terms of the body, 28–30; as conflict, 18–22, 154–61, 175; creativity within, 20; in hockey, 47, 152–87; objectification, 20; as productive, 17–20; resistance to, 19–23, 161–3, 175–6, 178, 192; subordination, 177–84; subversion, 19, 21–2, 175–6
lacrosse, 39–43; as expression of Canadian nationalism, 40–3; working-class and ethnic minority involvement, 42–3, 201
Langness, L.L., 110
language: as homophobic, 133–5; as misogynistic 133–5; as performance, 129–35
Lavoie, Marc, 145, 206
Lévi-Strauss, Claude, 11, 199–200
liminality, 111–19; as ethnocentric, 116
Lindros, Eric, 48, 184–5, 201–2, 207
Lyon, Bill, 202

McAll, Christopher, 189, 190

MacAloon, John J., 73
McArthur, Phillip H.,
    202
McCarl, Robert, 18–19
McLuhan, Marshall, 200
Mahovolich, Pete, 173–4
Marcus, George E., 9
Marx, Karl, 17, 18, 19,
    20, 145
mascot, 71–4
masculinity: as competi-
    tive, 144–5; in ethnog-
    raphy, 13; in terms of
    homosociality, 142–5;
    as limiting, 189; male
    preserve, 141; tradi-
    tional construction of,
    140–1, 188–9; as work-
    ing-class, 136–7
merchandise, as in Reds,
    67–8
Messerschmidt, Donald
    A., 200
Messner, Michael, 129,
    200
Metcalfe, Alan, 42, 43,
    201
modernization of sport: in
    Britain, 34–5; in Can-
    ada, 38–9
Morinis, Alan, 111, 117
Morrow, Don, 40, 41, 43,
    201
mythology of hockey, 3,
    47, 167–9, 179

National Hockey League
    (NHL), 6, 46; as cartel
    structure, 46; as
    monopoly, 46–8; rela-
    tionship with AHL, 51–
    4; in terms of salaries,
    186–7, 198
National Hockey League
    Players' Association
    (NHLPA), 47, 53, 152,
    206–7
nationalism: British
    nationalism and sport,
    34; Canadian national-

ism and hockey, 3, 32,
    47, 179; in terms of
    lacrosse, 39–43
Nietzsche, Friedrich, 119–
    25

outsider research, 5

Panaccio, Tim, 185
play, 16, 78–9; as cre-
    ative, 170–1; as flow,
    172; in informal con-
    texts, 173–6; as juice
    boy, 163–5; mythol-
    ogized, 167–9; as
    power, 176–8, 180–1;
    in the rebound game,
    165–7; as resistance,
    162–3, 175–6; in
    response to systemiza-
    tion, 169–72
player agents, 185
pleasure, in terms of rit-
    ual, 119–25
Potvin, Felix, 160–1
power, 21; in terms of the
    body, 26–30; in terms
    of British sport, 33–7;
    in hockey, 151–2, 169–
    70, 172; as illusion,
    176–81, 184–7; in play,
    175–6; in ritual, 103–4,
    119, 126
Professional Hockey Play-
    ers' Association (PHPA),
    53, 152, 206

Radner, Joan, 25
Raphael, Ray, 129, 140,
    206
Rapoport, Amos, 199
reading behaviour, 23–5
repression, sporting
    behaviour, 34–6
rite of passage, 111–19
ritual, 100–1; as dis-
    course, 103; as initia-
    tion, 101–26; in terms
    of liminality, 111–19;
    nudity within, 109, 113–

14; as transformation,
    118–19, 125–6, 189; as
    unifying, 110–11
Robinson, Laura, 4, 105
Rojek, Chris, 21
Rutherford, Jonathan, 13

Sanday, Peggy Reeves,
    103, 206
Saussure, Ferdinand de,
    23–4
Schoenberg, Mark B.,
    139
Sedgwick, Eve Kosfsky,
    142
semiology, 23–5
semiotics. See semiology.
Shogan, Debra, 27
Simpson, Tony, 141
Simpson, Wayne, 44, 46
Smith, Michael, 136, 186
Sohn-Rethel, Alfred, 29
spectacle, 72–6
Spivak, Gayatri Chakra-
    vorty, 5
Sprouse, Martin, 200
Stallybrass, Peter and
    Allon White, 72–6
Staudohar, Paul, D., 186,
    208
Summit Series, 3

Team Canada, 3
time out of time, 56, 202
Turner, Bryan S., 30
Turner, Rory, 202
Turner, Victor, 112–13,
    116

United Hockey League
    (UHL), 53

van Gennep, Arnold,
    111–12, 116
Vaughn, Garth, 201
Veblen, Thorstein, 14–15
Vigil, James Diego, 110
violence: expressed ver-
    bally, 77–8, 129–35;
    in practice, 89–90; as

pragmatić, 75–6, in
  ritual, 107–8
Visweswaran, Kamala, 13

Wagner, P., 99
Weinstein, Marc D., 136
West Coast Hockey
  League (WCHL), 53

Western Professional
  Hockey League (WPHL),
  53–4
Wheeler, Robert F., 33
Whitson, David, 3, 39,
  168; on humour in
  hockey, 169, 174; on
  the male preserve, 141

Williams, Raymond, 18
Wisenthal, David, 136
Wolcott, Harry F., 10

Yeo, Eileen 35, 200